Chapter 1

"I'm going to kill you!" Todd laughed.

"No...seriously!" Dave asked. He was slightly perturbed that Todd was not as serious as he was. "What if she's hideous?," Dave asked again. "Would you still be my wingman? Would you take one for the team?"

"How ugly *is* she?," Todd teased. He paused, trying to maintain his composure as tears ran down his face as he laughed at Dave's questions. "Let's just say you might find yourself walking home if that was the case," Todd responded, chuckling.

Todd would do a lot to help a friend in need, he thought, but he had his limitations. Admittedly, he was shallow. He judged people – girls – based on looks. He wanted to say he dated the prettiest girl around, even though he couldn't be called a trophy himself. Todd was in shape because he played baseball, but he wasn't some muscle-bound man. Women didn't swoon over him because he was tall, dark, and handsome. He wasn't tall; he stood barely 5'9". He was light complected with short, wavy hair.

Todd considered himself plain. Ordinary. Most girls in his life would say the same. Plain. And he was okay with that description. Today, for his friend Dave, he would be polite, and respectful to his blind date, but that was all. He wasn't going to lead her on just to run interference for his friend. He had morals; he was just shallow.

"Turn here!" Dave exclaimed. Dave was still miffed at his friend's response. He felt as if Todd's behavior was going to make or break his chances with his own date.

Turning into a subdivision, Todd revved the engine of his '91 RS Camaro unnecessarily. He loved his car and wanted to be seen in it. It was a reluctant early graduation gift from his parents. Well, actually, a reluctant gift from his mom, but one his dad insisted on giving him. His mom wasn't sure they should give such an expensive gift to a child with a history of failing to take care of anything he'd been given before. (This, by the way, included five other cars.) . It had been his father's idea to gift him a sports car. A sports car with a supercharged V-6 engine, mostly a means of reliving his own glory days: when *he'd* been the one to rev his own sports car's engine unnecessarily. Back then, it had been a '57 Chevy, and his dad had loved that car as much as Todd loved his, maybe even more since his dad still talked about the car 35 years after he had to get rid of it. A car such as his father's was not conducive to a couple starting a family. As loud as the '57 Chevy was, Todd would have been deaf before he drove one. Both parents were concerned with their speed-demon son handling such a powerful machine. From racing – and crashing – his green machine Big Wheel as a toddler to drag racing (or at least trying to drag race) the previous five cars – one of which had been a subcompact Ford Escort which caught fire after the attempted race – Todd didn't exactly have the best vehicular track record. His mom was fearful of the hypothetical piles of speeding tickets and increased insurance premiums Todd was sure to rack up. Still, Todd loved the cherry red car and its black t-tops. He loved the sound of the car flexing its muscle whenever he revved the engine. He loved the looks he got when he made the car purr. And he *really* liked the looks of admiration he got – mostly from girls – when the engine roared and the tires squealed.

"Pull over here," Dave said, pointing excitedly. "It's the house over there. How do I look?" he asked Todd, anxiously ironing his t-shirt with his hands.

"Dave. **DAVE!**" Todd shouted, trying to break his friend's focus on his wrinkled t-shirt. "I couldn't care less about how you look," he joked. "I'm more concerned about this hideous girl you're trying to hook me up with."

Dave ignored Todd, too concerned with his own image to care about what his friend was saying. Todd did not share the same concerns about his image as Dave did. As a senior in high school, Todd had matured past the point of caring how others viewed his appearance. He had only one concern in life: the plans he had for his future. He needed to figure out what he was going to do with his life after high school , and he needed to figure it out fast. He knew he was going to go to college, but he had no clue where. He didn't even want to go. That was his parents' vision for him, not his own. He was barely getting through high school and didn't figure college would be any easier. Though he'd received offers to play baseball for a few small schools, his reluctance to attend college and the resulting procrastination in accepting any of the offers caused them to expire. College or the armed forces were his parents' only options for him. If he chose the non-existent option three, he'd have to fund it on his own. In his own place. He could barely afford to put gas in his car, so taking care of himself in his own place was out of the question. Deep down, Todd knew college was probably the right move for him, but he didn't have a clue what he wanted to study. One thing was for sure, though: he was not going to major in math or science, the banes of his existence, but the two subjects his parents excelled in. The two things their professions encompassed.

Todd loved to read and write, but he didn't think that love could turn into a lucrative career. And even if he could, Todd had never worked hard enough to hone his skill so that he'd be great at them. He manipulated the aptitude test answers the school guidance counselors made him take to hopefully reveal that he was best-suited for an easy, high-paying job, but the results always said he should be a teacher or counselor: two middle-income professions. Todd had caused a great deal of stress to those who'd taught and counseled him; he didn't want to *be* one of those people for a living.

Todd, a decent enough member of his school's baseball team, lied to himself that he could go pro in the sport. Honestly, he could. He had a love for the game. He imitated almost every aspect of a major leaguer: their mannerisms, their superstitions, even their swings. He lived like a pro prospect, he just didn't copy the work ethic of one . That still didn't stop him from dreaming of playing in the Majors, though. Unfortunately, these dreams happened at home when he was supposed to be doing homework. The problem, like in many other aspects of his life, was that he didn't embrace the hard work and commitment it would take to make it to the Majors. Todd could hear his dad now: "The elevator to the top is out of order, that's why it's called climbing the **ladder** to success." But instead of climbing, Todd would work harder at trying to find the easy solution instead of rolling up his sleeves and working at being successful.

"Todd," his dad would also say, "you need to focus on achieving your goals with organization and critical thinking." Todd *did* focus. On two things, actually. Girls… and girls. He, like most teenage boys, was more concerned with getting laid, than with focusing on his future. He was young, dumb, and he was very naïve. Todd wanted to do it his way – the easy way – which somehow always wound up being the hard way, as if he were going to discover some new way of doing things after the hundredth time.

"Move it!" screamed a little girl on a bike, snapping Todd out of his preoccupied trance. She was being chased by another girl on a bike and was pedaling toward Todd at a ferocious pace. Todd tried in vain to jump out of her way. Annoyed by the presence of a road block, the girl leapt off her bike. Its metal spike smacked squarely into Todd's right shin, ripping his skin. The searing pain radiated through Todd's body. Oblivious to the pain she'd caused, the little girl laughed and turned her attention to what appeared to be a sibling running around the house. Cursing under his breath, Todd was reminded of why he hated kids. Just another reason why the school's aptitude test suggesting he was best suited to be a teacher was bullshit.

Looking down at his injury Todd again questioned why he was there. He'd never been a fan of blind dates, and he couldn't care less about what his or Dave's date looked like. He just wanted to be a good friend. Still, friendships had their limits. He'd reached his when the tiny cyclist used him for target practice.

Wearing a retro St. Louis Cardinals replica jersey and matching shorts, Todd often dressed in attire featuring a baseball team. His red and white Reeboks were the perfect accompaniment to his wardrobe. In his mind, it was perfect. In his mind, Cardinal red matched everything. Everything except the droplets of blood now running down his shin, ruining his tennis shoes.

Standing there bleeding, Todd noticed the number of bruises he had on his legs in addition to the more recent wound. Maybe wearing shorts hadn't been the best idea. Sure, most of the bruises were there thanks to sliding along the base paths during his last season of high school ball, and the others were from being a careless teenager, but jeans might've been the better choice for a date. He turned to look at Dave, still in the car brushing his hair. Todd reminded himself once again that he was there to be a good friend and contemplated his next move.

"Are you here for Sasha?!" yelled a voice from a house in front of Todd. Still focused on his injury, Todd ignored the question. "You should get that looked at!" yelled the voice again. Todd could barely make out what it was saying as the two kids who caused his injury carelessly kicked it as they came whizzing past him again. Todd wanted to scold the two hellions, but refrained until he could identify if they belonged to the mystery voice.

Todd couldn't see who he was talking to. The setting sun's glare was blinding him. As Todd walked closer to the house, he could make out a young lady, no more than twelve or thirteen years old.

"I'm sorry," he started, "what did you ask?"

"I was asking if you were here to see Sasha," she repeated.

"I guess so," Todd replied, joining her on her porch. Todd had no idea who he was here for, he just knew he was here to be a wingman.

"Do you have a band aid?" Todd asked, blood still trickling down his leg.

"I'm sure Sasha does. Why don't you limp your ass over to her house and find out," answered a woman in her twenties who was exiting the house. "You're dripping blood all over my property! Do you think I want to spend my evening cleaning up someone else's blood? Someone I don't know, or care to know?" she snapped.

It was quite apparent to Todd he was not welcome there.

"Akilah," started the young lady who'd first greeted Todd, "Aisha speared him with her bike."

"I don't care!" Akilah replied. "He shouldn't have gotten in her way!"

Akilah's attitude made Todd's blood boil, especially since someone she was related to had just put him in a great deal of pain.

Just as Todd was about to give Akilah a mouth full of his *own* attitude, the door swung open and out stepped another girl.

She appeared to be around Todd's age, and while she was definitely attractive, there was more to her than that. Todd sensed the loveliness of her essence. He felt coupled to her. Was this love at first sight? Had he just met his soulmate? He wanted to ask if he knew her, if they'd met before, but he already knew that if he had it had only been in a dream because he would definitely have remembered her.

"Oh my goodness! You're bleeding!" she exclaimed. Her voice was like a symphonic choir, every syllable like an angel's voice. He could have listened to her talk all day. Her concern for him was just the icing on the cake, proof that he'd just met the perfect woman. She stood around 5'6" and was about 110 pounds. She had a natural, sun-kissed, exotic tan, and her dark brown doe eyes were intoxicating. He wanted nothing more than to get lost inside of them. Her long black hair was slightly curly and blew slightly in the air as she moved.

"He's leaving," snorted Akilah as she pointed Todd off her porch.

"At least let me get you a band aid," the mystery girl said, disappearing back into the house.

Please be single, please be single, please be single Todd prayed silently as he stared at the girl's backside. He saw his whole life with her flash before his eyes. He just met the girl of his dreams, he was convinced of it.

"Don't stare too hard," Akilah snorted. "She doesn't date monkeys."

Todd was too mesmerized by the girl's beauty to be fazed by the insult. He waited patiently for her return, but Akilah wanted Todd gone and continued hurling insult after insult. Each was more venomous than the last. The more Todd ignored her, the more hateful she got. He wondered if the verbal assault was worth another glance at his mystery girl.

The door flew open again. As he gazed upon her he was convinced she was well worth the wait. His newly-found crush returned with a first-aid kit.

"Let me see your leg," she said. Her touch was magical, making every hair on his leg dance with goose bumps.

"Ouch," she said. "Whatever did this to you got you good." Todd was intoxicated by every word she spoke. He didn't care what she said, he just wanted to continue hearing her speak. She was quite a contrast to her evil sisters. He wondered if she was Cinderella and her little hellions and older sister were the evil stepsisters. They had to have different parents, Todd thought. Her gentle caress across the back of his leg as she tended to the front was euphoric, the moment perfect. Nothing could ruin…

"Ouch! Shit! Shit! Shit!" Todd yelled as the mist from the hydrogen peroxide spray stung his leg sharply. "Ahh! Ouch! Ouch! OUUUCHHH!," he wailed, jumping around in pain. The crowd of siblings behind Todd appeared to delight in his pain.

"Come here, you big baby," his nurse directed, giggling at his reaction to her treatment.

Blowing softly on his leg, Todd's intense leg pain was quickly replaced by more goosebumps and chills. The pleasure was indescribable. The tingling reached his midsection. Boner alert! Go down, go down, go down! he prayed. Todd was still a virgin, and anything, *every*thing set that thing off. Even sitting in class without a thought in his mind would cause it to pop up. Todd had mastered the art of hiding it with his books. Unfortunately, he didn't have any books with him right now. He needed something to cover it. Now. No one had *ever* touched him this way before, and his hormones were on overdrive.

He started to panic. Having an erection would make a horrible first impression. There's no recovering from that, he thought. Todd quickly turned his thoughts to Akilah. Her nasty attitude could cool *any* fire. She was cold and callous for no reason. He couldn't fathom someone being so venomous toward a stranger, but here she was.

Whew! Todd sighed. Focusing on Akilah worked. Boner gone. Crisis averted. Grateful for the care he received, he chivalrously helped the young lady who'd attended to his leg off the ground.

"Thank you so much," Todd said. "By the way, my name is Todd," he continued, trying to deepen his voice. His effort was a bit too heavy-handed, because the audience behind him chuckled. He didn't care. He still held the mystery girl's hand in his. It was soft, delicate. He glanced down, marveling at how wonderful their hands looked together. Todd was convinced they were meant for each other.

"Nice to meet you," she replied. "I'm Amani."

"She doesn't care who you are!" Akilah snorted, breaking their hands apart. The smack was sharp and vengeful.

"Get the fuck off my porch!" Akilah shouted, shoving Todd toward the porch steps. She kept ranting, but Todd couldn't decipher anything she was saying. She and Amani seemed to be arguing in their native tongues. Even their argument styles were different. Akilah spoke with venom on her tongue, while Amani seemed more compassionate. The two were nose to nose. Mostly it was Akilah in Amani's face with her sister backing down. Todd still didn't have a clue what they were saying, but he was pretty sure he *wasn't* being invited over for a family dinner.

"Hey!" Dave shouted, finally exiting the car. "You're at the wrong house. She lives over here," he said, pointing at a bright yellow, two-story house.

"I have to go," sulked Todd.

His interruption seemed to really set Akilah off. "Yeah. Take your ass over there!" she yelled.

With her full attention now back on Todd, she forced him off the porch, berating him under her breath the whole time. Todd purposely made her job of getting rid of him a chore. He leaned his head back in Amani's direction.

"It was very nice meeting you," he said in his most charming voice, adding a wink in an attempt to appear endearing. The effort produced the most adorable smile from Amani. He was smitten, and his heart melted.

Akilah's forceful shove off the top step caused him to crash back down to earth. In mid-air, Todd tried to figure out a way to land graciously. His momentum sent him sliding two feet onto and across the property's paved walkway. His body coming in contact with the gravel sent a jolt of blistering pain through his hands, elbows, and knees. His leg hurt, was now pounding and stinging, and the air had been knocked out of his lungs. He could hear laughter coming from the porch as he struggled to breathe. He could only guess it was Akilah basking in the glory of Todd's pain and embarrassment. He tried to get up off the ground but couldn't. As his body came into contact with the concrete walkway again he could feel a force on the small of his back, keeping him there. Confused, Todd tried lifting himself off the ground again, but was forced back down violently. Turning his head to try to see what was going on, he was once again blinded by the sun.

"Hey Abbas, my man," Todd could hear Dave say, "give my man a break." He could hear concern and fear in Dave's voice as it cracked. Todd felt more weight on his back. Breathing got harder, and the foot now between his shoulder blades was getting heavier and heavier.

"What are you two doing at my house?" the man Dave had called Abbas asked. His tone was just as venomous as Akilah's, maybe even more so.

Before Dave or Todd could answer, Akilah had joined the trio. Todd winced as his new cuts came in contact with his sweat and the hot pavement. Gasping for air, Todd choked a plea to the man named Abbas.

"Let me up," he begged.

"This one made Aisha crash her bike, and then he started flirting with Amani," he heard Akilah inform Abbas.

"You fucked up, asshole," Abbas declared.

Todd felt Abbas' foot lift off his back. Todd was sure he was going to slam it back down in the same spot any moment. Todd quickly rolled to his right just enough to escape. Finally he could breathe again. Barely. Todd was on his knees, trying to take in as much oxygen as he could.

Looking up, he gazed upon the man they called Abbas. From the kneeling position, Todd looked subservient to him. He could tell Abbas shared the same thought. There was a wickedness to him as he smiled down at Todd. They both knew Todd's life was in Abbas' hands. This frightened and angered Todd but empowered Abbas. Todd leapt to his feet. He'd never seen Abbas or heard anything about him, but Dave's reaction was enough to solidify Todd's understanding that Abbas wasn't someone Todd should confront. But there he was, standing eye to eye, face to face. They were close to the same height. Abbas, however, outweighed Todd by a good thirty pounds. All muscle. To Todd it looked as if he did a lot of push ups since his chest muscles protruded proudly through his shirt. Todd wondered if he'd worked on his chest somewhere in lockdown at a prison. Guessing he was a couple years older than the girls, Todd assumed he was the overprotective older brother. Todd was definitely not a fighter, but he still foolishly refused to back down.

As the two continued their staredown, Todd began to run in his head the several ways this could go:

1. They fight and he gets his ass beat in front of the girl he just flirted with. No big deal because he doesn't know her; he'll just miss out on getting to know her.
2. He wins the fight, but misses out on getting to know this beautiful woman because he just beat up her brother.
3. Worst case scenario, someone calls the police, he gets arrested for fighting, and loses the chance at another scholarship and his life because his parents will kill him.

"Let's go!" Dave demanded, grabbing Todd's shoulders and guiding him away from the confrontation. Todd breathed a big sigh of relief.

"Stay the fuck away from my house or the next time I'll curb stomp your ass," Abbas threatened.

"Whatever!," Todd replied, wishing he could have come up with a wittier comeback. He walked backwards, continuing to stare Abbas down and taunting him with hand and arm gestures inviting him to come get some. For added emphasis, Todd grabbed his crotch. Realizing he was no longer being held back by Dave, Todd quickly turned his attention away from Abbas and joined Dave as they walked up the driveway of the house next door.

"I just saved your life," Dave said.

"From *him*?!" Todd asked incredulously. "I think I could take him," he bragged. "*Where* I would take him, I have no idea," he joked.

"Abbas is bad news," Dave replied, ignoring Todd. "He's spent time in juvy. I know someone who had History class with him last year, at another school. He pistol whipped the teacher when he found out he was failing the class. Put him in the hospital. "Todd," Dave continued, "we're not built like him. He's a maniac. You and I, we're too scared to fall asleep in class. Imagine the mentality of someone who brings a gun to school and whips an authority figure with it. You really want to have a confrontation with someone like that?! If he pulls out a gun, you're on your own because I'll be running away."

"Their family just moved here for a fresh start," Dave continued, "but it looks like he still hasn't been rehabilitated."

"I still think I could have taken him," Todd replied, the confidence in his voice wavering.

"Really?" Dave asked, giving Todd an exaggerated eye roll. "Abbas would probably curb stomp you without batting an eye."

"What in the hell is that, anyway?" Todd asked curiously.

"Are you serious?" Dave asked incredulously. "How is it that you're graduating next week and you don't know what curb stomping is? If you'd have paid attention in Western Civ. you'd know it was a means of torture the Nazis used during World War II."

Todd had a blank stare on his face. He had no clue what Dave was talking about.

Dave rolled his eyes and sighed. "Remember? The Nazis would forcefully open their prisoners' mouths and make them bite the curb while someone stomped on the back of their head? Here that maniac just threatened to do that to you, and you're thinking you could beat him in a fight?! The little one beat you up with her *bike*, for crying out loud! And the older one threw you off the porch like a rag doll! You've lost how many layers of skin today because of that family? And then Abbas had you face down and was about to stomp a mudhole in your ass and walk it dry. Oh yes, I can see how you think you could win a fight. You're just lucky I was there to keep you from getting your ass kicked even worse! I bet the grandma was probably the next one gonna come out and kick your ass," Dave joked.

"Did you see their sister?" Todd asked, ignoring Dave's armchair Quarterback analysis of the evening thus far.

"Are you being serious right now?!" Dave said, mouth agape. "Get her out of your mind. A date with her probably comes with a death certificate and a toe tag," he warned. "Now focus. Before we go in here, remember to try and build me up. Tell her I'm a good guy," he continued. "Anything to differentiate me from whatever stereotypes she might believe about African Americans."

After meeting Amani and her family, Todd had no desire to meet Sasha, her friend, or to deal with any of the drama this meeting was sure to create. Dave had told him that Sasha was adopted. She was Black, her family was white. A prime example of the rainbow coalition at work Todd surmised. Dave had also said she had big tits, a big smile, and that she was racist. Apparently she didn't date Black guys. This hadn't stopped Dave from trying to win her over. He'd brought Todd along for two reasons: to distract Sasha's older sister Tasha from getting in their business. (She was apparently outspoken and not a big fan of Dave's), and two – and Todd thought this was a stupid reason – to see if Sasha was really against dating Black guys or just him.

Standing 5'7", Dave looked like an athletic version of Steve Urkel's alter ego Stefan. He carried himself as a confident ladies man, Todd thought. Dave considered himself a track star. He was more of a star than Todd ever was a baseball star, though Todd had been more successful. At their high school, no sports outside of football and basketball mattered. Track was a distant third on the list, and baseball wasn't even *on* the list. No one came to watch the team play, not even parents. Even golf and swimming were more popular than baseball. Todd thought this was a shame, because the baseball team had the better winning percentage of all the other sports during his high school career.

Dave's definition of a star might not be too far off since people actually recognized him as being on the team. A year younger than Todd, the two grew up next door to each other, they were not best friends, nor did they really have friends in common. They just grew up playing with each other and would occasionally hang out when their respective sports were not in season. Todd even got Dave a job where he worked. Dave issued a challenge to Todd to see if Sasha was racist or if she was just not interested in dating him. Todd liked a challenge, but not this one so much. It was a dumb plan, he thought. Try to see if your crush won't date you but will date your friend? What was he going to do if Sasha did, in fact, want to date Todd? Tell her "no thanks, you were an unwilling participant in Dave's social experiment?" But he came anyway, mostly out of curiosity. Pass up a chance to meet an African American that doesn't like African Americans? This would be entertaining.

Dave rang the doorbell and waited. The two could hear voices inside arguing as to who was going to open it. Dave began brushing himself off, making last minute alterations to his appearance.

"Dude you look like shit. Clean yourself up," he instructed.

"Eww! You're bleeding all over my porch!" screeched the lady holding the door.

Chapter 2

Standing in front of Todd was a very attractive young woman. Dave hadn't lied. Sasha was gorgeous, voluptuous, and her caramel-colored skin glistened radiantly in the sunlight. Her light hazel eyes sparkled. Todd could see why Dave was so enamored with her. He himself would pursue her if Dave wasn't interested in her. Plus he'd already met the girl of his dreams.

"My eyes are up here," she snapped. Dave's elbow to the ribs snapped Todd back to reality and he raised his gaze. Sasha was clearly a firecracker but stood just 5'3".

"Dave, why did you bring him to my house? We aren't a homeless shelter," Sasha snorted sarcastically. "There's a hose on the side of the house. Go clean yourself up." She pointed Todd in the direction of the hose and ushered Dave inside. Todd could hear her scolding Dave for bringing a bum to her house. Any attraction Todd had had toward Sasha disappeared immediately. His dad always said that beauty was skin deep, but ugly was to the bone. No amount of makeup can cover up an ugly personality. It was a stark contrast to Amani's sweetness. He already missed the gentle way she'd tended his injured leg. He wished she were here right now attending to his new injuries, but he'd probably killed that possibility by confronting her brother.

Walking toward the side of Sasha's house he felt as if he was the "help" being asked to clean himself up before he was allowed into the house. Sasha had a point, though. Why let a sweaty, bloody stranger into her house and allow him to sit on her nice furniture? In addition to being covered in gravel, dirt, and blood, Todd was pretty sure he also had a footprint on the back of his shirt. If the roles were reversed, he, too, would have reservations about inviting him inside. Todd hated that he had just defended her actions. He wanted to stay mad at her. He wasn't going to like her because he disagreed with her beliefs, but mostly because she dogged his friend Dave. He was still worked up from getting beat up by a kid, her evil sister, and maniac brother. Todd wanted to fight. Verbally, of course. He wanted to tell Sasha she was black and should look past this silly prejudice she has towards her own race. He ignored the rational thought that confronting her in this manner would probably cement her reasoning for not dating African Americans. Still, he rehearsed the arguments he was going to present in his head in case the subject came up. A cold chill shook him to his core. He could feel Sasha's neighbors watching every step he took. Todd wanted to give a menacing look back, but Dave's cautionary tale made him think twice.

He could see Abbas standing on his porch and mimicking Todd's earlier challenges of bringing it on. Todd shot him an exaggerated eye roll and tried to brush him off. Abbas pointed at Todd and raised his shirt, revealing a gun. This had never happened to Todd before. His never-back-down, face-to-face bravado was quickly replaced with that of a choir boy.

"A gun is definitely an attitude-adjuster," he thought nervously. "Don't make eye contact. Hopefully he's an honorable maniac, not one that shoots people in the back." Todd looked away quickly and hurried toward the hose. He heard Abbas call him a pussy, but he didn't care. He'll be whatever he calls him as long as it doesn't end with him being shot.

As the water from the hose hit his injured leg, Todd found himself thankful that his baseball season was over; the injury would be bothersome if he had to slide on it. It may still be bothersome in two weeks when summer league began. The anticipation of playing baseball excited Todd to no end. He loved the sport more than anything.

"What are you doing to my mom's flowers?" questioned a perturbed voice from behind him.

Startled, Todd shrieked, thinking at first that it was Akilah back with Abbas to finish him off. He dropped the hose on top of an array of marigolds, crushing them.

Turning around, he spotted a tall, thin, dark-complected teenager standing with her hand on her hip. Still trying to calm his nerves, Todd stuttered as he tried to find an answer to her question. Her stance looked fierce, and the sly smirk on her face revealed that she took comfort in scaring Todd. He paused, carefully measuring his words in his head. He didn't want to upset yet another person today; his body couldn't take it.

"I was told to use the hose to clean a cut on my leg," Todd said nervously.

"That doesn't explain why you're killing my mother's flowers," the girl snapped back angrily. Todd looked back to see part of the hose resting on top of some of the flowers. He nervously fumbled it as he attempted a rescue, trying to stand them up as if by a miracle their stems would heal.

"It's too late for that," the girl scolded. She snapped her fingers animatedly and tilted her head. Todd rolled up the hose and gently placed it on the ground next to the flower bed.

"I sincerely apologize. Is there anything I can do?" He was trying to appear as remorseful as he could.

"Yeah. You can give me money to replace them," the young woman answered, tapping her palm. "Who the hell are you, anyway?" she asked disdainfully. "Why did you decide to use our hose? We're not running a charity here. Unless you plan to help pay the water bill I suggest you take your ass to the gas station to clean yourself up; they have free towels and squeegees."

"But Sasha told me I could use…," Todd stammered.

"Sasha?" she asked, cutting him off. She looked both confused and annoyed. "Why are you here for my sister?"

Sisters, Todd thought. Of course. Only sisters would attack him with the nearly the same insensitive question as to why he was there.

"Sasha doesn't even *like* Black guys," she continued.

I guess that answers Dave's question, Todd thought.

"My friend Dave," he started, but was interrupted again.

"That kid needs to quit," she said. "He has *no* chance with her. He keeps coming around here like a lost puppy. I see this time he brought a stray with him." She paused. "After my mom finds out about her flowers he'll have even less of a chance with her, she said." She held her hand out again, waiting for the money Todd still hadn't given her.

Todd felt like he was being extorted. I'm going to kill Dave, he thought, slightly perturbed that he was being set up with this girl. Todd reached in his pocket and pulled out his wallet. He knew he had lunch money he could give her, not so much for the flowers, but to hopefully quell her attitude.

"Let me see," she exclaimed, snatching Todd's wallet out of his hands.

"Hey!" he snapped, reaching for his wallet back. The look she flashed him made Todd freeze. He felt like a gazelle angering a lioness. She removed the velcro banding and began inspecting the contents. She pulled out his public library card.

"Nerd!" she cried, tossing it to the ground.

"Hey!" he started to object, but she shot him a look that reminded him that *she* was in charge.

Next she pulled out his school ID. She gazed at it intently, as if she were a bouncer at a club. "Humph!" she snorted sarcastically. I would have shot whoever took this picture." She tossed it to the ground next to his library card. Todd was in unfamiliar territory. He was a little upset by her critique of his picture. He'd tried desperately since middle school to take the perfect school ID picture. He thought he'd finally gotten it this year. I guess I was wrong, he thought. He was also surprised that he cared what this stranger thought about his looks, especially when he rarely ever did. Then again, it's easy not to care when no one's ever judged you by your appearance. Or, in Todd's case, too naive to notice whether he'd been judged that way or not.

"Oh snap! You were a boy scout?" she asked, laughing hysterically as she pulled out his old boy scout ID. In the picture, he was in his Cub Scout uniform, and this was the first ID he'd ever had. It was as old as his wallet and had been one of the first things he'd put in it. He refused to take it out, especially since it reminded him of all the fun activities he'd done with his dad when he was a Scout.

"You were a cute kid," she added.

"Thank you," Todd said with a smile. Maybe she's not as bad as I thought, he considered.

"Were!" she emphasized. "Time hasn't been kind," she added.

Todd began feeling his face as if he could feel the imperfections to which she was referring. He'd had enough. "Who *are* you?" he asked. He assumed it was Tasha, the young lady he was supposed to be keeping busy as Dave tried to win Sasha over. He prayed it wasn't her, but who else could it be?

Tasha ignored his question and continued rifling through Todd's wallet. "Wishful thinking," she said, pulling out the condom Todd kept stored there.

"Hey, put that back!" he demanded. Tasha ignored him.

"Why?" she asked. "You're not going to use it on me." She tore the wrapper open, pulled the condom out, and threw it on the ground with the rest of his items. Todd figured he'd be a little more upset about the condom if he had prospects in his life to use it on, but he didn't. This actually saddened him. He just realized he hadn't had a real relationship during his high school years. No one he would consider his high school sweetheart.

"Encino man!" Tasha suddenly squawked, pulling out a movie ticket and startling Todd from his wandering. "Apparently you don't have good taste in movies. One ticket? Guess you couldn't find any one desperate enough to go with you," she laughed sarcastically. Todd was growing tired of being her punching bag. You're here for a friend. You're doing this for Dave, he repeated to himself.

"This should cover it," Tasha declared, taking all the cash Todd had in his wallet. "$9. *$9?!*" She looked him up and down. Todd could feel her judgment of him, and it wasn't flattering. "Boy! You need a job."

"I have a job," Todd barked.

"With only $9 in your wallet you need a *better* job," she retorted. "If you got mugged the robber would feel sorry for you and probably put money *into* your wallet. No wonder you were using my hose; you can't even afford water!"

"I didn't expect to get robbed of my $9," Todd responded.

"I didn't rob you," Tasha said. "Think of it as an investment in a better garden." Todd knew that money would not be used for her mom's garden. He also knew he would still be blamed for the damaged flowers. "I'm Tasha, by the way."

"I know," Todd said.

"Good. And before you get any ideas, I'm not like my sister, I do date Black guys, but I would not date you."

"What's wrong with me?" Todd asked, offended.

Tasha scoffed at the idea. "Look at you! You look like shit. Obviously whoever kicked your ass proved that you can't fight. I need a man who can protect me, not get mugged with me. I need a man who's willing to buy me flowers, not destroy my mom's flower garden."

"That was an accident," Todd interjected.

"And that, sweetheart, is why I wouldn't date you." She walked up to Todd and slowly caressed his cheek with the back of her hand. She leaned in seductively and whispered, "Honey, I need a man who's attentive to everything he touches. A man who takes care of his woman's property <u>and</u> needs. And Darling," her tone quickly changed back to normal, "You aren't that man." She turned her hand over and tapped the cheek she'd just been caressing, punctuating her point.

"Follow me, go inside, gather your boy, and get the hell out of my house," she demanded.

Todd followed her around the side of the house. He peered next door, desperately hoping to catch a glimpse of Amani. "Don't be looking at my ass, either," she warned.

Todd hadn't been paying any attention to Tasha. He wanted to be spiteful and say something like "I didn't know you had one," but he kept his mouth shut. He was a thousand percent sure Tasha would hit him if he did.

Entering the home, Todd could hear the blaring sounds of a Color Me Badd song. Dave and Sasha were sitting on the couch singing along with the music and laughing when one of them messed up the lyrics. Todd had to admit, they would make a cute couple. All the signs were there. She subconsciously mimicking his movements, flirtatiously laughing at his jokes, playfully slapping his knee. She tossed her hair, and smiled when he would glance up at her.

Shouting over the music, Todd commented on how cute they looked together. He wasn't sure if he was heard or ignored.

"Oh my gosh!" Sasha shouted, jumping off the couch. She ran over to the tape player and turned off the music. "You poor soul, Dave told me what happened to you next door. I didn't know that was why you were bleeding."

Tasha, who had begun walking away, stopped in her tracks. "Wait! *They* did this to you?" she asked, pointing in the direction of her neighbors. The two sisters focused their attention on Todd. Both were all ears.

"I think one was an accident," Todd began, pointing at his bandage. "This happened when the little Evel Knievel slammed into me on her bike. Rudely, but on accident." Ponting at his knees, elbows, and hands, Todd continued. "These happened when I was thrown to the ground from their top porch step. I think I slid five to ten feet thanks to the force," he said. "Face first," he added for emphasis. He knew he was laying it on thick, but he wanted to keep both girls' attention, especially since they seemed engrossed by his tale.

"He has a footprint on his back from where Abbas stomped on him," Dave interjected, trying to steer Sasha's attention back to him. "I had to save his life," he added.

"He stomped on you?" Tasha gasped, concerned, She outlined the footprint Abbas had left on the back of his shirt. She was still in shock of how cruel one person could be towards another.

"The parents are even meaner," Sasha added. "The way they yell at my friend…"

"Amani?" Todd interrupted excitedly.

"Yes," Tasha replied, frustrated. Her seductive touch became a slight shove and she turned her nose up at Todd.

"They seemed racist," Todd added. "One of the sisters called me a monkey." The sisters gasped.

"I can't stand the hatred in this world," Sasha said.

Looking at Dave, Todd nodded as if to say *I'm making a move*. "I agree," he began. "It's a shame that in 1992, people are still willing to judge someone based on their skin color or a stereotype. They should get to know the person as a person."

Tasha snickered. She could see right through Todd's ploy. Sasha completely ignored his spiel. "Amani and Amna are sweet," she chimed in.

"Yes," Todd agreed. "Amani tended to my injury, and I'm thinking Amna was the one who spoke to me first. She seemed nice, and Amani was so gentle. She took really good care of me."

"Your boy is headed for dangerous territory," Tasha retorted, rolling her eyes and walking away.

"I think my sister might've started to like you until you started drooling over Amani," Sasha explained.

"You wouldn't know it from the way she berated and insulted me outside," Todd said.

"Todd, my friend, did you not go to elementary school?" Dave asked. "You tease the one you like. That's just how she flirts," he added. "No one is going to seductively start caressing your back just for the heck of it."

Just then the doorbell rang. "Get that, Tasha!" Sasha yelled, but Tasha had walked up the stairs toward her room.

"You're closer. You get it," Tasha yelled back.

"I can't! I have company," Sasha replied.

"I'll get it," Dave volunteered, disappearing around the corner.

"You two really do make a cute couple," Todd said.

"Who?" Sasha asked. "Me and Dave?" She chuckled. "He's like a brother to me. He's just a friend. I have my heart set on Bryan Abrams from Color Me Badd."

Todd wanted to roll his eyes, but he was worried she'd give him another tongue. "I'm pretty sure your 'brother' is interested in something more," he added jokingly. Sasha's face twisted; she appeared sickened by the thought.

"Todd! It's for you," Dave called, peeking around the corner and smirking.

"For me?" Todd asked. He stared at Dave, hoping for a clue as to who was there for him, but Dave ignored him and plopped back on the couch. "Who even knows I'm here?" he wondered out loud.

"I thought you might need another Band-Aid," came a soft voice from the doorway. It was Amani. He could live a hundred lifetimes and would never forget the sweet sound of her voice. He sprinted around the corner toward the door. Behind her, the sun created an angelic silhouette around her. She looked heavenly. Am I dreaming, he wondered.

Blushing, Todd responded, "I *am* in need of medical attention. I need 50 CC's of your smile," he teased. Amani looked away bashfully. Todd was grinning from ear to ear.

"Will you take good care of me?" he asked. The two blushed and smiled, taking each other in.

"I would love to," she replied softly.

They stood there in silence, staring into each other's eyes. From the moment Todd had walked to the door and his eyes met hers, a spine-tingling warmth coursed through his body. His palms began to sweat, stinging the cuts on his hands. He didn't care. He didn't even notice. The hair on his arms stood up as if it was trying to leave his body. As their pair stood there, smiling at each other, Todd felt a feeling he'd never felt before. Was this love at first sight he wondered again? He was in trouble, and he knew it. He wanted nothing more than to be in Amani's presence forever.

Just when he thought nothing could ruin the moment, the warmth of being this close to her rushed toward his midsection and he giggled. "Anything I say right now is going to sound so cheesy," he said.

Amani chuckled sweetly. "Who said you have to say anything?" she asked? Her voice sent erotic shivers down his spine. Todd felt like the old cartoon where the male hears his love's words or smells her perfume and floats through the air toward it.

"Hey, girl!" Sasha said from behind Todd. She pushed past him, gave her friend a quick hug, and ushered Amani inside.

"What brings you here? Oh. Let me introduce you to my buddy Dave and his friend Todd."

Dave winced at the introduction. "Buddy?" he said softly. It was an awkward moment.

"Hey," he said sullenly. Todd just stood there, the same puppy dog smile on his face.

"We met," Amani replied. "Hey Dave," she said, not taking her eyes off Todd. "I just came by to give you another Band-Aid and to apologize for my brother and sisters' behavior. They…"

"No need to apologize," Todd interjected. "Your little sister could hit me with a bus, your older sister could throw me from a mountain, and your brother could shoot me in my back if it meant I got to meet you."

"Aww," Amani replied, blushing. Todd melted at the smile she offered.

"Ugh. I'm going to barf," Sasha teased.

Dave continued sulking on the couch. Todd couldn't help but feel sorry for him. "I have a great idea," he began, trying to liven the mood. He was still looking deeply into Amani's eyes. "Let's all go to the movies tomorrow night. Get to know each other." He secretly hoped Dave and Sasha had other plans so it could be just him and Amani. There was nothing in particular that he wanted to see; he just wanted to be with her. Maybe there was a scary movie out that they could go to so Amani would jump into his arms during the surprising parts.

Amani's expression changed. She looked panicked. "I...I...I can't," she stuttered. An uneasy feeling rocked the pit of Todd's stomach, so much so he almost doubled over. What if she had a boyfriend? He hadn't even thought of that possibility.

Sasha looked back at Dave, who had perked up at the prospect of a double date. "I don't think so," she blurted, crushing him.

"I have to go," Amani said suddenly. She turned on her heel and fled quickly.

"Wait!" Todd called after her, but it was too late. The door had already closed behind her before he could follow her.

"Y'all have to go, too," Sasha barked. "My mom will be home soon and she'd be pissed to find me alone with two black guys."

Chapter 3

The car ride home was a quiet one, a stark contrast to the excitement there'd been on the way there. The promise of an enjoyable late afternoon had fallen flat. Really flat. Dave turned off Todd's car radio when Shanice's "I Love Your Smile" came on.

"Man! This shit sucks!" he whined. "Me and Sasha had a great time. She was laughing at my jokes, she opened up to me about her life. We had a real connection! She even said she thinks I'm a great guy."

"You are," Todd agreed. "You're quite a buddy," he teased.

Dave shot him a nasty look. "Zip it, Todd," he snapped. "I can't believe she won't give me a chance because I'm Black," he sulked. "Me!" he exclaimed. "What's wrong with me? *This* Black man," he continued, "is a straight-A student and a track star. I have a job. I'm respectful. She'd be *lucky* to date a guy like me. And that b.s. comment about not having two black guys in her house when her mom gets home??..." Dave was too upset to finish.

Todd was only half listening; he had his own broken heart to mend. "Did I just have a Cinderella moment?" he asked. "She just ran out of Sasha's house as if the clock struck midnight."

"Leave that alone," Dave said, hitting his fist into his palm. Todd could tell Dave was concerned for his wellbeing. "What is *wrong* with you? You got your ass beat by her family. Do you think you're going to be invited to dinner? You are not Sidney Portier and life is not like the sitcoms we watch on Friday nights. If Abbas catches you flirting with his sister the situation won't be hilariously wrapped up in thirty minutes. Sasha said Amani's family doesn't allow her to date someone from outside their faith. They take that seriously. Very seriously. **Deadly** seriously. So let it go."

"Her family tree is like a cactus," he continued.

"A cactus?"

"Yes. It's full of pricks," Dave replied.

"I think you're being overly dramatic," Todd said dismissively. Dave sighed, rolled his eyes, and sat in silence the rest of the trip home.

When Todd pulled up to his house the pair hopped out of the car and headed to their respective houses.

"Thanks for trying to hook me up," Dave said. "Sorry you got your ass beat in the process."

"I didn't get my ass beat," Todd replied.

"Your leg and the footprint on your back say different. You have so many bandages on you you look like a mummy."

"Who beat you up?" Todd's dad shouted from the garage. How is he always around to hear things I don't want him to know, Todd thought.

"I didn't get beat up," he said.

"Yes he did, Mr. Glass. He got stomped out," Dave laughed.

"You're *about* to get stomped out," Todd's dad replied. "I thought I asked you to cut the grass."

"I'll cut it tomorrow, Dad," Todd said.

"Tomorrow is too late," his dad shot back. "The county collects yard waste in the morning. Plus it's been a week since the last time you cut it. As fast as it grows it needs to be cut twice a week," he scolded. "I work hard every day to put a roof over your head. clothes on your back, food in your belly, and a car for you to get around in. Do we have a nice home?" he asked.

"Yes." Todd said cautiously. He knew a lecture was coming.

"Then help me keep it taken care of," his dad said. "And after you're done mowing, clean yourself up. I can't have your mom thinking I never taught you how to defend yourself."

It was getting late. The last thing Todd wanted to do was cut the grass. It took over an hour! All he wanted to do was play some Sade and chill in his room. Her soft, melodic music would echo the pain he was feeling after the woman of his dreams ran out of his life. I can't sulk over Amani while cutting the grass, he thought. He also knew he wasn't going to get away with just mowing; his dad would expect him to edge the yard and pull some weeds, too.

Todd watched as his dad pulled some fertilizer out of his trunk. Something *else* Todd would be expected to do…without being asked. If he didn't, he knew his father would wake him up in the middle of the night to make him.

"Hey, Dad. Wait up. Why can't we get a riding mower?"

His father paused and looked as if he was seriously considering Todd's request. "Why do I need a riding mower? I have you," he quipped, turning and entering the house.

Cutting was a struggle. Every drip of sweat stung his cut leg, his sinuses were acting up, his nostrils filled with mucus, and the congestion made it hard to breathe. Blades of grass stuck to his sweaty body as he struggled to get them from the lawn mower to the yard waste bag.

"Heavy duty?" Todd growled. "Heavy duty my ass. This bag isn't worth the paper it's made of" he complained as the bag started to rip. The bottom of the bag began to tear as Todd dragged it to the curb. Well, it's the garbage man's problem now, he thought.

The sun had set completely by the time he'd put all the lawn equipment away. He was glad tomorrow was Friday and that he didn't have any weekend plans except work. Plus, he was one day closer to graduation. Exactly seven days to freedom. No more pencils, no more books, no more teachers' dirty looks he thought as he recited Alice Cooper's "School's Out" in his mind.

"Where have you been?" Todd's mom asked as he entered the house.

"I was outside cutting the grass," he said, opening the refrigerator. His mom couldn't have missed the sound of the lawn mower, so Todd waited for the other shoe to drop. He'd learned from experience that his mom's seemingly innocent questions were never really innocent. "Didn't I ask you to go to the mall and get a pair of slacks for graduation? A lot of people are coming into town; I'm not going to have you looking like a derelict when you walk across the stage."

"I'll do it tomorrow before I go to work," Todd lied. He knew he'd probably wait until he'd been reminded several more times to get the task done. Not out of defiance, just because he was lazy and didn't feel it was a priority.

"Didn't I also ask you to finish mailing out your graduation announcements? *And* these college applications?" Oops, Todd thought. He'd completely forgotten.

"Todd!" she began, then stopped. Todd waited patiently. "You need to get your life together. Your future starts when you walk across that stage. High School Graduation isn't the finish line; that's when life begins!" Todd could tell she was beyond frustrated with him. "You can't stay here the rest of your life working at that restaurant," she continued. "You need to get an education beyond high school, work on getting your own things. Your dad and I can't always be your safety net."

Todd was only half listening; he was more interested in finding food.

"Before you eat, go take a shower," his mom said. "You stink."

"Okaaay, Mooom," Todd responded.

"Without the attitude, Son," she snapped. "You're not too old to get spanked."

"Todd!" he heard his dad chime in. "Have you heard of a man named Napoleon Hill?"

"The French monarch who shot the nose off the sphinx?" Todd asked.

His dad grumbled something under his breath about the results of not doing homework, and shook his head. "He's known for saying 'strength and growth come only through continuous effort and struggle.' Can you do fifty push ups effortlessly, or will you struggle?"

"Effortlessly, of course," Todd boasted.

"Let me see," his dad said.

Todd dropped down to the ground. He didn't understand why his dad was asking him about push ups, but he knew he needed to get them done.

"I see Todd's in trouble again," teased his little sister Tiffany, appearing in the room. Tiffany, only four years younger than Todd, was wise beyond her years. Or at least wiser than Todd. Tiffany was both angel and demon. To their parents and her teachers, she was an angel. The good kid. Got good grades, kept her room clean… did all the stuff Todd was always getting in trouble for not doing.

Unfortunately, Todd only saw her evil side. To him, Tiffany was a demon. They were opposites in every sense of the word. If you didn't know them, you wouldn't know they were related. She was outspoken. He was reserved. She was adventurous, he was cautious. She liked to strategize, he was reactive. Luckily for her, but unfortunate for Todd, she got away with everything.

It was his own fault. All their parents' attention was focused on Todd. Rightly so, he thought. He got caught doing a lot of dumb stuff. At times, Tiffany would brazenly do things because she knew she could get away with it. If she didn't she'd just say "Todd told me to" and he'd get in trouble for corrupting his sister.

"50!" he shouted. "And I barely broke a sweat."

"What do you want to do for a living?" his mom asked.

"He's going to be a bum," Tiffany teased.

"Don't you have something better to do?" their mom snapped.

"And miss this? Nope!" she replied with a laugh. Todd shot his sister an evil look and mouthed, "I'm going to kill you."

"Go get ready for school tomorrow," their mom ordered.

"I got my clothes ready for the week on Sunday," Tiffany assured her mom. "I'm not Todd, remember?" she added, sticking her tongue out at her brother.

"Then go get *his* clothes ready for tomorrow," their mom responded. "Ironed!" she added. Tiffany sighed in protest and flipped Todd off as she walked away.

Todd was miffed; he'd never be able to get away with a response like that. Not without some sort of repercussion. But he knew it, too, was his fault. Once again, his parents were more focused on him and his antics than anything his sister was doing.

"Do you plan on doing the journalism program again?" his mother asked. Todd, who'd once expressed an interest in being a play-by-play announcer for the St. Louis Cardinals (his favorite team), had participated in a minority journalism program the summer after his junior year. He'd truly enjoyed the program and had learned a lot. Then it dawned on him. The line of questions from his mom, her interest in his future… he'd forgotten to sign up for the program! It was probably too late to sign up now. An opportunity gone, he thought.

"Can you do another 50 pushups?" his dad asked out of the blue.

"Yeah, I guess," Todd said, confused. He figured another lesson was coming but he didn't know what it could possibly be.

He dropped to the floor again. After the first ten he was eager to prove his strength to his dad. He felt his muscles tighten up after twenty. It amazed him how he was struggling just two weeks after his baseball season ended. He made it to 50, but the last ten were difficult. Slowly, he eased himself off the floor. It had been a long day: school, then the assault by Amani's family, and finally yard work.

"Easy peasy," he said softly. He was out of breath, but tried to mask his exertion by holding his breath. "Why are you asking me to do so many pushups?" he asked, heading back to the refrigerator.

His dad sat down at the kitchen table, took a deep breath, and paused. Todd waited for him to say something. This was his father's way of getting Todd to pay attention. Sometimes he just had to wait a few seconds, sometimes a few minutes. This time the wait was long…and excruciating.

Finally, his dad said, "Todd, your mom and I are getting tired of thinking for you, cleaning up after you, and making sure you have a pot to piss in and a window to throw it out of. Get me a glass of Kool-Aid," he said. Todd's dad often would interrupt his own lecture, with small demands out of the blue. Todd just ignored the obscurity of it. He always assumed it was his dads way of ensuring Todd was paying attention.

Todd was used to his dad's weird pauses and off-topic requests, so he wasn't fazed and stood to get the Kool-Aid.

His dad continued, "What do you want to do for a living?"

"I don't know," Todd said, instantly regretting it. He knew better than to answer any of his parents' questions with those three words. He knew they expected him to already have his life planned out and that they were going to call him out on it because he didn't.

"Next week," his mom began, but paused, struggling to articulate her thoughts. "You are eighteen. You graduate next week. You should have some sort of clue as to what you will be doing to sustain yourself in life. We're tired of asking you to do the same thing over and over again." She almost went on, but paused when his dad gave her his "I've got this" look.

"I think I want to be a broadcast analyst," Todd blurted out. In truth, he *wasn't* sure this is what he wanted to do, but it sounded nice. It was something that might get his parents off his back.

"How do you plan on achieving this goal?" his dad asked.

"I don't… I'm not… I…" Todd stammered. He couldn't say 'I don't know' again; they'd kill him! Is death-by-lecture a thing, he wondered?

"You had a great opportunity with the minority journalism program but you didn't follow through by signing up again this year. Do you realize the networking and connections a program like that could produce?" Todd stayed silent. "Luckily," his dad continued, "I pulled some strings to get you signed up, but the rest is up to you."

"Great," Todd thought. He'd purposely not signed up for the program so he could have his summer free of obligations. He wanted to enjoy himself, not immediately start his adult life.

"As for the pushups," his father continued, "you have until fall to figure out what you're going to do with your life and the direction you're going. Coming home half beat up, not pulling your weight around the house, refusing to fill out college applications because you want to be lazy… The way I see it, you're headed one of two places: prison or the Army. Doing push ups will prepare you for both."

Todd heard a chuckle come from around the corner. Tiffany was eavesdropping. "Todd's going to jaaaiil, Todd's going to jaaaiil," she sang.

"By the way, some little girl called you while you were outside," his mom said.

"Okay, Todd replied," half listening. "Who was it?" he asked, already headed away from the room and desperate for a shower.

"Some girl named Eman... Aman... I don't know."

"Amani?!" Todd asked, sprinting back into the kitchen and nearly knocking his mom over. "What did she say?"

"She asked to talk to you."

"Did she sound sweet?" he asked.

"I said you were busy," his mom answered, ignoring his craziness. "She said, 'Tell him,' – what's her name again?" she asked.

"Amani. Her name is Amani," Todd said.

"Well then she said 'Okay,' and then I hung up."

"But how did she *sound*?" Todd asked. "Why didn't you come get me? Did she leave a number?"

"Todd, I'm not a secretary. You're lucky I got *that* much information for you."

"Thanks, Mom," Todd said, planting a sweaty kiss on his mom's cheek. He skipped off gleefully to take a shower while his mom wiped away his disgusting kiss.

"That right there is your problem!" his dad yelled after him. "If you put this much energy into everything else in your life as you appear to be into this young lady, your mom and I wouldn't have to worry about you so much."

But Todd was already upstairs.

Chapter 4

The next morning, Todd made his way to the bus stop sluggishly. He hadn't slept well. The combination of the previous day's injuries, lawn work, pushups, and thoughts of Amani had made for a restless night. After nearly 13 years of running up the hill to where the bus had picked him up since he was a 6-year-old kindergartner, mostly because he was almost always running late, today he was actually on time. Then again, it was Friday, and less than one week until graduation. This gave him extra energy and motivation. Plus, Tiffany had gotten his clothes together for him.

"Hey! Are you protesting something?" a voice yelled from behind him. It was Dave.

"What are you talking about?" Todd responded, confused.

"Your outfit, man. Yellow shorts and an orange polo? Even *I* know that's a fashion faux pas."

"Damn it, Tiffany!" Todd exclaimed. This had to be her way of getting back at him after their mom made her iron his clothes. He glanced down at his retro Cardinals Fossil watch. He had very little time to go back and change. Todd wished he didn't care how he looked or what people said about him, but his peers would make his last week of high school a living hell if he showed up in something they considered unfashionable. "I'll be back," he groaned. "Save me a seat."

Sprinting back home, Todd wondered what he could wear. He'd left clothes in the washing machine a couple days ago. He hurried down the basement stairs and grabbed the oversize, wet load of clothes from the drum. Frantically, he searched for something that didn't smell of mildew. He finally decided on a pair of jeans and a shirt. I've got 8 minutes! he exclaimed to himself. Plenty of time. He contemplated the fastest way to dry them. The dryer would take at least twenty minutes. The oven, fifteen. The microwave! he thought. He tore up the stairs and headed for the kitchen. He threw the shirt in there first and set the microwave to three minutes. He then headed to his dad's closet to see if there was anything he would wear in there if the microwave didn't do the trick. Both his parents were already off to work and his dad had dropped his sister off along the way because she'd had to be there early for a class project. Todd thought about purposely missing the bus and taking his car to school, but without a school parking pass, he'd get a ticket unless he parked in one of the surrounding neighborhoods. But then he would have to worry about his car getting towed.

Before he could ponder further, he heard the microwave ding. His shirt was done. Racing back down the stairs, he found it had worked. His shirt was dry. Dryish. Time for my jeans, he thought. He threw them in and set it for five minutes.

Running back up the stairs, Todd rummaged through his dad's closet some more. He came across a slim fit violet Ralph Lauren purple label polo shirt. "Perfect!" he exclaimed, throwing off his damp shirt in favor of his dad's $400 one. I *know* this matches my shorts, he thought. They're the same colors the Lakers wear. Todd admired the quality of the material of his borrowed shirt as he headed toward the mirror to check himself. He felt as if Hollywood had come to town.

His self-adoration was brought to a quick halt when Todd heard crackling sounds coming from the kitchen. Panicking, he flew back down the stairs, praying the sound was not that of the metal on his jeans scorching the microwave. His prayers were not answered. As he threw the door open, a sickening smell overwhelmed him.

Turning to the kitchen sink in search of a dish cloth he could use to clean up any evidence that he almost burned the house down,

Todd heard the sound of his school bus on the next street. I'll fix all of this when I get home from school, he decided.

Rushing for the door, Todd grabbed his bookbag and shut and locked the door, all in one motion. There was only one way he was going to catch the bus. He ran across several backyards, through the woods, and popped out of a clearing just as the bus was approaching. Out of breath, Todd collected himself and strutted onto the bus so everyone could see how amazing he looked in his dad's expensive shirt.

"Looking good!" someone shouted from the back of the bus. Todd felt like royalty.

"Hey you have a leaf stuck to you," a freshman said as Todd walked past him looking for an open seat. Before Todd could look down, the kid yanked on the branch attached to the leaf, pulling on the shirt's fabric. It snagged. Todd froze in shock. The rip was blatantly obvious given the material's perfect stitching.

Gasps filled the air as the freshman dropped the branch, straightened in his seat, and looked straight ahead as if it would make Todd forget what he'd done. Anger canvassed Todd's face, and the look he shot the freshman could have bored a hole through the back of his head.

Suddenly, the bus jerked forward, breaking the tense moment and causing Todd to nearly lose his footing. He returned the focus to his dad's shirt as he clumsily continued his way down the aisle.

Finding a seat across from Dave, Todd fixated on his already ruined day, a day in which he had two final exams and work later on that night. His dad's shirt was ruined, and the microwave probably was, too. What else could possibly go wrong?

"So I gave Amani your number," Dave said. And just like that, Todd snapped out of his woe-is-me attitude, replacing it with a bluebird-on-my-shoulder one. He hadn't even realized Dave had been talking to him since he'd sat down. The whole time since he sat down across from him.

"What?" he cried, interrupting whatever monologue Dave was engaged in. "What did you say?" he asked.

"I said, Sasha asked me to give her your number so she could give it to Amani. She felt bad running away last night."

All of Todd's cares evaporated in an instant. Yahoo! he thought. He wasn't the reason she'd run out so suddenly. And she'd called to tell him so! A huge smile spread across his face. Todd's plan for cramming for his economics exam on the bus ride to school had just been thwarted by thoughts of a missed call from Amani and her determination to get his phone number. He opened his book bag, ripped out a piece of notebook paper, and began scribbling a note to Amani at a frantic pace. Years of doing last-minute homework assignments on the bus had refined his penmanship so it looked no different than when he wrote sitting still.

By the time he got to school he was a page into a love letter to a girl he'd met just twelve hours earlier. He hurried through the halls to get to his classroom. The handful of students who'd arrived early were deep into their books, cramming as much material on financial management, budgeting, investing, and savings as they could in the last few minutes before the final. Todd had planned on doing the same, but had been side tracked by his love letter. He couldn't care less now about the final exam in this class, or in any of his classes. According to his calculations, he'd pass the course as long as he got a low D on the final. Passing was all he was concerned about. His rank among his 500-plus fellow graduates was plummeting rapidly. He still pushed aside all thoughts of transcripts, scholarships, and his future in favor of having fun. He'd been cruising through school since midterms. If it hadn't been for his parents forcing him back on track in several of his classes, graduating may not have been a reality.

Test-performance and class participation had never been a problem for Todd when he studied the material, but homework was a foreign concept. When progress reports were sent out his parents realized that Todd had been lying to him on all those evenings he'd said he didn't have any homework. He was grounded for several weeks as he made up tons of incomplete assignments and essays in an effort to raise his grades high enough that he could graduate. His *parents* should be the ones earning his diploma for all work they'd done to get him there. His mom had spent many a late night typing the essays Todd was still in the process of writing, and his dad tried over and over and over again to go over Todd's missing math assignments. And while Todd *still* didn't understand those problems, he <u>did</u> know his parents deserved the Nobel Peace Prize for not killing him through all of it. Ever misguided, though, Todd felt all that hard work should be rewarded and that he should be able to take it easy the last two weeks of school.

His goal his senior year had been to keep his grades high enough that he could play baseball. Now that the season was over, his academic concerns were riding on fumes. His practical side said he needed to keep striving for the best marks possible, especially since he hadn't been accepted to college yet. Hell, he still needed to apply! Todd often changed the subject when conversations with classmates turned to talk about the future. It seemed like everyone around him knew where they were going and what they planned to study, and if they weren't going to college they had jobs lined up, careers, trades, or the armed services. Todd's contingency plan – well, really, his *only* plan – was community college.

The bell ringing distracted him from the letter he was still writing to Amani.

"Books under your desk!" the teacher said. Todd was miffed. He wanted to keep writing, not take some stupid high school final. He breezed through the test but couldn't say how well he'd done since he'd barely read the questions. And he certainly hadn't double checked his work. He did remember going over some of the material but put little thought into anything else. It was his senior year, after all. Wasn't he *supposed* to slack off a little? Deep down, Todd knew doing this was for those who'd busted their asses off the previous three years, something he hadn't done. He was an average student in every sense of the word and always wondered how much he could have achieved if he'd worked harder. Now he'd never know.

He hadn't been very involved in high school at all, come to think of it. He'd only gone to a handful of school dances and never had a real girlfriend. The only school activity he'd been involved in was baseball. In fact, his only "claim to fame" in high school was talking on the phone to different groups of friends every night. Their main goal had been to see how many people they could get on a three-way call. Their highest number had been 16. School was ending in less than a week and Todd could feel life threatening to pass him by. He was scared, and he was lost. He knew he had to do *some*thing to plan for his future, but that feat felt impossible. How does one plan for their future when they have no clue what they want to do?

"Mr. Glass. Mr Glass? Todd!" his teacher shouted. Todd was shaken from his daydream.

"Yes, sir?" Todd replied

"I expected more from you on this," his teacher, Mr. Bethel, said, holding Todd's graded exam out to him. Todd was so deep in thought, he hadn't realized his teacher had probably been standing over him for quite a while.

He glanced at the exam. He'd gotten a C-. Todd was pleased. His teacher clearly wasn't.

"You left three questions blank, Todd. Answering just two of those correctly would have given you an A-" Mr. Bethel was clearly disappointed in him, but Todd didn't care. He was officially done with the class now and wanted to focus on what he considered more important matters. Like his letter to Amani.

"So! Let's see what was drawing your focus away from your final, shall we, Mr. Glass?" Mr. Bethel commented. He snatched Todd's letter and began reading it out loud.

"*Amani,*" he began. "My my, Mr. Glass, she has a very exotic name. But you should capitalize the 'a' at the beginning.'" He continued, "*Words cannot express the desire I have to get to know more about you.* Interesting, Mr. Glass," Mr. Bethel teased. "Our Todd here is reaching out to a mystery woman."

As he resumed reading the letter, Todd sank low in his chair. Expressing his thoughts and emotions was hard enough for him. Having them shared with his classmates was tortuous.

"*Who knew that after only a few spoken words and stolen glances that I would fall completely head over heels in love with you,*" the teacher read.

"You Simp!" shouted out one of his male classmates.

"Shut up, Brad," a female student retorted from the other side of the room. "I think it's sweet that he's sensitive enough to express his feelings for this girl."

Sensitive? Todd sulked. That's not what I was going for. He was going for romance.

"*Just a smile from you*," the teacher continued, "*would melt my cold heart and make me see the world with so much more color.* What are you trying to say here, Mr. Glass, the teacher asked.

"He's saying he's whipped," replied a male student. All the other guys burst out laughing while the girls seemed annoyed by their immaturity. Todd covered his head with his hands, embarrassed beyond belief.

"I think he's saying he sees beauty all around now that her presence has opened his heart," one girl chimed in.

"I think so, too," another girl agreed.

"I think he's saying he's a dork," one of the guys joked. "Women want a man to take charge," he continued. To tell them what they want, and to tell them where to go."

"And *that's* why you're single, Clarence," a girl snapped from the back of the room. "Todd," she began, "tell her that her smile is the light that illuminates all the joys in your life.

"Honestly," Todd said, "I heard it in a song. I've been gathering song lyrics and mashed them together to make her feel special."

"My boy's gonna get laaaiiiid!" cheered Brad. The boys in the class high-fived each other while the girls called them pigs and dogs.

"Is that all guys think about?!" yelled one of the girls.

Renee, the head cheerleader and Todd's crush since middle school, walked up to Todd. "I think it's sweet that you're writing a love letter to this girl. Listen to the girls in class; we have more in common with your crush than these single dogs do. Plus, they need to learn that a man showing his sensitive side demonstrates inner strength. I wish someone would write me one," she added.

This felt like a smack in the face to Todd since he *had* sent her heart grams for Valentine's Day. For three years in a row!

"Just tell her how she makes you feel," she continued. "Use words from your heart, not from the radio. Tell her how you'd like to get to know her better and you'll be okay," she concluded.

Todd took her words to heart and tore the letter up when his teacher gave it back to him. He was going to start over with *his* words, not ones from old Motown songs. What is a sugar pie honey bunch, anyway, he thought as he read part of the letter.

At lunch, Todd headed to the library for peace and quiet so he could write. .

    Dear Amani,

He made sure he capitalized her name this time.

> *I fell in love with you the instant I laid eyes on you. I have been blessed just to be in your presence. My heart has finally found who it's been searching for. It only beats for you and has been in a constant flutter as it waits to see you again. I never knew such beauty existed before I laid eyes on you. And while you **are** incredibly beautiful, there's more to you than that. I will pray to every god, make a wish upon every falling star, and pack my pockets with four leaf clovers as I hope for the chance to see you again. I pray you will honor me with the privilege of getting to know everything about you. Until that day. I will see you in my dreams.*
>
>   *Sincerely,*
>   *Todd*

Taking Renee's advice had been a great idea, and Todd was pleased with the letter he'd written. He hurried through the halls, trying to catch Dave before his lunchtime. He wanted to ask him to ask Sasha to deliver his note to Amani.

When he finally found Dave and handed him the note, Dave began to read. A confused look appeared on his face, and his lips twisted into a kind of contemptuous smile.

"You sure you want to give this corny shit to her?" he asked.

"Definitely," Todd replied. "Why wouldn't I?"

"It's sappy!" Dave answered. "You should tell her how hot she looked," he continued. "This reads like you're trying to get a job with Hallmark," he teased. "What even is this shit? Your heart's in a flutter? That is so lame, dude."

"Please," Todd pleaded. "Just give this to Sasha to deliver to Amani."

Dave put the note in his pocket, said "Okay," and walked off. Todd felt guilty for not sharing Dave's sorrow over Sasha not having any interest in a relationship with him – misery loves company, after all – but he was too thrilled that his note would finally be in Amani's elegant hands.

The rest of the day was a blur. Another mediocre result from a final exam, and another lecture from a teacher disappointed that he wasn't reaching his full potential. Then P.E. – a class Todd called recess for upperclassmen – and then Speech. Todd had given his speech earlier in the week, so today's assignment was trying to stay awake for 55 minutes as his classmates took their turns.

As he sat there listening to his peers drone on and on, Todd daydreamed that he was spending time with Amani. He fantasized about going to the movies, having picnics in the park, and making out. When the dismissal bell rang, it was time for him to go home and repair everything he'd destroyed that morning. And he had to do it before anyone else got home, most importantly his sister. She was always on the lookout for ways Todd had messed up. It was how she made her money, by blackmailing him. And since Todd messed up all the time, business was good. But no matter how much he paid her, his parents still found out about whatever it was he'd done. Todd often wondered if she was playing both sides. He suspected his parents were paying her more to snitch.

The bus ride home was peaceful. Todd wondered if Dave had been able to deliver his note to Sasha. He wasn't on the bus to ask, though, since Dave and the track team were heading out of town for a meet. The closer Todd got home, the more anxious he became. He had two issues, and both were pressing. One was returning his father's shirt back to his closet with a repaired snag. Two was removing any evidence that he almost burned down the house trying to use the microwave as a dryer.

As he entered the house, Todd could still smell the odor of metal burning. Removing his dad's shirt, he quickly rummaged through the refrigerator and cabinets for a lemon and some vinegar. Thankfully, his mom kept both in the house at all times: the lemon to fight colds, and vinegar for cleaning. Todd had ten minutes to fix everything before his sister's bus dropped her off.

He quickly filled a bowl with water, vinegar, and lemon juice. He placed it in the microwave and turned it on for five minutes. He then ran upstairs with his dad's shirt. He rifled through his mom's sewing kit, and found a needle and a needle threader. He pushed the wire loop through the wrong side of the fabric near the snag. Then, he threaded the snag through the wire loop, pulling it carefully back through.

"Success!" he cheered, putting the shirt back in his dad's side of the closet. Todd had criticized his school for forcing students to learn how to sew and crochet. He deemed it a waste of time. Now he praised them for helping him obtain this very practical life skill.

At that moment, he heard the microwave ding. He sprinted down the stairs and grabbed baking soda out of the pantry, sprinkling it onto the surface of the microwave. With a little elbow grease, he was able to erase all evidence of the messes he'd made. He was grateful for the tricks he'd learned from his weekend cooking job.

"What did you *DO*?" he heard Tiffany ask accusingly. Todd was startled; he hadn't heard her come in. The Ninja that she was, Tiffany had mastered the art of popping up silently and catching Todd doing things he shouldn't be doing like sneaking girls in the house and hiding bad report cards, just to name a few.

"I didn't do anything," Todd replied.

"There's no scenario in this universe in which we come home to a lemon-scented house because you felt the need to randomly clean something," Tiffany said. She looked around the room, eyes widening. "Lemons, vinegar, and baking soda," she said. "Hmmm. I bet you destroyed something and are trying to cover it up. I hope I'm there when you get caught. I've always wanted to be an only child!"

Chapter 5

Sprinting through the loading dock of the Plaza Mall, Todd had less than two minutes to clock in for work. Like most things in his life, he didn't take his job as a short order cook seriously; his parents had made him get a job as soon as he turned sixteen. Their reasoning was that it would teach Todd responsibility. Mostly financial responsibility. But Todd hadn't learned the lesson; he wasted all his money on who knows what and had nothing to show for it. Todd thought of having a job at sixteen as a punishment. And it was all because of his dad.

His dad had a job when he was 16, too, and Todd always thought he'd needed one to help feed his family, though that notion likely came more from the way things were portrayed on TV than reality. His dad was always droning on and on and on to him and Tiffany about all the jobs he'd had when he was young. He made it seem like there must have been more than 24 hours in the "good ol' days" because he was able to take care of all his chores, work several jobs, and easily handle all his other responsibilities, too. Based on the endless stories he'd told, Todd imagined his dad waking before the sun, plucking the cows and milking the chickens at the same time he delivered newspapers and helped Todd's grandfather at his garage.

"The early bird gets the worm!" he'd always say, to which Tiffany would usually respond, "The early worm usually gets eaten or winds up in the night owl's tequila." Their dad would ignore her and reiterate how, as a youth, he'd chop down trees, use the wood to build furniture, and save burning buildings from babies, all while never missing an assignment and maintaining a 4.0 GPA. Or something like that.

Todd almost never focused on the things his dad had to say about life when he was young. During the school year, Todd worked only on the weekends, a rule his parents insisted on so that work wouldn't interfere with school. The summer months were different; Todd worked whenever he could.

Green Leaf Kitchen was a small franchise of casual dining restaurants. There were fewer than ten across the country, all modeled after restaurants like Denny's, Big Boy's, and Shoney's, and located next to or attached to a large pharmacy chain. Their specialty was cheap breakfast- and hamburger-type fare. But unlike their more well-developed counterparts, their success came from their strawberry pies and coldest draft beers.

In the two years Todd had worked there, most of the other chains in the fleet had sold their properties to independent owners or just closed. When Todd started working there, one of his responsibilities was frosting the beer mugs. He never quite understood how a frosty mug made the beer better or made it cost an extra dollar, especially since the frozen glass created more foam and forced more beer down the drain. And no matter how much the owners spent on advertising, patrons were still few and far between. It was Green Leaf Kitchen's identity crisis that kept customers away. The ambiance was a mix of a luncheonette and an old steakhouse. One section had stools and a countertop, similar to an old soda fountain shoppe. It was bright and vibrant there, and was located near the front of the restaurant. And while the owners were trying to capture the feeling of wholesomeness of yesteryear, it was the nineties now; kids today thought the decor too old fashioned.

The rest of the restaurant had a steakhouse feel (without the steak). Dark cherry wood was all over the place, the lights were kept dim, and soft rock played over the PA system, giving everything a haunted library ambiance. The entrance featured a giant glass window, perfect for passersby to see how empty and boring the interior was. There was no natural light since the restaurant was placed in the middle of the mall, and the carpet was a burnt orange color. This, combined with the light peanut butter-colored, faux leather booths created a fairly nauseating 70s and 80s feel.

The kitchen was open and gave patrons a partial view of their meal being prepared. Todd would often create an exaggerated flame on the small grill when diners ordered something grilled to create the illusion that their meal was being grilled to perfection. In reality, many of the cooks used the flat iron stove and then used the grill to score the meat so it had the *look* of having been grilled.

The owners were conflicted as to who they wanted their customer base to be. In the morning, they were frequented by senior citizen mall walkers. Many of them were regulars who only wanted coffee and conversation, since they were on a fixed income. Not very profitable, and they created the illusion that the restaurant was a happening place to be… for old people. Most of the mall patrons were teenagers. Besides several department stores, the majority of the stores targeted teens. And while these teens were in school throughout the day, Green Leaf's only patrons were mall employees on a quick lunch break. In the evening, the restaurant tried to cater to families. The only problem was families didn't visit the malls together anymore. After the sun went down, the Plaza was crowded with teenagers. Todd called them mall orphans. Parents would "abandon" their kids for a couple hours to do whatever they needed and would pick them up right before the mall closed.

In contrast to the restaurant, the mall played trendy music over its PA system. There was natural light and plants during the day and even trendier music and neon lights at night. All this made Green Leaf Kitchen look even more like a fish out of water to potential diners. Teens wanted to eat finger foods that they could take with them and be seen by whichever cool kids were there, not eating a sit-down meal hidden in a dark establishment. Todd often thought about suggesting to the owners that they play trendier music, improve their lighting, and alter their menu to attract a younger audience, but he'd never actually done it.

The current menu featured meatloaf; liver and onions; and smothered, open-face sandwiches to go along with the burgers and breakfast items. Todd had never heard anyone under the age of forty ask for liver and onions. Before he started working at Green Leaf Kitchen, he had never heard of an open-face sandwich. To him, it was just a meal on top of soggy bread. With these kinds of items, Todd could see why no one his age was tearing down the doors to eat there. Even the breakfast items churned Todd's stomach. The pancake batter was left sitting out in the hot kitchen all day, requiring him to stir it every fifteen minutes to break up the crust that would form on top.

Todd always stopped short of presenting his suggestions because he liked the slow, easy pace. Green Leaf Kitchen was usually as quiet as an empty church, and Todd liked it that way. Easy money. He didn't mind earning his $3.85 an hour sitting on his butt. Plus he didn't want anyone he knew seeing him dressed up in a greasy white collared shirt, greasy black slacks, and even greasier shoes. Working at Green Leaf was like attending a social gathering for its employees. Students from different local high schools worked together, discussing what was going on in their worlds. They would discuss the latest trends, music, relationships, and sex.

Todd preferred working evenings. That was when the cool kids would work. Since he worked all day on Sunday he would start working with older, more veteran employees followed by the younger generation. He didn't mind the older coworkers; he just couldn't relate to them. They would give him what they saw as worldly advice, telling him stuff like 'If you want to be happy in life, make an ugly woman your life' and 'Don't worry about anything, it will all work out in the end.' Todd never listened. He wasn't about to take advice from someone thirty years older than him who worked in the same place he did. He did know, he didn't want to end up like them and often wondered how the older employees could support themselves, much less a family, on $3.85 an hour, plus tips. But without any concrete plans for his future, Todd was risking being stuck working at Green Leaf Kitchen forever.

When Todd started there, he'd just assumed his older coworkers worked there because they had zero ambition. But now with graduation rapidly approaching, he could see they were people who couldn't keep up as life passed them by. He was naive, and was just now beginning to see all the responsibilities adulthood brought with it.

The only advice Todd ever listened to came from the prep cook, Ms. Savannah. Ms. Savannah was a large woman with short curly hair. She looked like Mrs. Butterworth brought to life. She was in her late sixties, had been around and seen much. She'd worked at Green Leaf Kitchen since its inception and was like Todd's guru, in the loosest sense possible. Her words of wisdom and especially the colorful way she expressed them made sense to Todd. Ms. Savannah never just gave advice; she would make an observation and let Todd form his own opinion. She could be crude, and she didn't care who was around to listen or if her words were hurtful.

He vividly remembered Ms. Savannah calling one of their coworkers a trollop because of the outfit she wore to work. The outfit was modest for a teenager but would be questionable for anyone older than that, especially if they had any size to them.

Ms. Savannah told the coworker – in front of a small crowd, no less – that she knew better than to wear an outfit like hers out in public, that she looked like a lady of the night. She proceeded to tell the boys around, including Todd, to look out for women like her. "Not even a condom can keep you safe," she'd stated. "For a woman like her," she would tell Todd, "a condom was just a bridge for crabs." The image was now cemented in Todd's mind. Todd used to find the girl attractive, and may even have pursued a relationship with her until he noticed her regular trips to the pharmacy next door. And thanks to Ms. Savannah's trollop description, Todd absurdly assumed she was buying antibiotics and pregnancy tests.

The most insightful advice Ms. Savannah ever gave him was about respect. She would tell him to stop respecting those who don't respect you. If someone enters a room you're in, doesn't speak to you or they ask how you're doing, and leave before you can answer, they do not respect you and you should not respect them. Most of the time, Ms. Savannah's motives in the advice she'd give came from being a minority and from a place of concern for how others treated minorities. She never held back in her descriptions of non-minorities, and she usually made people so uncomfortable they found it easier to avoid her. Todd would also chuckle when Ms. Savannah would respond "Yes Sir, Massa sir", when asked to do any task outside those she usually did. She found it hilarious that her rhetoric made others feel uncomfortable. And while Todd knew her antics were disrespectful, they were funny! In moderation… He also knew their bosses (and other non-minorities) were worried she'd play the race card. With the civil unrest happening in California because of the Rodney King verdict, everyone was walking on eggshells when it came to race relations. Everyone except Ms.Savannah. Todd still didn't understand why the owners didn't fire her. Doing so would be uncomfortable for a couple minutes, but wouldn't it be worth it to be rid of the hassle of a disrespectful employee?

All the "controversy" notwithstanding, Todd took Ms. Savannah's advice to heart and used it daily. But he often wondered what happened to her to give her such a jaded view on life. Todd's dad used to tell him that people are who they are because either their minds have been broken or their hearts open. It was obvious Ms. Savannah was broken.

"How's it going?" asked Todd's boss Tim. But before Todd could respond, Tim was gone. So much for respect, Todd said to himself.

The owners – Rick and Tim – were complete opposites. Their operating styles were so vastly different that Todd often wondered how they managed to be business partners. Todd preferred Tim, an ambitious, friendly shister. He made lots of promises he couldn't deliver on, or would forget about. Todd wondered how much money he owed people because it was often how he started conversations. "Hi, Todd, do I owe you money?" was as likely to be his opening line than anything else. Todd wondered what would happen if he'd say, "Yes, you owe me money" sometime.

Mostly he liked Tim because he let his employees do – or, rather, get away with – whatever they wanted. Tim was tall and slender, and was always on the go. He had so many deals going and ideas germinating that Todd had to remind him of promises he'd made. The biggest of these was paying Todd under the table. Tim had approached Todd about the idea to hide business expenses from someone he owed money to. Todd didn't quite understand it. He just knew that no matter what he made each day, Tim would take two dollars out of it for what he called taxes if anybody asked. Todd knew it was suspicious, but it was far better than waiting every two weeks to get paid. Plus, Uncle Sam would take way more than two bucks so Todd was happy to oblige with his pay arrangement. This way he got paid daily.

Todd was not a fan of Rick's, the other owner, mostly because he took five dollars out of Todd's pay for taxes. Though both he and Tim were in their late thirties, Rick looked older. A lot older. And he was always stressed, mostly due to his many gambling debts. Rick mostly bet on the ponies but would gamble on anything from the Olympics to high school sports. Shorter and rounder than Tim, Rick tried cutting costs whenever he could, which often led to bigger problems. Once, thinking he might cut down on water costs from all the dishwashing they did, Rick replaced all the metal utensils with plastic ones. It worked for three hours until a plastic tine from a fork broke off in a customer's meatloaf and they swallowed it. Doing so impacted the customer's intestines and the lawsuit they brought was financially devastating. Thankfully for Rick and Tim, Buster Douglass knocked out Mike Tyson at 42 to one odds and Rick's winnings covered the financial constraints from the lawsuit.

Another difference: while Tim didn't mind his workers lounging around or goofing off when things were slow, Rick would not tolerate anyone sitting down. "If you're on the clock you'd better be cooking, serving, or cleaning," he would say. If he was paying you, he wanted to get his money's worth. The "Masta" Ms. Savannah referred to was mostly Rick. On days Todd worked with Rick, he always had a towel in his hand and pretended to be wiping something down at all times. He could not fathom how Rick never called him out for constantly wiping down the same spot when he would look in Todd's direction.

Thankfully, Tim was working tonight. Todd needed an easy shift after a stressful week of finals. But since he hadn't stressed over finals, he really just wanted to be lazy, gossip, hang out, and get paid.

Looks like a great crew tonight, he thought. The servers were Marla, and Anne, Josie was hosting, and Crystal was working the counter.

Marla was a single mother in her early twenties who was both sweet and funny. Her stories about her infant daughter added to Todd's disdain for having children. Ever.

Anne, a promiscuous lady in her late thirties, was trying to discover the fountain of youth through younger men. The younger men, mostly teens, didn't mind, they just wanted some action to brag to their friends about. In some states, dating minors she did would be considered illegal. She was the one Ms. Savannah had referred to as a trollop. Anne could turn any casual topic into a highly sexual one. Sometimes it was too over the top.

Josie, a sixteen-year-old cheerleader at a rival school, fit the stereotype of a ditzy blonde.

And Crystal, an eighteen-year-old Todd would describe as a rebel, despised Todd to a degree he didn't understand. But after seeing that she treated everyone the same way he just figured she hated life and wanted everyone to be as hateful as she was. Misery really does love company, he thought.

Kendrick was in the back on dishes. He seemed to idolize Todd. He played second base for a rival school and was always talking to him about techniques and stats. Todd never paid him any mind since his stats weren't comparable to Todd's and Kendrick's school record was abysmal. He did like Kendrick for his admiration of the game they both loved, though.

They all sat in a corner booth, enjoying food and drinks that Rick would have definitely charged them for. Everyone was laughing as they discussed various television shows and urban legends they'd heard about in school. Anne shared what she would do to each of them if given the opportunity, creeping them out in the process. And Marla brought up what her child pooped out – including its color – creeping Todd out.

Every now and again, a customer came in and interrupted their conversation. The crew groaned about having to get up and work, but would then sit back down and complain about what an inconvenience customers were.

This evening was a little different for a Friday evening in the spring. The flow of customers was light enough to not be considered busy but was too busy to be considered dead. Todd looked at the time on the clock in the kitchen. 8:02! An hour and a half left until we close, he thought, miffed that time was dragging so slowly. He began to clean up the kitchen. After two years of working there he knew the flow of traffic would be one or two customers looking for a dessert or appetizers followed by a couple of shoppers walking in to use the restrooms since Green Leaf's restrooms were considerably cleaner than the mall's. Then there'd be another lull. And then the night would end with someone – maybe a group – coming in at the last minute with a full order and would take their time leaving. Todd wasn't in a rush to do anything this evening; he just wanted to be anywhere but in the hot kitchen.

"Todd, you have a customer at table six here to see you," Crystal said.

Todd was confused. Who could possibly be there for him? He rarely told anyone where he worked because not only would they expect free food, but he also didn't think his job was cool enough to talk about. Not like the tennis shoe or clothing stores his peers would actually want to be seen in. Green Leaf Kitchen was so far off teens' radar that most of his classmates weren't aware that the Plaza even *had* a casual dining restaurant. Todd didn't understand how this was possible given how close it was to the main entrance.

The only people who might visit were usually his parents, mostly his dad to see if Todd was actually at work. A couple of times he hadn't been when he told his parents he was. But he doubted they would be visiting since they didn't visit the mall on the weekends. Too many mall orphans. It could be Tiffany, but she never wanted to be seen with Todd in public. He was a loser who cramped her style.

"Where's table six?" he asked. Frustrated that she'd had to learn the sections of the floor so why shouldn't everyone else, Crystal pointed in the direction of the table.

"She's cute," Marla chimed in.

Todd peeked his head around the corner to see who his cute visitor was. "Oh shit," he muttered. He crouched down so as not to be seen.

"What's his problem?" Josie asked.

"Some cutie came to visit him so he's acting like a wanted fugitive," Marla joked.

"That's the girl," Todd whispered. "That's her!" The trio of women had blank stares on their faces. "Cinderella!" he exclaimed.

"Ohhhh!" they answered in unison, glancing around the waitress station to grab another look at his guest. Earlier, Todd had asked them what would make his mystery woman run off like she did. As was typical of the group, they'd teased him with responses like her pumpkin was double parked or she had to get her glass slipper windexed. Only Crystal's had stung: that once she could see him in better lighting she ran away in fear.

Dropping to one knee as if he were in a football huddle devising a play, Todd gave them an abbreviated version of the same story they'd heard repeatedly already. "I met this girl named Amani. I told her I liked her. She ran off. I wrote her a letter, and now she's here and I look like shit!" he exclaimed.

"I'm glad she's here," Crystal began. "Maybe now you'll have more context to this story rather than the version I've heard six million times already," she said sarcastically with a roll of her eyes.

"If she came to see you, I don't think she cares what you look like," Marla reassured him.

"You look good enough to eat me, I mean eat," Anne joked, walking into the middle of the conversation. "What's going on?"

Todd was about to begin the rundown of his interactions with Amani when Crystal put her hand up to his face to silence him. "Please Todd," she started, "I can't hear you tell this lame ass story again. This is Green Leaf Kitchen, not some damn episode of *Melrose Place*. Stop trying to turn your boring ass life into a drama. News flash: we don't care. Just grow a pair already and talk to her!"

Standing upright, Todd brushed himself off and walked awkwardly toward table six.

"Hi, Todd," Amani said, her voice soft and flirtatious. Todd smiled goofily and said hello back, his voice cracking.

"What are you doing here?" he asked, confused.

"Wow," she replied, chuckling. "I got this letter from you from Sasha and felt like I should come say hello. But if you don't want me here…," she began feigning a rise from her seat.

"No, stay!" Todd responded quickly. "I mean, please stay," he mumbled, trying to make his voice deeper. Amani giggled sweetly. "I'm glad you're here," he continued. "I was just shocked you knew where I worked."

"I think your friend Dave told Sasha and Sasha told me. Have you met my sister Amna?" Amani asked, elbowing the girl sitting to her left.

"We've met," Amna said, appearing nervous.

"When?" Amani asked, confused.

"When Aisha speared him with her bike," Amna replied.

"Ugh. Don't remind me," Todd joked, rubbing his leg.

"We can't stay long," Amani said. "Abbas dropped us off to pick up a few things." Todd tried hard to keep his poker face on, but his blood began to boil as soon as she said her brother's name.

Sensing his displeasure, Amani tried making an excuse for him. "He's just very passionate and overprotective," she said. Todd ignored her.

"And your older sister?" he asked.

"She's just a bitch," offered Amna. In Todd's eyes, Abbas and Akilah were *both* asses.

"In our culture, women are subservient to men," Amani began. "We're seen as property. Possessions." Her voice was low, her tone somber. Todd could tell the subject saddened her. He hated that she felt she needed her to defend her siblings. "Akilah has been arranged to marry someone that she doesn't quite know, and it's affecting her…" she continued, then paused, clearing her throat as she tried to find the right word. "…mood," she concluded. "And Abbas," she paused again.

Todd could tell she cared deeply for him, but was constantly making excuses for the things he did. She took a deep breath and exhaled slowly before she spoke. The pain on her face broke Todd's heart. "It's frowned upon to have a man that is not part of our culture in our lives," she said finally. "It's seen as if that outside man is trying to control our culture's women, or lead them to stray from our way of life."

"I don't want to control you," Todd explained. "I just want to get to know you." The two locked eyes as a smile spread across their faces.

Amna rolled her eyes exaggeratedly then nervously excused herself from the table. Todd wasn't sure if she left to give him time alone with Amani or if it was something else. Timidly, her voice soft, as if she didn't want others to hear, she said, "I'm going to look out for Abbas." Good, thought Todd". Two's company, three's a crowd. Once she left, he and Amani quickly forgot she'd ever been there. They were lost in each other's eyes. They didn't need to say anything; their hearts said enough. The moment was perfect. Todd knew he should probably say something, but words escaped him. He didn't want to sound corny or cliché.

"I have to go," Amani said, and Todd wondered if she could hear his thoughts, if his failure to say something witty or romantic had made the moment uncomfortable. "I just wanted to say thank you for the kind words," she added.

Todd quickly placed his hand over hers. "I don't know how to say what I need to say," he started. "All I know is there's something about being with you that makes me feel whole. I feel like an empty vessel when you're not here. I know I just met you, but I feel like our souls have known each other for a lifetime and are electrified that they've found each other again" As Todd regurgitated song lyrics and lines from sappy rom-coms, he hoped he was touching Amani's heart. His hope was buoyed when Amani blushed.

"Wait here," he said, hopping up from his seat quickly, almost knocking it over. He made a mad dash for the kitchen just in time to grab the chicken breast off the flat stove. He threw it on the grill for a few seconds to allow the racks to score the meat.

After dowsing it with teriyaki sauce and a generous helping of sauteed onions and mushrooms, he added it to a plate of mashed potatoes and gravy and garnished the plate with a sprig of parsley. He set it on top of a metal shelf under a heat lamp and tapped the bell to let Anne know her order was up. Then he quickly ran to the back of the restaurant to a small break area and inspected himself in the mirror. He almost tripped over Kendrick, who'd clearly decided to take a late break and was now snoring loudly.

Running back through the dish washing area, he grabbed a fresh towel and sprayed himself with some water, wiping any remnants of kitchen grease off his face. As he hustled back through his work area he shoved a couple of sprigs of parsley into his mouth to freshen his breath, spitting them out before he got to the dining area.

No, no, no, he thought as he approached table six. All his coworkers were talking to Amani! This can't be good, he thought, approaching the group.

"Anne, your order is up," he said, hoping to clear the table of the unwanted guests.

"I guess it's time for us to go," Josie said as she and the others went back to their duties.

"Remember what I said!" Crystal snapped, giving Amani an I-have-my-eyes-on-you gesture as she exited.

"Sorry about that," Todd apologized.

"Oh it's okay," Amani replied. "I had a wonderful conversation with your friends."

"I can only imagine what they said," Todd replied sarcastically.

"They were telling me how wonderful a person you are," she said, this time placing *her* hands on top of Todd's.

Todd turned in the direction of his coworkers as they quickly ducked behind the counter. Though the job wasn't going to sustain him for life, Todd shuddered to think of the day he had to quit. The job itself was mundane and tedious. Todd could not see himself affording the lifestyle to which he'd become accustomed by working for Green Leaf Kitchen, but the people made the work fulfilling. He would definitely miss the people the most.

"Oh," Amani interrupted, "Your friend with the jet black hair threatened my life if I ever break your heart." Todd was shocked. He never knew Crystal liked him, let alone would come to his aide.

"So let's not put our lives in jeopardy," he started. "How about you allow me the pleasure of taking you on a real date. Not here," he added quickly, "I know the cook." The customer who'd just received their smothered chicken glanced at Todd suspiciously before taking a bite of his food.

"Me dating outside my culture could be dangerous," Amani warned. "I can get in a lot of trouble just talking to you right now."

Todd didn't understand. "We're just talking," he said.

"Me running off to meet a boy like this could be disastrous. You think my brother is bad? He's a teddy bear. My dad is a million times worse," she said.

"I'm willing to take the chance," Todd replied, brushing off her warning. "I'm assuming I can't call you, but you can call me anytime," he added. Then he quickly jumped up and ran toward the waitress station as Amna came back to the table.

"Abbas is here," she told Amani. Todd scribbled his number down on a napkin. As he returned to the table to give it to Amani, he was alarmed to see a look of fear on both their faces.

"Abbas?" he asked. They didn't have to answer. He could tell by their body language. "Call me?" he asked.

Fascinated As if she were turned on by the hint of danger, Amani sat in silent, hard thought.

"Please," Todd begged her.

"Okay," she replied hesitantly, her face still full of fear. "It'll be later tonight," she added. Probably after midnight. I don't want to disturb your household, though…" she started.

"Don't you worry about that," Todd replied. "I'll wait for your call." He was worried about her calling so late at night and disturbing his parents and Tiffany, but it was a risk he was willing to take.

Amani got up from her seat and threw her arms around Todd, much to Amna's consternation. She was dismayed that her sister would display affection in public with her brother lurking around the mall somewhere. Todd tried to pull away from the embrace, not because he didn't want it, but because of his greasy appearance.

Amani ignored his attempt to extract himself – and the grease – and pulled him closer. Todd could feel life's stresses leave his body. If he died right then and there it would have been a life well-lived. He could hear the clandestine sounds of acceptance and approval from the waitress station. Everyone except Crystal.

"It's only a hug, people!" she exclaimed.

"A hug leads to sex!" Anne cheered.

"Yes, but sex leads to a baby," Marla chimed in.

"Let's go," a nervous Amna said. "You're going to get us killed." She and Amani hurriedly exited the restaurant just as Abbas neared its entrance. Todd watched as he forcefully grabbed his sisters' arms, practically yanking them off their feet. Todd clenched his fists and headed into the mall to come to their aid.

"Stop!" Josie demanded, stepping in front of Todd and blocking his path. For the first time since they'd started working together she did not have a smile on her face. She was apprehensive, concerned.

"This is a family matter," she said. "Let them work out their own issues. Plus, I know him. Well… I know *of* him. He's not someone whose bad side you want to be on."

It took every ounce of Todd's resolve not to run up to Abbas and punch him in the back of the head. He watched helplessly as Abbas dragged his sisters out the door. He was beginning to understand that Amna wasn't kidding when she said they could be killed for associating with someone outside their culture and was concerned by the fact that no one seemed to care about what he'd just seen. Gone were the days of white knights rescuing damsels in distress. Then again, with a guy like Abbas, interfering would not be as simple as slaying a dragon. Maybe this was a premonition. No matter what happened between Amani and Todd, no one was going to come to their rescue.

Chapter 6

Todd rushed home after work. Usually, he and his coworkers would join other mall employees in the parking lot to decompress and to try and one up each other with stories of unruly customers. These sessions tended to last a while and could probably go through the night, but Public Safety usually ran them off after an hour or so, not because a bunch of teens were gathering peacefully, but because someone usually started drinking and smoking. And although the allure of traveling down the rabbit hole that were stories of working retail was tempting, Todd wanted to be sure he was home well in advance of Amani's possible call.

He wished he had his own phone line so he could receive phone calls at any time. His parents didn't allow phone calls after 9 PM during the week and 10 PM on weekends.
As he showered, Todd wondered how he could field a call from Amani without disturbing his family. With his parents already in bed, it was too late to turn the ringer off on the phone in his parents' room. And although Todd had quick reflexes, he knew

they weren't fast enough to answer the phone without his parents hearing anything. His fear wasn't the call waking his parents up, it was what they would do once they were awakened. They'd threatened both he and Tiffany before about enforcing their phone rules. And they'd embarrassed both of them by answering calls that came in after 9 by saying, "Todd and Tiffany aren't allowed phone calls after 9. Do not call back" and then hanging up. This was social homicide for a teenager. An embarrassment like that would fly around school like wildfire and die a slow, painful death. Tiffany had been devastated when it happened to her. She'd walked around for days asking "How could you do that to me?" Their mom had replied unapologetically, "If you won't respect the rules, I'll enforce them."

Finally, Todd had an idea. Moviefone! he thought excitedly. I'll just call Moviefone! When Amani calls, call waiting will alert me. I'll just click over to answer her call and no one in the house will be the wiser.

He ran downstairs to the family room, grabbed the yellow pages to find Moviefone's number and dialed.

"Hello! And welcome to Moviefone!" the automated greeting said. Todd was just as excited as the guy who'd done the recording. His plan to receive a call from Amani without disturbing anyone seemed poised to work!

For what seemed like hours, Todd listened to the automated voice excitedly rattle off descriptions and showtimes for *Aliens 3*, *Sister Act*, *Reservoir Dogs*, and *Encino Man*. After hearing the same information several times, Todd was able to recite the Moviefone greeting, each movie description, and their respective showtimes verbatim as well as the directions to the theater and hours of operation. He turned on the TV to break the monotony of the recording. It was past midnight now, and many of the local television stations went static between midnight and 2 AM. The very few cable stations that had content mostly showed news 24 hours a day, infomercials featuring beauty breakthroughs, or holiday club vacation advertisements. Todd settled on a station showing a film about avengers who fell in toxic waste. The low-budget film was bookended by in-studio comedy skits featuring the show's overly-obnoxious hosts yelling "USA Up All Night."

When he started drifting in and out of consciousness Todd finally decided to hang it up. Literally. It was 3 AM. If Amani had had plans to call Todd, he assumed she either fell asleep or had second thoughts.

Just as he sat up on the couch and began looking for the phone's cradle, Todd heard the faint tone of another call beeping through. He bolted upright, cleared his throat, and fixed his face as if the person on the other end could see him. Clicking over to the other line, Todd said "Hello?" in his manliest voice. He could barely hear whoever was on the other end, but recognized the faint whisper as Amani's. She sounded nervous. Todd knew calling him was a big risk for her, and he greatly appreciated it. Even if she hung up at that very moment, Todd would say it was worth staying up all night just to hear her voice.

"I'm sorry to call so late," she apologized.

"No need to apologize!" he replied, "I'm thrilled that you did." He then told her about his MovieFone idea and the hours he'd spent listening to the automated messages.

"It must have been excruciating listening to the same information over and over again," she said.

"I'd do worse to have a chance to talk to you," Todd replied. "Like listening to Time and Temperature," he teased. They chuckled, and then there was a long pause. Neither knew what to say. They didn't have mutual friends, they went to different schools, and they'd only happened to meet each other by chance. Neither wanted to ask the usual, awkward "getting to know you" questions.

To break the silence, Todd reached for one of his sister's *Seventeen* magazines and started asking Amani questions from that month's quiz about how sun safe you are. He continued reading the "Hot talk, Cool talk" and "Relation" sections. The snippets led to more open discussions about life and their future. Once the conversation got started it flowed naturally. Todd looked up and saw the sun rising.

"Oh my goodness! The sun's coming up! I guess time *does* fly when you're having fun!"

"I need to get off the phone," Amani said. "My father and brother will be getting ready for work and I can't get caught on the phone with a boy. I love talking to you, Todd, but this has to be the last conversation we have."

"What? Wait!" Todd cried, confused. He racked his brain trying to come up with reasons why she shouldn't cut him out of her life. "You come into my life, you leave abruptly, then you come back again but leave just as quickly." Todd wasn't just confused; he was hurt. "What is happening?" he asked. "I thought we were having a great conversation. I think we have wonderful chemistry," he argued.

Amani took a deep breath and began to weep softly. "My family left our home country to escape the violent persecution of our family's religious and cultural beliefs. We chose America, a land supposedly founded on the right to freely practice religious culture, but we've been met with hostility and hatred. My brother took matters into his own hands and brought a gun to our old school because he felt the lessons the teacher taught ridiculed him. My father's goal now is to adhere to our beliefs and values regardless of what others around us say. He's very strict. Some outsiders would say he's an extremist, especially in his views about women."

She paused for a moment to gather her thoughts. Todd could tell she was upset. When she continued, her tone changed from a soft whisper to a loud one. "Ironically, him having five girls has been a curse. Imagine being me. Try living in a society where women are seen as the equal to men, but being raised in a home where we have to be subservient to them. And not just the two that live in my house, but *all* men. It's a curse to me. I see my friends' moms free to do and be who they want while I watch my mom being treated like my dad's and brother's slave. I can't say either way is wrong because religious truth is up to the believer. I just wish I was allowed to live my life and choose my own path. I love my dad and brother, but I do not like them. Todd, you have the luxury of dating anyone you desire. My life will be arranged for me by my dad."

"Amani," Todd interrupted, "If I can't date you then we're in the same situation." As soon as he said it, he instantly regretted it. He was trying to be cute, but she was being deadly serious.

"How do you figure?" she snapped. She was obviously upset. Todd knew their situations were not the same, but he was determined to figure out a way to be with this girl. "What can I do so that your dad will accept me?" he asked, trying to move past his previous statement.

Without hesitation, Amani answered, "Be born a Muslim."

"Amani, I'm willing to do whatever it takes for as long as it takes to be with you. Besides, what's the worst thing that can happen if we date?" Todd asked.

"Death!" Amani cried starkly.

"Sounds a little extreme," Todd replied sarcastically.

"They're called honor killings," Amani snapped, upset that Todd was making light of everything she was telling him. "They're real, and they're a part of many cultures around the globe. Men like my father and brother are willing to kill to protect their dignity and honor and that of their families. So Todd," she concluded matter-of-factly, "They will kill you, me, and anyone else they believe has brought shame to their family. Are you willing to die for me?" She was in tears, and Todd could hear the pain in her voice, how emotionally exhausted she was discussing her life in the US.

"As much as I love the prospect of having a loving relationship with you, Todd, I don't think you understand the risk involved. You seem nice. And I'm extremely attracted to you. I think about you all the time. Your note melted my heart. It captured how I wish people could see me. I'm just not willing to jeopardize my life for anyone."

"Keep it down!" came a voice from somewhere behind Amani, and then the line went dead.

Amani's question echoed in Todd's head as he held the receiver in his hands. It was a lot to take in. Was he willing to die for anyone? His life was just beginning; he wasn't ready for it to come to an end. The dial tone broke Todd's concentration. He was exhausted. He contemplated going to sleep – he had to be at work at noon – but it was Saturday. Cleaning day. He thought about doing his share of the work and then hitting the sheets for a couple hours, but he knew he wouldn't be able to sleep after being told that there was no chance for him and Amani to be a couple. Just as he was getting used to being told he couldn't date someone based on his color he was being told he couldn't date someone because he wasn't Muslim.

It was ironic to him that growing up, he was forced to say the Pledge of Allegiance every day in elementary school. Children all over the country pledged that they would be one nation under God, indivisible. But as he grew older, he realized that wasn't the case. The older he got, the more divisible he saw how this nation – this world – really was.

Chapter 7

Todd's alarm screamed, echoing throughout his room. The day he'd anxiously awaited since kindergarten was finally here. The week leading up to what was supposed to be his big day had been a blur. Senior pranks, obligatory goodbyes, and yearbook signings were all distractions from the last minute tasks his parents needed done for the family coming in for his graduation ceremony. Todd had been tasked with mopping, waxing, and shampooing every surface of flooring in the house. Dusting and disinfecting every surface was Tiffany's duty. Todd silently protested having to clean. After all, he was the guest of honor. They should be cleaning up for him. He would never share his thoughts with his parents, though, for fear that he'd sound ungrateful, especially with his grandparents, aunts, uncles, and cousins traveling such a long way.

His older relatives were ecstatic to see the eldest of their younger generation graduate from high school. All week, Todd had observed his classmates become emotional over their last of every high school experience. They'd cried over their last school lunch, their last test, their last classes. None of it had affected Todd; he hadn't shed a tear. Not even the end of his high school baseball experience made him cry. The only thing that might have brought him to tears was having to do it all over again.

Everyone would be arriving soon. Todd had just enough time to get dressed and go get a haircut before he had to entertain his family. Since no one except him, his parents, and Tiffany lived less than six hours away, seeing them was usually exciting. Until now. He dreaded the questions he knew they'd ask about his future. He knew it was inevitable that someone would ask where he was going to college. His response was more than likely going to be community college. His procrastination left him very little choice for anything else.

"Todd! Get up!" his mom yelled from downstairs.

Let the fun begin! Todd thought, forcing himself out of bed.

"Didn't I tell you to make sure you took your slacks and shirt to the cleaners?" his mom asked. With all the other details he'd been attending to, Todd had completely forgotten. He didn't know how to respond; his parents already knew the answers to any question they asked, anyway.

"I decided to iron them myself," he said.

"Oh that makes sense," his dad replied. "I was wondering why they were balled up in the back of your car." Todd was grateful his dad had said that, mostly because he had no clue where he'd left them.

"I'll iron them when I get back from getting my hair cut."

"No," his dad interrupted. "When you get home you're cutting the grass. I shouldn't have to tell you this every week!"

"You're right," Todd said. "I gotta go. You know how crowded barbershops get."

"It's Friday," Tiffany said as she made her way out the door for her last day of school. "It won't be that busy."

"Enjoy school!" Todd teased. Their school district allowed seniors to finish three days ahead of everyone else. Todd didn't know why. Maybe it was so they could welcome out-of-town guests who were coming for graduation? Or maybe it was so they could decompress a bit after struggling through thirteen years of school. Either way, it was the best part of being a senior and Todd loved rubbing it in Tiffany's face.

"I have a great idea," their mom began. "Why don't you drive your sister to school?"

"Why can't she take the bus?" Todd whined. He knew he was overstepping his boundaries, but he was pretty sure she wouldn't kill him since his grandparents were arriving in a couple hours. Or so he hoped.

His mom shot him a look. "I don't know where you're going to be this fall, but it won't be here," she said. "You two need to spend some time together."

"Why?" complained Tiffany. "Fourteen years is long enough."

"When your mom and I are no longer here, it'll be just the two of you," their dad added. "I know you think he ain't shit at times, but he'll be all you've got."

Todd considered his dad's comment. He imagined him and his sister in the nursing home together playing pinochle and reminiscing about their childhood. Two siblings who didn't get along when they were young but we're best friends now.

"If he's all I have left when you two are gone, then I failed in life," Tiffany said. "Take me with you!" she teased. "I'll take the plot next to yours. I plan to get married and have kids," she continued. "The whole nine yards. As far as this loser is concerned, I'll swing by whatever street corner he's panhandling on and give him some spare change."

"Make it a dollar," their mom teased.

"Let's go, you little brat," Todd said. "I'd hate for you to be late."

After dropping his sister off at school, Todd hurried to the barbershop. His sister was right. The scene was completely different during the week. Most Saturdays it was a madhouse with patrons of all ages trying to get a haircut to look good for a night out or for the upcoming week. Amid the chaos you could hear conversations about local sports teams, relationships, fashion, personal experiences, money, music, and food. Everyone had an opinion and they were all conflicting. And since everyone wanted to be heard, they'd shout so everyone in the shop could enjoy what it was they had to say.

Depending on what time you got there, getting a haircut could be an all-day thing. Todd often wondered why barbers didn't use an appointment system like hair stylists did. The first-come, first-served business model didn't seem to work that well.

Today was different, though. There were three barbers there, and none of them were working. They were tidying up their work stations and preparing for the day. There were five customers inside, but they weren't really customers. For one thing, they were always there, and they never got a haircut or a shave. Three were bald and the other two were on their way to bald. In all the years Todd had been coming here, he never remembered any of the men having hair, or enough of it to warrant getting a haircut. They were just there for the free coffee and an audience for their soapbox rants. Today they were discussing their predictions for the NBA finals. Jordan versus Drexler was the source of much debate.

Todd waited patiently by the door for his favorite barber to wave him in: Ms. Rose. Ms. Rose had been cutting his hair for as long as he could remember. This was the third shop he'd followed her to so she could keep cutting his hair. Ms. Rose was a small woman with a big personality. In a male-dominant field, her stature was gigantic. She was quick-witted with a fierce enough tongue to humble anyone who needed to be brought down a peg. She was barely five feet tall, and weighed just about one hundred pounds.

"Boy!" she snapped, noticing Todd standing at the door. "What are you doing out of school?"

"I graduate tonight," Todd answered. He stood and allowed the others their walks down memory lane: "I remember when you was yea high." "You can't be that old," and the like.

Ms. Rose looked Todd up and down, shaking her head in disbelief. "I don't buy it," she said. "You can't be old enough to graduate high school, because that means I'm a lot older than I tell people I am." Everyone in the shop chuckled. "What are your plans for the future?" she asked, placing the cutting cape around him.

Before he could answer, one of the older gentlemen began giving Todd advice. "You should go to college," he said. "You can't go too far without a degree nowadays."

"Nah… College is too hard," one of the others chimed in. "All you need is hands-on training somewhere."

"Too hard?" the first man asked. "Stupid people graduate from college every year. If they can do it, I'm sure he can."

"Join the Army," the third said. "Three hots and a cot!" he added.

"That's prison," the second man retorted.

"Either way, you're getting fed!" his companion replied.

"What do you want to be, young man?" the first gentleman asked.

"I have no idea," Todd answered.

"That's why you need the military, son," the third gentleman said. "They'll make a man out of you. If they can make penicillin out of moldy bread they can surely make something out of you!"

"Become a postal worker," the fifth man offered. The whole room erupted in laughter. "Fuck you!" he responded, hopping up to leave. Todd noticed he was wearing a postal worker's uniform and had a bandage wrapped around his leg. He had a very noticeable limp.

"Watch out for Kujo!" yelled one of the barbers.

"Kujo? He was probably bit by Benji." The room erupted in laughter again. And just like that, the group was on to another subject. They went from protecting themselves from a dog attack to wondering if they could knock a bear out with a bat. It never ceased to amaze Todd the insane range of topics discussed in the barbershop.

"All done, sweetie!" Ms. Rose said, handing Todd a mirror. He carefully inspected his haircut, though doing so was just a formality. Ms. Rose always did a fantastic job.

"I may not be the smartest person walking across the stage," he remarked, "but I'll look good doing it!" He paid Ms. Rose, thanked the men gathered for their clichéd congratulations, and headed home. He hoped for a thunderstorm that might wash away tonight's outdoor ceremony.

Chapter 8

"F through H, line up here" Todd's homeroom teacher directed. Mrs. Apple, Todd, and a group of fifty students lined up in alphabetical order outside an empty classroom. The graduating class was preparing for the ceremony in locations throughout the school. Todd marveled at how different the place felt in the evening. Maybe it was because 1500 other students weren't there. Or maybe it was the reality that this was officially the end of his public school journey. He was steps away from officially crossing over into adulthood, and he wasn't ready. Whatever the feeling was, being in the school now gave Todd a different vibe and made him feel uneasy. He did his best to ignore it as Mrs. Apple went over the itinerary for the ceremony:

"We will walk to the football field together in a single file line. You will all remain standing until the rest of your classmates are standing in front of their respective seats. Then we'll have the invocation. You all will remain standing during the playing of the *Star Spangled Banner*, then you'll sit to listen to a welcome speech by your class president, two poems by fellow students, an introduction of the faculty by your class vice president, a speech by this year's honored faculty member, the introduction of the choir by your class secretary, and then a performance of your class song." I didn't even know we *had* a class song, Todd thought. "After all that, your class treasurer will introduce the administration." Todd marveled at how there could be so many important players at his school that he'd never met or even heard of. Maybe he should have focused more in high school than he had.

The ceremony had yet to begin and Todd was already over it, but Mrs. Apple kept going. Principal Miller will then announce the class awards and scholarship winners. The presentation of your class colors, class flower, and the reading of your class motto will follow."

A motto, flowers, colors… How much did I miss these past four years? Todd wondered. He began to regret not being more active in high school but changed his mind when he thought about having to be an active participant in this ceremony that more than five hundred people were going to witness.

Taking a deep breath, Mrs. Apple continued with the evening's itinerary. "Your salutatorian and valedictorian will speak next, followed by the presentation of your class. That's when you'll receive your diplomas. The choir will sing *America the Beautiful* and your high school career will be complete!"

Is all this really necessary? Todd thought. He wasn't even outside yet and he was already sweating. He was wearing his black graduation robe, of course, and underneath it a cyan collared shirt and black slacks. His school's colors were black and gold and he wondered why they hadn't opted for robes in the lighter of the two colors. His only saving grace was the fact that the sun would set halfway through the ceremony.

"I would've been better off dropping out and getting my GED," joked the classmate he'd be sitting next to during the ceremony. Todd knew her name was Emily, and though they'd shared the same homeroom since junior high, he didn't know anything else about her. He didn't even know what her last name was, though it had to be close to his in the alphabet. This was the most interaction he'd ever had with her.

"It all seems a bit much," he replied.

"Just think of it as sitting through a movie that's entirely end credits," she joked.

"Let's go!" Mrs. Apple cried, clapping her hands. "Your audience awaits." Todd rolled his eyes at her enthusiasm. She was even more excited than the actual participants were!

As the graduating class of 1992 made its way to their seats they were met with a steady stream of applause. *Pomp and Circumstance* played on a continuous loop. The crowd of over a thousand joyous family members filled the stands. Rows of white plastic folding chairs were soon to be filled with his classmates. Todd strained to try and catch a glimpse of his family. He'd plastered an exaggerated smile on his face – one that showed his teeth – because his mom had threatened his life if he ruined any photo ops by the fact that he wasn't smiling.

"You've taken years of school pictures with no smile or with some stupid look on your face," she'd said. "My reward for getting you to graduation had better be a huge smile on your face. Or else," she'd warned.

When he was finally able to sit, Todd read and reread the graduation program that had been left on each seat. He tried to guess how long each portion of the ceremony would take. Though he had no real plans afterward, he was still in a hurry to finish.

"Are you going to the graduation lock-in?" Emily asked him. The lock-in was an indoor celebration for all the graduates where there would be a dj, a hypnotist, games, and swimming. Todd was still up in the air about being locked in a school he'd spent the past four years trying to get away from.

"I'm not sure," he answered. "Are you?" He couldn't have cared less about her answer. It wasn't like after four years of going to the same school they were going to become besties.

"Hell yeah, I'm going!" she replied. "I'm going to make out with my boyfriend under the bleachers and see what the boys locker room looks like." Todd chuckled.

Thirty minutes into the ceremony he was growing more and more restless. He had to sit perfectly still in his seat to keep the chair from sinking into the soft ground of the natural grass on the football field. He checked the program after each new speaker. He was bored stiff and wondered if this was what college lectures were going to be like. He hoped to heaven it wasn't because he hadn't paid attention to a single thing.

Finally, the valedictorian, Winthrop Andrews, was ready to give his speech. "Todd, is it?" Emily started.

"Yes. We've been in the same home room for six years," he said, slightly offended that she didn't know his name. Though if he saw her in a different setting besides school, he'd have no clue as to who she was. Emily brushed off Todd's little protest.

"*I* should have been asked to give the valedictorian speech," she whispered.

"Were you an honor student?" Todd asked, curious.

"Oh hell no!" she snorted. "Not even close. I just know I would have written a livelier speech than anyone up there. Plus mine wouldn't be so drawn out. They're just saying a lot of words that no one will remember or care about ten minutes later."

"Yeah. It makes no sense that a student with zero life experience is deemed qualified to give us advice on our futures," Todd agreed.

"Exactly!" Emily exclaimed. "See? He's telling us the key to success is individuality. It's bullshit to tell 500 17- and 18-year-olds who are all dressed the same to be an individual," Emily mockinged.

"Shhhh!" Mrs. Apple hissed.

"What?" Emily snapped back. "Are you going to give me detention? Drama teachers…" Emily said, rolling her eyes.

"If I were up there," she continued, "My speech would take thirty seconds. 'I would first like to thank the Funk and Wagnall Encyclopedia company, mostly for giving me something to read so I can give this speech today, while everyone else was off having fun." Todd laughed to himself since he didn't have a huge social life, either.

"Next, I would like to thank my arms for being by my side, my fingers to count on, and my feet for supporting me." She and Todd giggled as the valedictorian droned on.

Ten minutes later, Emily said, "I bet no one outside of his family could tell you a thing he said."

"Alright! It's time!" Mrs. Apple whispered. "Follow the row ahead of you!"

She is *way* too excited about all this, Todd thought. In the last four years, the only "connection" he'd had with Mrs. Apple was to collect his report card from her four times a year. He'd never heard anyone else mentioning having a connection with her, either, so he was truly baffled by how thrilled she seemed about all this.

As Todd neared the stage, little thoughts entered his head. What if he falls? What if he drops his diploma? What if no one besides his family cheers? He and Emily were almost there. As the announcer read the names of those ahead of him, Todd's stomach began to churn and his face flushed. He felt like he might pass out. He no longer was hot; he felt chills. A sandwich he'd eaten earlier burned his throat and he thought he might vomit. Todd had never been one to experience stage fright, but suddenly he'd developed a huge case of it. He took a deep breath.

"Here we go, Emily!" he said, trying to give her a boost of confidence and hoping she'd do the same for him. Instead, she turned toward him, shot him a hateful look, and mouthed the words "Fuck you" just as they announced the name Erica Glad. Embarrassment consumed him. Her name was *Erica*, not *Emily*! He couldn't believe he **didn't** know the name of someone he'd spent the past six years with in homeroom. Then again, his biggest concerns were not the names of the others in his homeroom but the failing marks on his report card.

"Todd Glass!" the announcer called. Todd froze, still preoccupied by the fact that he'd messed up Erica's name.

"Go!" the classmate behind him hissed, shoving him forward. Todd almost fell on his face right there. He was not accustomed to his new dress shoes. Not yet scuffed, they created a slick surface with each step on the stage floor. To keep from looking completely foolish, he did an impromptu pirouette. It was the only thing he could do to regain his composure from his classmates' slight shove. Todd walked up to Principal Miller, shook his hand, grabbed his diploma, and hurried off the stage. Nearly three quarters of the way down the steps, he stopped abruptly. He'd forgotten to smile! He froze; looked out into the crowd; flashed a big, fake smile; and walked off. Hopefully his family had gotten the pictures they wanted.

As he headed back to his seat, Todd kept the stupid grin on his face in an effort to prevent catching the ire of his mom. He knew his grandparents weren't going to save him this time because they, too, would want a picture with him smiling.

Erica was angled away from him when he reached his seat. Thankfully, the ceremony was almost over, but sitting next to a classmate he'd offended still wouldn't be pleasant. *Maybe she'll cool down by our ten-year reunion*, he thought.

Opening the diploma folder Dr. Miller had given him, Todd was shocked to find it empty. Panic filled him. Had he miscalculated his credits? Did he not graduate? Would his mom get another opportunity to take a picture of him smiling at next year's graduation?

"Hey! Mine is empty," Todd could hear a classmate complain.

"They give you the real thing after the ceremony so we don't mess it up out here" somebody else replied. When the announcer finished reading names and presented the graduating class of 1992, Todd tossed his cap in the air halfheartedly. It was over. This chapter of his life was finally over. He was officially a graduate. A true adult. And he wasn't ready. A graduate for only thirty seconds and Todd was ready to be a high school freshman all over again.

He saw his classmates celebrating all over the football field. They looked eager to start whatever the next phase of their lives would be. They appeared to have direction. Todd was lost. He wasn't ready to be an adult. He knew he should live his own life and stop trying to compare it to others, but it was hard not to when *every*one else appeared ready for the next step and he wasn't. Where do I even go to get my diploma? he wondered. Not only am I lost in life, I'm lost on this damn field. Am I the only one looking to leave? He felt alone. His family was there somewhere but hadn't found him yet. It was time for him to blaze his own path. His first move as a graduate? Find a bathroom. His nerves had wreaked havoc on his stomach and he had to poop.

Chapter 9

"Hey, graduate!" said a soft voice from behind. Not knowing the voice, and not expecting a greeting to be directed toward him, Todd ignored it and kept walking.

"Todd!" the voice yelled. Turning around he saw it was Sasha. Todd was disappointed to see she was alone. He half hoped Amani would be there, even though he hadn't heard from her since she hung up on him early in the morning.

"Hey, Sasha," Todd replied monotonously. He was still on his mission to find a bathroom and having a meaningless conversation with Sasha was delaying him. He was also still insulted by the way she'd made him and Dave feel like they were potential rapists and crooks the last time they'd been together. What right did she have to judge him?

"How's it feel to be free of this place?" she asked, not noticing how irritated Todd was.

Todd was hesitant to answer. He felt uneasy talking to her and feared every word would be scrutinized and judged. But he decided to be kind because his grandparents were there, and they thought he was an angel. He didn't want to disappoint them by being rude. He also felt uncomfortable talking to Dave's crush. Bro code #1 was never, *ever* talk to your friend's crush or ex. Especially a racist one. Though nothing was ever going to happen between him and Sasha, he didn't want someone to see them talking and start some rumor that they were in a relationship. "It feels good," he said. "I gotta go. You know. Family and pictures and stuff."

"I have a message for you," she said, stopping Todd as he tried walking past her. "Amani told me to tell you something," she continued.

Todd wasn't sure he wanted to hear whatever Amani had to say. She'd already cut him off twice, and her family is not only rude; they'd kill him if he got involved with her. My best bet, he thought, is to run far away from her, but, as usual, he was thinking with his heart and not his brain. Maybe I *should* hear her out, he thought irrationally. He didn't *really* want to cut Amani out of his life. What's wrong with just being friends? He longed for the euphoric feeling he got when she touched him. The memory of the chills he got from just being near her had been permanently etched into his soul. He was addicted. The high he experienced the moment he met her had him now and forever chasing the white dragon.

"Oh, alright," he sighed. "What's the message?"

Sasha could tell he was curious and took her time delivering the message, making sure to pause for effect. She smiled as Todd's eyes danced for the bit of information she had. "Amani told me to tell you she's sorry," she began. Her face twisted, pained that she was delivering an apology to someone she didn't like. It was clear she wasn't accustomed to saying the word 'sorry.' "She said she was scared because of the way you make her feel."

"Really?!" Todd asked, incredulously. He was confused. "Why run away from someone that shows interest in you? What else did she say?" he asked. That little message wasn't enough to warrant his playing the fool again for a girl who didn't know what she wanted.

"I don't know," Sasha replied. Her tone revealed that there was more to the message and that she was taunting him. She pulled a crumpled up note from her jeans pocket, and paused again for effect before opening it and reading: "I'm choosing to live in constant fear with you rather than constant regret without you." Sasha looked at Todd, trying to judge what he was feeling. Todd just stood there, confused and trying to decipher what the heck Amani was talking about. It finally dawned on him that she wanted a relationship.

"Have you caught up yet?" Sasha teased. Todd was embarrassed that it took him as long as it did to understand where Amani was going with her not, but, then again, he hadn't been expecting to hear from her at all. "She also said something about calling you tomorrow night because you have your lock-in tonight. And she said she expects a full recap of showtimes and descriptions." Todd chuckled as Sasha shrugged her shoulders, missing, of course, the inside joke.

Sasha suddenly appeared bored with the conversation as Todd's interest level began rising. She turned to leave, but Todd called out, "Wait'! Is that all she said?" he asked.

"Yes," Sasha answered abruptly.

Todd wondered how the conversation had actually gone. He was curious about the tone Amani had used as he imagined her telling Sasha what to say.

"There he is, Mom!" Todd heard Tiffany exclaim. In a matter of seconds, Todd was ambushed by his entire family, each of whom gathered him into a huge hug. Everyone but Tiffany. He was relieved that no one made mention of his spin or his missing smile.

"I'm so proud of you!" both his grandmothers said in unison.

"Now life begins," added his dad.

"...but don't take it too seriously because you'll never get out of it alive," joked one of his grandfathers.

"Go get your diploma and we'll meet you back at home before we head to dinner," his mom directed. Todd wondered how she knew he didn't have it yet.

After getting his diploma from the table staffed with secretaries and using the restroom, Todd felt lighter and full of energy. He couldn't tell if it was the bathroom break or the news about Amani. It could also be the dozens of congratulatory remarks he received from strangers as he'd made his way through the crowd moments earlier. Either way, he was thrilled to be a graduate. He felt a huge weight had been lifted off his shoulders, and as he stole a glance in the car window he found himself enamored with his appearance. He wanted to show it off. More than anything, he wanted more people to make a big deal about his moment. Todd liked the spotlight, and this was the perfect time for him to extend his fifteen minutes of fame.

He hopped in his car and headed for The Plaza. One quick pit stop, he told himself, then I'll head home. He pulled into a parking spot and decided, for once, to walk in through the front door. He actually *wanted* to be seen, gleaming in his accomplishment, a stark contrast to when he came to work. Todd walked directly to The Green Leaf Kitchen. As usual, the restaurant was empty and his co-workers were sitting in the corner booth chatting.

"Hey Todd! What's up?" Tim greeted him. He had already turned his back to Todd when he stopped and faced him again. "Did I forget to pay you?" he asked.

"No, I just stopped by to say hello," Todd said. He was talking to himself; Tim had already walked off. "What's up, guys?" Todd said to the others.

"Hey what's up?" they said, continuing their conversation. Todd was irked that no one made mention of the fact that he was wearing his graduation robe. He sat there listening to the group complain about work for a while before excusing himself to head home. He was disappointed.

I guess my dad was right, he told himself. His day would say, "Todd, people are selfish. They only care about themselves and don't have room for anyone else. So instead of chasing after selfish people's attention, take care of your own self." But Todd still felt defeated. He headed toward the door that led to the mall but stopped short of the exit and removed his graduation robe. I guess I look silly wearing my robe outside of graduation, he thought.

Todd headed back into the mall and toward the parking lot. Several teens ran past him. Something must be happening, he thought. Two things teens have a knack for: sensing when a fight is about to occur, and knowing when something is being given away for free. A fight, Todd realized, seeing a group of teens surrounding two men. He could hear the group cheer, the 'Oohh's' and 'Whoa's' as they hyped the combatants. Todd had been taught to stray away from fights that didn't involve him. His dad always used a cousin as an example of how an innocent bystander could lose their life by being in the wrong place at the wrong time.

In between breaks in the crowd, Todd recognized one of the assailants as Abbas and made his way toward the commotion. He had to see this. Sorry, Dad, he apologized silently.

To Todd's surprise, it appeared Abbas was the victim in the situation. The other guy was talking about Abbas' mom, his appearance, and his haircut. Then the guy shoved a finger in the middle of his forehead. Todd was stunned that Abbas just stood there and took it. Suddenly, Akilah appeared and pushed her way through the crowd. She grabbed Abbas and began dragging him away from the commotion as the crowd booed. His tormentor hurled one last insult, but Abbas still didn't react. Todd wouldn't have messed with the guy, either. He was over 6'5" and almost a hundred pounds heavier than Abbas. He looked like an NFL linebacker. One punch from him would cause some major damage.

Todd started to walk away when the linebacker called Abbas and Akilah camel jockeys. Abbas stopped, and everyone in the crowd grew silent. Todd could see fire in Abbas' eyes. He forced himself from Akilah's grasp but stood in place.

"That's right!," yelled the bully, "Let your bitch save your life. Or maybe she should leave with me so she can feel the power of a real man."

Abbas had had it. As he walked toward his aggressor, Todd heard Akilah scream. "No!!" Todd held his breath as he waited to hear what Abbas was going to say, but no words came out of Abbas' mouth. He let a vicious left hook do the talking and followed it with a peppering of punches to the guy's rib cage. A devastating haymaker dropped him.

Todd stood silently, thinking about what Abbas might have done to him the other night. His tormentor was lying motionless on the pavement. Todd was awestruck; the fight lasted less than ten seconds! Todd's dad had always told him not to hit a man when he's down and out. Apparently Abbas had been raised with different values because after he kicked the guy in the ribs several times, he jumped on top of him and pounded his face relentlessly. The crowd that had originally called for bloodshed, gasped in horror as each punch spilled more and more blood onto the ground. Some of the spectators cried while others walked away. Todd wanted to throw up. He felt he was witnessing what might become a murder if someone didn't step in soon. As if on cue, Todd heard the wails of mall security scooters approach.

The few spectators left scattered across the parking lot, hoping to avoid being questioned as witnesses. Todd stared in disbelief at the slab of meat that was left of the once-menacing instigator. Todd felt pity for him as he faded in and out of consciousness. For the second time since Todd had met them, Akilah had to drag her brother away to stop him from inflicting even more damage. Todd sent a silent thank you to Dave for sparing him the same fate as this guy. All he'd done was call Abbas names and insult his mother and his hair cut, Todd thought. Imagine what he could do to me if he caught me touching his sister. Amani's warning reverberated through him as he saw security yell over a walkie talkie for paramedics. He tried to convince himself that he'd fare better against Abbas, but knew he was kidding himself. Todd's fighting style was to swing wildly until he got tired and just hoped he landed a couple blows.

Todd watched in horror as security picked up a couple of the victim's teeth. Abbas was a brawler. His punches had direction and landed ferociously. Todd knew he needed to think seriously about taking Amani up on her offer of a relationship. His sisters and his faith were Abbas' obvious triggers. And it was a hair pin trigger at that.

As he turned to head back to his car, Todd glanced one last time at Abbas' victim, who was now being tended to by paramedics. As horrible as it had been to witness, he'd needed to see it. The man was terribly hurt and hadn't yet regained consciousness. Todd was conflicted as to whether he should stop and give a statement to security but decided not to get involved. Abbas knew who he was, and saying something to authorities might set him in Abbas' sights. He *definitely* didn't want that. But he was conflicted. "What if this was you?" he thought. "What if you were the one lying on the ground after having been beaten to a pulp? You'd want someone to say something to help catch who'd done it, wouldn't you?

Todd's good-natured side and the values he'd been raised with won. He threw the car in park and hopped out. He made his way back to the scene. The victim was conscious but was struggling to tell the police his side of the story. His face was severely swollen and jaw was definitely broken; he spit blood with every word he spoke. He looked like a bruised, split tomato. Todd felt nauseous.

When he got within earshot of the group attending to the victim he heard him tell the authorities he was attacked for catcalling his aggressor's sister. Todd glanced around and was shocked to see that Abbas hadn't left the parking lot. He was observing the scene from far away. Todd made eye contact with the officer who was jotting notes but never broke his stride. I don't need these problems, he told himself, deciding not to make a statement after all. I need to learn how to fight, he thought, turning around and heading back to his car. And I need to get home if I'm going to go to the lock-in later.

Chapter 10

"One last hurrah!" yelled Tony, a classmate of Todd's since Kindergarten. Todd hadn't been sure he wanted to go to the lock-in. On one hand, he felt like he should be there in case something memorable happened. He didn't want to be the one person who wasn't there when something happened that he'd want to see. On the other hand, he wanted to be around his grandfather from his father's side of the family.

His grandfather was a huge fan of baseball and helped develop Todd's passion for the game. When Todd visited him during the summer they would stay up and watch baseball on television and talk about the league. It was one activity Todd knew he would always cherish when he himself was old and sitting in a nursing home. Todd wasn't sure how many years his grandfather had left after recently being diagnosed with Alzheimer's disease. How long would he have until he could no longer remember Todd? Or anything else?

Todd hated that he didn't know his mom's father. He'd passed away when Todd was very young so he felt it very important to make memories with all his remaining grandparents while they were still here, especially since he knew they were the reason his parents hadn't killed him yet.

Watching a baseball game with his grandfather sounded better to Todd than going to the lock-in, but then each of his grandparents sat down to 'rest their eyes' when they all returned from dinner. His grandparents never slept. They were always just resting their eyes or checking their eyelids for cracks. But since their synchronized snoring said otherwise, Todd decided to go to the lock-in.

Ribbons, balloons in the shape of 1992, confetti, and generic student-made posters were on display at the front entrance of the building as Todd approached. Mrs. Apple was still extremely excited and greeted each person as they came in.

"The pool's open, students," she called, "And the hypnotist will be performing at midnight. Grab some food, put your name into the raffle, and have a great time!"

Todd regretted coming almost immediately, but was locked in. He decided to make his way to where he could check out the items he could win in the raffle. The PA system had been left on to allow music to play throughout the school. Milli Vanilli was currently blaring throughout the halls. Todd wasn't a fan, but he did have to admit their songs were catchy.

There were plenty of activities spread out throughout the school: swimming, basketball, volleyball, singing, dancing, and eating. All activities Todd enjoyed, but nothing he wanted to do all night. There were several gift baskets assembled for the raffle. One was labeled the Spirit Basket and featured notebooks, folders, pens, and pencils, all with the school's logo on it. Todd snickered at the thought of anyone being interested in high school memorabilia after they'd graduated. He'd barely finished his thought when he was shoved aside by a group of girls eager to win the Spirit Basket.

"I *have* to win this!" one of them declared beginning to choke up. "I'm going to miss high school and all of you sooo much!" she cried, giving each of her friends a hug. Todd didn't know if he should laugh at her or nominate her for an Oscar. Making eye contact with Todd, her tears dried up in an instant and she plastered a big smile on her face. "Sign my yearbook!" she said in a bubbly, cheerleader-y voice. Todd had no clue who she was but grabbed her pen, anyway, and wrote the thing he had in everyone else's: "May the best of your past be the worst of your future." She read what he'd written then gave him a sideways glance.

"Sign mine next!" said one of her friends. "But make mine more personal." Todd scribbled that he knew she would make an indelible mark on the world and that he couldn't wait to see her in ten years. She was thrilled when she read it, and Todd was pleased since he had no clue who she was, either.

He signed the remaining friends' yearbooks the same way he'd signed the first's and continued checking out the remaining raffle baskets. The next one had a sports theme that featured generic Cardinals memorabilia like a pennant with the Cardinals' logo on it as well as Cardinals pins, stickers, and notepads. The next basket was full of cosmetics like Lip Smacker fruity lip balm, 3-D butterfly hair clips, and Sun-In hair lightener. Todd walked past it quickly.

There were a couple other baskets, but none that caught his eye. As he wandered through the empty halls of the school, Todd was struck by how eerily silent it was. The corridors were empty and dark, and though they weren't closed off, Todd felt like he was breaking the rules by walking down them without a note from a teacher.

The halls had a different vibe now than the one they'd had the past four years. Before graduation, he'd felt they were leading him down a path to his future. Now, deserted as they were, they felt like they weren't there to lead anymore. They felt retired and useless. As Todd walked, he could hear the faint sounds of laughter. He half expected someone to jump out and scare him. He peered into the empty classrooms he used to make it to just before the tardy bell. He could see a few of his peers had broken in and used the rooms to say their goodbyes in a more "intimate" setting. Todd couldn't imagine having sex in the same classrooms in which he'd studied Algebra and Biology, but to each his own. They had their end-of-high-school To Do lists, and he had his.

Making his way to the opposite end of the hallway from which he entered, Todd counted down: "Five. Four. Three. Two. One." And he was off, sprinting down the hallway as fast as he could. It was the first time in four years he could do so without a teacher yelling, "There's no running in the halls!" or, "Slow down!" As he finished, Todd wondered how many detentions he could have avoided had he been able to run down the halls so he could get to class on time.

And then suddenly, he wanted to go home. Now. He felt trapped. During the school year, being stuck in the building had been okay. Not great, but okay. He'd had a purpose for being there. It was different tonight. He had a choice, and he should be able to come and go as he pleased. He was free, yet he was still there and he wasn't allowed to leave. He was locked in. The you're-no-longer-obligated-to-be-here-but-can't-go bothered him. It was as if the building had a hold on him. Eighteen, a graduate, and still not allowed to do as he pleased.

Why am I here? – really – he thought. He wasn't like Erica, who was, no doubt, somewhere in the building making out with someone. He couldn't care less about any of the other activities going on. He could play sports and swim this summer at the YMCA, if he wanted to.

Back in the Commons now, Todd walked past the buffet. On it was an array of sugary carbonated drinks – fruit-flavored Slice, Jolt Cola, and Surge among them – and snacks like Doritos, Jumpin' Jack Tortilla Chips, Chocodiles, Cheetos Paws potato chips, pretzels, and pizza. A teen's dietary heaven. Todd would normally have gorged himself on the buffet like his peers, but he was still full from the dinner his family had had at his favorite steakhouse: Stuart Anderson's. Or as his father used to teach him to say *I have filled my palate quite adequately*.

Not hungry, but bored, Todd decided to grab a Bar None, and a curious Mango Fruitopia. He wasn't going to eat or drink it; he just needed a sense of security to bring him comfort in a place he didn't want to be.

Todd left the cafeteria and joined up with a couple of his now-former teammates.

"Hey, Todd! How's it going?" they asked. Todd had been keeping his distance ever since the team was eliminated from District play. But now there was nowhere else to go so he relented. There was an awkward silence within the group.

Todd had a hard time with the team's outster from the playoffs. Todd had made the last out with the tying run in scoring position, so he blamed himself for the loss. He didn't know which was worse: making the final out and his team being eliminated by a rival school or making the final out in his final at-bat of his high school career. Yeah. Definitely the latter. There was no next year coming up in which he could vindicate himself. And Todd had felt like he'd been safe! He *knew* he'd landed on first base before the ball arrived, and no one was ever going to convince him otherwise. A sharp ground ball between shortstop and third had been bobbled briefly, giving Todd just enough time to beat the throw. He was past the first base bag when he heard the ball hit the mit. Hearing the umpire call, "You're out!" had struck Todd to his core. And having to watch the other team celebrate your failure/their win was worse. All he could do was stand motionless just past the first base bag, bury his face in his shirt, and cry into it. Even though he'd gone four for five in that game, he knew he'd let his teammates down. The moment had been tailor-made for him to be a hero, a moment athletes dream of, but he'd failed.

"You playing summer ball?" John asked Todd. John had been the team's shortstop and had been poised to be the tying run in that final game. "We could use you," he added, trying to sound encouraging.

The others nodded their heads in agreement, throwing in phrases like "It won't be the same without you" and "We can't win without you." Todd smiled, but wanted to change the subject. He wanted to play, but not on the team he'd played on the past three years. It was a combination of three schools, one of which was the school that knocked them out of the playoffs. He wasn't sure if he was ready – or would ever *be* ready – to play on the same team with them.

Chapter 11

The doors opened at 6 the next morning. Todd was the first person out. He hurried to his car and drove away. Never again, he thought. I'd have to be desperate to ever step foot in that building again.

It was a beautiful morning. The sun was rising and the birds were chirping as they fought to pull worms from the ground. Todd removed the T-tops from the car and drove away. He was at peace and kept the radio off, enjoying the sounds of his town waking up on this beautiful Saturday. Todd had taken the weekend off from work to enjoy his family, but wasn't in a hurry to get home. He enjoyed the quiet of the late spring breeze as he drove.

The tranquility didn't last long. His mind began to wander, to consider all he had to do come Monday. About life. It was the weekend but come monday he needed to begin working on the next chapter in life. What do I want to do for the next fifty years? Baseball had always been part of his answer, until the district game. His confidence was shot. He thought about being a play-by-play announcer, but he didn't like the way his voice sounded. He'd learned a lot and had made plenty of connections last summer in the Minority Journalism Program, but he wasn't fond of writing. He didn't like kids, so teaching was out of the question. Math and science weren't going to be part of his life, he declared. Ever. Sales. Maybe I can do sales. But what could I sell? Cars, maybe. Real estate? Maybe. He quickly shot them all down when he thought about being assertive and possibly having to give presentations. He felt like a boulder had just dropped into the pit of his stomach.

Baseball. Baseball was his only option. He wasn't good enough to get drafted by a major league team, nor was he good enough to get a Division 1 scholarship. Todd was getting tired. He had been up locked up all night and was ready to get some rest. One thing I'm *not* going to be, he told himself, is a criminal. If being locked up in an open school gives me fits, I can only imagine what it would be like being in a cell.

Todd slept for a couple hours until the phone in his room began ringing. He ignored it at first, sure that someone else in the house was going to pick it up. After the fourth ring, Todd flipped over and answered it himself.

"Hello?" he croaked.

"Hello," came the reply. "Is Todd available?"

"This is he," he said, still half asleep.

"Hi Todd," the caller giggled. That gave it away, and Todd was immediately wide awake.. "I'm sorry," Amani apologized. "I didn't mean to wake you."

"Oh it's okay!" he said. "I can sleep anytime. I'd rather talk to you," he added.

"Honestly, I'm not sorry," she confessed. "You sound very sexy when you're just waking up."

"Good to know," he said, trying to keep his voice sounding the way it must have when he first woke up. It didn't work.

"I was calling to see if you wanted to see me," Amani asked. Todd sat bolt upright in his bed.

"Definitely!" he answered, his voice full of excitement. He hoped Amani could hear his smile through the phone. "When and where?" he asked.

"Do you work tonight?" she asked.

"No, I took off all weekend with my family in town for graduation and all," he explained.

"That makes sense," she replied. "Well, maybe another time then."

"No!" Todd shouted. He cleared his throat and tried to regain his composure. "I mean, no. No one else is here," he clarified. "They're probably out shopping or something, so I would love to meet you somewhere. How about a park?" he suggested. "That way we can walk around in the open but still be away from anyone who might cause us problems if they see us together."

Amani was hesitant for a moment but soon relented. "Okay," she said. They arranged a time and place and ended the call.

Todd hadn't barely hung up the phone before he got in the shower. Afterward, he dried off and sprinkled a few dabs of baby powder on his chest and midsection. Rolling on some Ban Powder Fresh antiperspirant, and putting on some clean socks, he felt like a million bucks. He threw on a short-sleeved shirt and a pair of jean shorts, spritzed a mixture of Cool Water and Joop cologne behind his ears and was out the door.

He couldn't get to their rendezvous point fast enough. He rolled through every stop sign and sped through every yellow light. A trip that would normally have taken him twenty minutes took just nine. He drove more casually once he entered the park. Be cool, he told himself, trying to appear collected in spite of his nerves. "Be a duck," his dad would always tell him. "Remain calm on the surface but paddle like hell underneath."

Todd glanced at himself in the rear view mirror. He looked cool on the outside, but his heart was pounding a mile a second. He spotted Amani pacing outside her car. She looked nervous, as well. Somehow, this made Todd a little less anxious. He drove over to where she was parked.

Todd had never been one to make the first move, so he shocked himself when he hopped out of his car, walked over to her, and hugged her tightly. He was even more shocked when she hugged him back. A feeling of familiarity overcame Todd, as if he knew that being in her arms was where he should always be. Time stood still.

Todd didn't know how long they held each other, nor did he care, but the steady panting of a jogger as he passed by snapped them back into reality. They laughed. Todd wanted to hug her again. The world felt right when he was in her arms. Still, he opted not to. The mood wasn't right standing in the middle of a parking lot. Plus anyone could see them there. And while he suspected no one knew they would be at the park, he wasn't willing to take a chance. He was constantly reminding himself that their lives were on the line when they were together; they couldn't get relaxed and reckless.

"Hey, let's walk down to the river," he suggested. He hoped the path was dry. The park had several hiking trails; one of the less commonly-used ones led to the Missouri River. Not many people took it since it tended to flood in the late spring and early summer. Todd had heard tales of joggers who got trapped on an island that earlier in the day had been a gravel path.

The two journeyed in silence. They had a lot to say, but were too shy. The only sound came from the rustling of leaves blowing in the wind combined with the occasional snapping of twigs as they walked. Todd reached hesitantly for Amani's hand. Their fingers locked. It was perfect.

"This is beautiful," Amani said, marveling at the body of water before them. Todd agreed. The water was calm. Serene. The sun glinted beautifully off the river. The distant croaking of a toad and the soft buzzing of a dragonfly were the only sounds.

Todd unlocked his fingers from Amani's so he could readjust his hold. Her fingers were now in the palm of his hand. "Thank you for spending time with me today," he said. She smiled, and she blushed.

"The pleasure is all mine," she replied.

Awkward silence followed. There was so much nervous energy between them, but Amani's eyes invited Todd to make a move. Still holding the fingers of her left hand in the palm of his right hand, Todd wrapped his left arm around her waist, drawing her closer to him. He leaned forward, closed his eyes, and kissed her softly on her lips. She smelled divine. Intoxicating. Her lips touching his sent butterflies fluttering through his entire being.

He kept his lips on hers for the briefest of moments, but she parted her lips slightly and leaned in, inviting him to kiss her deeper. Her lips were warm, soft. He could taste their shared breath. She moaned lightly as he pulled her deeper into him. Todd could feel their hearts beating in unison. It was magical.

They kissed until the sound of a speed boat cruising by interrupted them. "Wow!" Amani said. "That was my first kiss." Todd didn't say anything; he didn't want her to know that she was only the second person he'd kissed. This one had meant much more to him and would be more memorable.

Silently, Todd grabbed Amani by the waist again, this time moving behind her. He nestled his head between her clavicle and neck and kissed the nape of her neck. The warmth of his lips must have electrified her because her hair stood on end and he felt her get goosebumps.

Todd chuckled. "Does this mean we're officially a couple?" he asked. His warm breath tickled her neck again. She moaned softly and fell into him, grabbing the arm holding her waist and pressing it tighter against her. She exhaled deeply.

"I am one of very few women in my culture who actually gets to have a first kiss with a man they truly want to kiss," she said.

She turned, looking up at him and smiling. "I want to experience a lot of firsts with you." Todd leaned down and kissed her again. They stood in silence, beaming because they were linked as a couple.

"I never imagined that I would find love," Amani said. She wiped a tear from her cheek. Todd turned her around so that they were face to face. Both her eyes were full of tears.

Todd was speechless. He wanted to console her with the right words, but nothing would come to mind. He wasn't sure if she was crying because she was happy starting a relationship with him or tears of sadness because that relationship would face so many obstacles. He assumed it was the latter, and the thoughts brought pain to his heart and tears to his eyes.

Todd didn't usually show a lot of emotion, especially when he was sad, so he was shocked by the tears in his eyes. Pets had died, relatives had passed, and Todd hadn't cried.

The last time he remembered crying was when he saw the movie *The Fox and the Hound*. He loved that movie – it was one of his all time favorites – but he refused to ever watch it again. Todd couldn't help but cry when the hound tells the fox that they can't be friends and the old lady smuggles him to safety. His situation with Amani reminded him of the movie. Society telling him he and Amani couldn't be together was soul crushing. How could love between two people be wrong? he wondered.

"Awww," Amani wept. "I'm sorry," she said with deepening sadness. Slowly, and so, so gently, she wiped the tears from Todd's face. She placed her hands on his cheeks and guided his head so it was just inches from hers. "I never want you to shed a tear for me," she said.

Before Todd could say anything, she leaned in and planted a huge kiss on his lips. It lasted longer than a peck but was shorter than anything intimate. It was her way of calming him, but it wasn't working. Todd was still shaken by the way of the world. He couldn't understand the hate in the hearts of mankind. They held each other tightly, two lovers against the world. Time slid by, but neither seemed to notice.

Todd, still tired from the previous night, broke his hold to cover his yawn. "What time do you think it is?" Amani asked nervously.

"I forgot my watch," Todd answered causally. He didn't want the moment to end.

"I have to go. Now!" Amani said, panicking. She immediately headed for the parking lot.

It took Todd a moment to remember this was going to the norm in their relationship. They were going to have to look over their shoulders constantly, to always be cognizant of the time. His life was going to be filled with even more uncertainty now. He sighed. The stress punched him in the gut. Hard. He began to feel the same constraints he'd felt last night during the lock-in. He needed freedom in his life, but a relationship with Amani was going to provide everything but. Had he bitten off more than he could chew? Was this a turning point for him? If he stayed at the river to let her run off alone, life would definitely be easier. But would he be happy?

He'd never felt an instant bond with anyone the way he had with Amani. If he took the path that included her, he'd be following his heart, but life was sure to be turbulent, filled with drama and danger. Because of their religious and cultural differences there would be no Christmas, no Easter, no gatherings at her family's house. He... *they*... will constantly be looking over their shoulders, their lives will constantly be in danger.

Todd was not comfortable with drama; he mostly stayed away from tense situations. So why am I going to chase after her? he asked himself. All the points he'd just considered were valid, but he was choosing to ignore them. The heart wants what it wants. This may be the dumbest decision he'd ever made, but he didn't care.

Todd had to maintain a slow jog to keep pace with Amani's hurried walk. As she exited the trail, she broke into a sprint toward her car. Thrusting the key into the ignition, she turned it and waited impatiently for the time to display on the dash. By the time Todd finally caught up to her, Amani had already thrown the car in reverse.

"I'm ten minutes late!" she yelled. Todd jumped out of the way as she slammed the car in drive and peeled out of the parking lot.

Todd stood and watched her drive off. He felt empty, but also relieved. When they'd been together, every noise had made her tense up. He'd felt it, and her uneasiness caused Todd to tense up, as well. He was conflicted again. Did the good of being with Amani outweigh the bad?

The screeching of a car's tires broke his concentration. He looked up to see Amani's car flying around the corner. What's going on? he wondered as she jumped out. She ran up to Todd, jumped in his arms, and held on. The kiss she gave him was loving and impactful.

"I never want to say hello without a kiss, and I never want to leave you without kissing you goodbye." And just like that, she sprinted back to her car and drove off. Todd got into his car and looked at the time displaying on the radio. Time really *did* fly when they were together. He'd thought they'd only spent an hour together, but it had been almost three-and-a-half. He had to make an appearance at home. His grandparents were no doubt missing him by now.

"Todd, what's this I hear?" his grandmother asked. "You haven't applied to any colleges?"

Todd glanced at his mom, who was standing at the stove preparing dinner. She shrugged her shoulders with a sly smirk on her face. Todd grimaced at the idea that his own mother would sell him out like that.

"I'm weighing my options," he replied.

"That's not good enough!" his other grandmother added.

I've been set up, Todd thought. I'm surrounded by parental units from two different generations. The lectures they're going to give me are going to be unbearable, he thought. He searched for an excuse that would get out of his situation but came up empty. He couldn't use work as an excuse; everyone knew he was off. The phone wasn't ringing, so he couldn't be saved by a phone call.

"I know where *I'm* going," Tiffany bragged.

"*That*'s my granddaughter!" his grandmother beamed.

Todd rolled his eyes.

"There's a letter for you on the baker's rack," his dad said.

Todd turned around and grabbed it. Lincoln University. Todd knew of the school. It was the nation's first degree-granting Historically Black College and University. He also knew it was in Pennsylvania. So far away, Todd thought. He didn't remember applying to the school or showing any type of interest in it, so he was curious why he was getting mail from them.

"Thanks, Dad," he said. "I'll open it upstairs."

"Why not open it with us?" his grandma asked.

Todd relented and opened the letter in front of everyone.

"What's it say?" his dad asked.

"There's a Lincoln University in Missouri?" Todd asked.

Tiffany snatched the letter from his hand. It was from Lincoln University in Jefferson City, Missouri. "Probably another rejection letter," she teased. "Wait!" She started mumbling the words in the letter. "They want you to come play baseball for them! But why? You aren't that good." She paused before continuing. "There's a new student orientation later this month. It also says you can register early for classes. They're going to pay your tuition, but room and board is on you.

"That's amazing!" exclaimed his grandparents almost in perfect unison.

"Call them now!" his mom cried.

"It's Saturday, Mom," Todd reminded her. "I'll call on Monday."

"If you expect to continue breathing, I suggest you do," she threatened.

Chapter 12

"I'm going to miss you," Amani said with heartache in her voice. He didn't say it, but Todd was going to miss her more.

Over the past couple of weeks he and Amani had spent as much time as possible together. They usually went on outings to the river, secluded picnics in the park, or to a quiet corner in the library. They talked about their lives, their dreams, their goals, and their love for one another. They held each other as if they would never get the opportunity to do so again.

Because they never had much time to spend, Todd would bring a timer along to allow them to maximize it. Also, Todd never knew when Amani was going to be available. His life mimicked that of an on-call employee. She'd call, he'd drop everything to go meet her. He didn't mind; he reveled in every moment he was blessed to spend with her. They were moments beyond description, both good and bad. As much as he loved being in her company, Todd could never fully enjoy it. He was constantly checking the time to see when they had to go, constantly observing who was around and if they were safe.

He spent every moment away from Amani waiting impatiently for her call. It was tortuous. He spent hours… days staring at a phone that wasn't ringing. He'd pick it up every couple of minutes to make sure it was still working. If Tiffany was on the phone he would remind her that he was expecting an important call. Every call that wasn't Amani left Todd disappointed, despondent. He spent sleepless nights on MovieFone hoping that her call would click in. He missed out on everything because he was waiting for her. He skipped summer league baseball games, practices, and the summer journalism program his dad had pulled strings to get him into, just so he could spend precious moments with her. He complained to himself as he waited for the phone to ring.

Had he turned into one of Pavlov's dogs? Had he, like the dogs, been conditioned to start salivating at the sound of a bell? (Or, in his case, the ringing of the phone.) To Todd, the reward of Amani's voice or, even better, her presence, was as much a treat for him as food was for Pavlov's dogs.

He stifled the questions lurking within him. Was it really worth it in the end to be with her now? He feared he was mortgaging his future for present-day plans, but he justified it, telling himself that that's what college was for. I'm just delaying my plans for my future for a couple months. I'll make it up in college, he would tell himself. He tried convincing himself that it was summer and that he deserved to enjoy it, but he knew he was lying to himself. He was raised better than that. Every time Todd procrastinated, he would hear his dad's voice: "Everything you do now is for your future. Good or bad!"

He hated that he was letting teammates and friends down, but he wanted to be selfish for once and do something for himself. Though he loved baseball, he loved the time spent with Amani more. He tried burying the guilt that he was letting himself down. For someone who believed he could one day play for the St. Louis Cardinals, he wasn't doing anything to make it a reality. He hadn't done anything to improve as a player or to be more visible to scouts.

He had decided to put all his eggs in one basket and attend new student orientation at Lincoln University. They wanted him, and he felt he could make the most of this opportunity. He honestly had no other choice. His parents said community college was out of the question since both wanted him to go away to school, to experience life on his own. Lincoln was perfect for him because he would only be 90 minutes away from St. Louis…and Amani.

He really didn't want to go away this weekend for the new student orientation, but he had to. They required him to take placement tests and register for classes. He was also supposed to meet an assistant coach who had apparently seen him play in his last game.

After a long hug that neither wanted to end, Todd kissed Amani goodbye and hit the road. He stopped off at the nearest gas station to fill up and to buy a state map. He had no clue where he was going. He just knew the University was in the middle of the state.

This was the first road trip he'd ever taken by himself. It was the start of his life on his own. He wasn't ready. After he'd spoken with the registrar's office earlier in the week he was sure Lincoln didn't want him anymore. He'd asked if he could register over the phone and if he could skip the placement test and start at the bottom. The representative in the office had clearly not had time for Todd's shenanigans and told him he'd either need to take the placement test or find another school to attend.

There was one word that summed up why Todd was so disinterested in his college orientation: Amani. He found out she was going to be left in charge of her sisters that weekend while her parents and older siblings went out of town. So visiting Lincoln meant Todd was going to miss the chance to spend a limitless amount of time with her. It was as if the universe had put a fork in the road and he had to decide which path he'd choose. If it were up to him he would choose Amani a million times over. But it wasn't up to him. His parents insisted he go to college, and Amani was willing to risk her life to be with him.

Todd pulled into the campus. A big 'Welcome New Students' banner flew over a brick Lincoln University sign. The letter Todd had received indicated there was going to be a welcome picnic today, testing tomorrow, campus tours on Sunday, and registration on Monday. Todd only wanted to be here for the placement test, but his parents insisted he do it all. They said it'd be fun! Spending the night in a dorm was not what Todd considered fun, but here he was.

He pulled into the park on campus at which the welcoming party was being held. It rested on the campus' highest peak and offered marvelous views of the city. Views Todd ignored.

"What's up, home skillet?" a young man said as Todd hopped out of his car. "Kansas City or St. Louis?" The kid had a huge smile on his face and Todd was sure he was faking it so he could sell the school to those attending the events that weekend.

"What?" Todd asked, confused.

The young man chuckled. "My bad! Most of the students here today are local like me," he began. Since I don't recognize you, you must be from either St. Louis or Kansas City."

"I'm from St. Louis," Todd responded. "What's it like being a local?"

"Oh snap!" the kid said suddenly, marveling at Todd's Camaro. "I'm totally buggin' over your car!"

"Uhhh… thanks," Todd said. He was about to give him more details, but the kid ran off to greet someone else.

Surveying the area, Todd noticed he was one of very few potential new students who didn't have a parent with them. *I guess not every parent is ready for their child to be on their own,* he thought. He also noticed that all the greeters had the same exaggerated smiles on their faces as the kid who'd greeted him, and each was wearing brown khakis and a blue and gray shirt that had the letters "LU" on the front and "Volunteer" on the back. Todd felt like he was at a Disney theme park. They all appeared to have memorized the same script: *Ask where they're from, show interest (but don't spend too much time talking with them), and keep smiling!...*

Todd walked around the park. Some of those in attendance were running around on the playground as if they were attending an elementary school orientation. Under the pavilion were heated games of Spades, Biz Whist, and Uno. Off to one side a spirited game of dice was being played. A DJ was playing a variety of urban contemporary hits, while a group of potential students were in the background doing the electric slide. There were burgers and hot dogs grilling on a barbecue pit and the smell was enticing. The scene reminded Todd of a cookout without alcohol or fights. It surprised him but also made him proud. It was nice to see a bunch of people his age having fun together without drama.

Suddenly, Todd felt a surge of pride pass through him. He was going to be attending an HBCU the same way others in his family had, and he surprised himself by feeling excited to carry on the tradition. Todd casually encircled the food but didn't want to grab anything since no one else was eating.

"Mr. Glass," he heard someone shout. Someone Todd assumed was another volunteer was headed in his direction. And though he was wearing the same exaggerated smile on his face, this one wasn't wearing the same attire as the others. He had to be a coach of some sort. Who else would wear those too-tight athletic shorts and Champion shirt? His socks – a colorful red, white, and blue striped pair – were pulled up his calves. "I'm Coach Raymond," he said, shaking Todd's hand vigorously

Coach Raymond was a portly, middle-aged man who stood about as tall as Todd, but weighed close to one hundred pounds more. He was top heavy, but his legs were slim. Athletic, even. Todd guessed he'd once been an athlete himself many years ago, though the weight he'd packed on over time made that hard to tell.

He spoke with a loud, gravelly loud voice. "Welcome!" he said loud enough for everyone in attendance to hear. Todd felt like a celebrity as the coach wrapped his arm around him and guided him around the area. "Let me show you around," he said exuberantly.

Todd could smell the distinct smell of Mint-flavored Skoal every time Coach Raymond spoke. He already had chew in his mouth but packed more in between his cheek and gums. He looked like a chipmunk packing food in preparation for winter.

"We are so excited that a kid with talent decided to join our team. When I asked around and found out you were still uncommitted to another program I reached out immediately. We were shocked to find a left-handed bat with your talent right in our own backyard."

Leftie? Todd thought. He'd dabbled as a switch hitter but definitely didn't want to be labeled as one. He began to wonder if Lincoln University had recruited the right person, but felt it was in his best interest to keep his mouth shut and begin working on becoming a left-handed dominant hitter.

"Coach Hunter is on a recruiting trip, otherwise he'd be here to welcome you, too." Try as he might, Todd was unable to dodge the bits of chewing tobacco that flew out of the coach's mouth with every 't' and 's' he uttered.

"Hey!" he yelled at the person behind the grill. His tone made everyone around him jump, including Todd. "What is *this*?" he asked. Todd looked around to see who else was witnessing the scene. "There are several food faux pas that are unforgivable in this world," the coach continued. "One: hamburgers and pizza are never to be eaten with a fork and knife." A crowd began to gather, and Todd chuckled at the idea that his first college lesson was going to be a lecture about food at orientation.

"Two!" the coach shouted. He wanted everyone to hear him, and everyone did. "Ranch dressing does not belong on a pizza."

"As if!" shouted a girl in the crowd. A few others disagreed with him. Todd thought he was right, but Tiffany would have a fit. She put Ranch on pizza and ketchup on eggs. Both were travesties according to Todd.

"Three!" Coach Raymond continued. "No steak should be grilled hotter than medium rare." Todd disagreed; he always ordered his meat well done to avoid seeing blood.

"It's not blood!" yelled someone in the crowd as if they could read Todd's thoughts. It was a parent arguing with another parent. "It's mostly fat and water."

"Well-done steaks kill the flavor of the meat," Coach Raymond asserted. "And finally," he said, climbing on top of a picnic bench. "No person over the age of eighteen should *ever* put ketchup on a hot dog." Todd laughed. He'd never known anyone with so much passion about food. *If he's this passionate about hot dogs, I can only imagine how passionate he is about baseball*, Todd thought.

He began to wonder about the head coach and the caliber of the other players. Just then, Coach Raymond walked up.

"Hey Coach," Todd said, trying to grab Coach Raymond's attention before another food debate began. He could hear rumblings from several parents discussing the dismissal of ketchup while Chicagoans put the entire kitchen sink on their dogs.

The coach looked at Todd, disappointed. It was clear he wanted to continue debating food rather than convince Todd to play ball for Lincoln.

"How's the team look?" Todd asked.

"We're in a rebuilding year," the coach said dismissively, still focused on the food debate.

Rebuilding? Todd was hesitant to join a team that labeled itself as rebuilding. To Todd, the word 'rebuilding' was code for 'we sucked last season so we're replacing all the old players.' It usually also meant another couple years until the replacements would be competitive.

"How many freshmen are joining me?" he asked.

"Just one," the coach answered, looking past Todd.

"How many transfers?"

"None."

Given his answers, Todd wondered how this constituted a rebuilding year. He was also leery of the coach's vague answers. Todd had a feeling he was hiding something, but it didn't really matter. Todd was all out of options. It was either here, the military, or commute to an HBCU in Ohio and live with his grandparents. They thought that would be wonderful, of course, but living with your parents while you were in college was a no. Living with your *grand*parents while you were in college and trying to have some freedom was a *hell* no.

Todd was just about to ask how many games the team won last year when the coach reached down, grabbed a hot dog and practically shoved it in Todd's mouth. "These are the good ones," the coach said. "Ice does not belong in wine!" he bellowed at a group of parents, and turned away to argue about food with them.

Coach was right, Todd thought. The slightly burnt ones *are* best, he considered, savoring the dog.

He thought about the itinerary again. It called for the welcome picnic on Friday, placement test on Saturday, Family Welcome Fest on Sunday, and registration for classes on Monday. Todd decided to do it all on Saturday.

After the picnic, he spent a restless evening in a cold dorm on an uncomfortable cot. The volunteers assured him dorm living would be better during the actual semester since the dorms were cleaned and renovated during the summer. On Saturday, Todd breezed through his placement test. He tried to do the best he could on the Reading and English sections – his favorite subjects – but not on the Math and Science portion. He actually zoned out on those questions, filling in the bubble letters randomly and hoping he'd fail so he could be placed in an easier class. He knew he'd be pursuing a Bachelor of Arts degree, anyway, in an effort to minimize the science and math requirements.

Once he finished the test he guessed as to what the results would be and filled out his schedule accordingly. He added alternatives in case he couldn't get into his first choices, signed the schedule, placed it on the academic advisor's desk, and headed back home. Unbeknownst to his parents, he'd borrowed their radar detector so he could drive as fast as he wanted without getting another ticket. The points on his license were stacking up and his parents were rapidly getting tired of paying increased insurance rates.

Todd wanted nothing more than to maximize the time he could spend with Amani. He didn't have any obligations since he'd already used the new student orientation as an excuse to miss yet another summer league game. Not that his teammates were missing him. Apparently Kendrick, his coworker at Green Leaf

Kitchen had been filling in nicely. Todd didn't mind. He is a collegiate athlete now. Let the summer league go on without him, though he *could* use the league to practice being a left-handed hitter. Todd had other thoughts on his mind. Amani.

Chapter 13

"Welcome to the newest chapter in your life," Todd's dad said.

"I can't believe your dumb ass got into college," Tiffany teased.

"Language…" their mom warned. Todd was slightly annoyed that his mom chided Tiffany for her language, not for calling him dumb.

As they approached the campus, after a two-hour-long car ride full of lectures and advice, Todd apprehensive about being a college student but relieved that he would finally be able to escape the car. He was still unsure about attending college. He'd struggled in high school; how was college going to be any different? He also missed Amani. It had only been two hours since he'd kissed her goodbye but it felt like twice that long.

Jefferson City was small and featured three prominent locations: the State Capitol building, the state penitentiary, and the state's largest high school that sat right next to Lincoln. Todd marveled at how much bigger it was than the one he attended.

As they rode through the campus, Todd was amazed at how many hills there were. His treks to class were going to suck. The campus was beautiful, though. He wished he had paid attention to it during the new student orientation in June. The tree-lined streets accentuated the historic brick buildings beautifully. From afar, the campus was hidden by all the trees. The closer they got, the more the hill revealed. The campus' rich history was ever present, and its Georgian-style buildings had an understated elegance.

The university itself was historically unique as it was the only post-Civil War school for black students founded by black soldiers. Todd was a big fan of history and was inspired by what Lincoln had become in just over a century.
"Watch for your dorm building," Todd's dad instructed.

"The ball field!" Todd exclaimed, pointing out the university's baseball diamond. As much as Todd did not want to be there academically, he was excited to be there as a baseball player.

"Remember," his dad started. Todd could feel an *ism* coming on. Todd and his sister secretly referred to their father's lessons as *isms*. Some were straightforward, others were meant for you to think deeply about. Some were long, some were short, but they always had a good point, and were delivered with much love. "You're not here to be a ball player; you're here to get an education."

"Mandela once said, 'education is the most powerful weapon you can use to change the world,'" he continued. "If you can't change the world, at least change your address. It's time for your mom and me to have some fun. Me and your mom want to walk around the house naked," he joked.

"Ewwww," Tiffany complained. "*I'm* still there! No one is trying to see your SAG awards," she protested.

"SAG awards?" their mom asked. "As in the Screen Actors Guild? What does that have to do with anything?"

"Your saggy titties, and dad's saggy balls," Tiffany said, laughing hysterically.

"Saggy or not, they got you here," their dad replied.

Todd could not believe the language his sister was able to get away with. He got yelled at if he used the word 'heck,' but Tiffany could say whatever she wanted in any context she pleased and not face any consequences.

"But also," his dad continued, "my money is a terrible thing to waste. Don't spend all your energy playing a game when you need to be using it to get an education."

Todd heard what his dad was saying but couldn't pay attention; he was still trying to get the image of them naked out of his head. He thought about defending his dreams of playing ball, but decided against it. While he wanted to argue that the scholarship he'd earned to play baseball was helping him get an education, he knew better than to go toe-to-toe with his parents because he usually lost.

Todd couldn't help but be upset that his parents hadn't believed in his dreams of being a professional athlete as much as he did, but he was painfully aware of why. He hadn't worked hard enough to make those dreams come true, and everyone who knew him could see it. But he was in college now, and things were going to be different.

"It won't be a waste if I become a successful ball player," he retorted.

Todd's dad slammed on the brakes, put the car in park, and turned around in his seat. *I should've stayed silent*, he thought.

"Do I have to hear Todd get lectured?" Tiffany whined. "I actually have realistic dreams," she added. "First I wanted to be Minnie Mouse, but then I grew up. Now I want to be a teacher so we don't have a generation of clueless men following stupid dreams like Todd," she joked.

"This will benefit you, too," their mom snapped, preparing to join in on whatever lesson Todd was about to get.

Todd wasn't paying attention to whatever they were getting ready to say. He was more embarrassed that his dad had parked the car halfway up a hill in the middle of campus.

His dad took a deep breath, exhaled, and paused for effect. He stared at both his kids, making sure he had their undivided attention. This never worked. Todd feigned attention but would try to ignore his dad. He didn't think he needed to be lectured and would daydream that he was somewhere else. Still, his dad's words always managed to make their way into Todd's brain. And though the advice was always good advice, Todd always chose to ignore it. And because he always had to do things the hard way, he set himself up for nightmare after nightmare.

"Todd, even you don't believe in yourself. If you did, you would've said 'When I become a baseball player.' Not if. Your words have power, Son. When you believe in yourself, your words will manifest success."

"Life is like a camera," he continued. "Focus on what's most important." He looked directly at Todd when he said this last part, emphasizing the words 'focus' and 'most'

Turning to Tiffany, he continued. "Capture the good times, develop from the negatives, and if things don't go well, take another shot!" He paused for what seemed like an eternity.

"Okay," Todd replied, wondering if his dad was still looking at him and waiting for Todd to acknowledge what he'd just said.

But without saying another word, his dad put the car in gear and continued toward their destination. His words spoke volumes, but Todd decided to mute them.

"There it is!" their mom shouted, pointing at a sign that read Martin Hall.

"Everybody out!" their dad cried. "Open up the trailer, Todd. I'm going to go inside and find a bathroom. Those cheese puffs are taking revenge on my colon."

"Dad! Please!" Todd begged.

"What?" his dad asked. "Am I embarrassing you?"

"Yes!" Todd said.

"Who cares?" his dad said. "I don't go to school here. No one knows me! And who here hasn't taken a shit at some point in their life?" he concluded. "Tiffany?" their dad called out.

"Yes?" she replied.

"Pull my finger!" he demanded.

Laughing, Tiffany gleefully pulled his finger. "Ahhh…." he sighed, releasing a long, soft fart. " " Holding in a fart can kill you" he informed Todd confidently. So can releasing one in the general public thought Todd holding in his breath. Now that he had been utterly and completely embarrassed, Todd scanned the parking lot to see who might've heard everything that had just happened. No one appeared to be paying attention.

Sensing his son's anxiousness, his dad wrapped his arms around Todd and drew him in close. "I'm going to make this short because the commode is calling my name, but stop caring what others think of you," he advised. "Your life isn't yours if you waste it caring what others think about it."

As soon as he'd been let go, Todd headed in search of a residential advisor with the location to his room and a key to get into it. He climbed five metal stairs and pulled open one of two large glass doors so he could enter the residence hall lobby. It was 90° outside, and the humidity had caused the doors to the air-conditioned building to fog. The blast of cold air was a welcome relief.

The small lobby had a futon-style couch that, thanks to its burnt orange and brown semicircles, looked like it came straight out of the 70's. Adjacent to the futon were two wicker chairs. To the right of the entrance was an office that had a bank teller-like window in it, metal bars included. A hand-written sign instructed visitors to walk around the corner to sign in. As Todd headed that way he saw two pay phones, both occupied. One user was asking his parents for money, the other was asking his girlfriend – or what seemed like ex-girlfriend – for forgiveness. Todd knocked on the open door and waited. The small office contained a card table that was functioning as a work desk as well as several yellow file cabinets that lined the walls. Inside the office to the left was a wall with tiny mailboxes. The space was small, cramped, and cluttered.

"May I help you?" asked a middle-aged woman sitting behind the desk. She hadn't bothered looking away from her perfectly manicured nails. Todd assumed she was a receptionist, though he wondered how she could get any office work done with such long nails.

"Yes," he responded. "My name is Todd Glass. I'm moving in today."

"Freshman?" she asked.

"Yes," Todd responded.

"I don't understand why freshmen wait until the last minute to move in," she complained to herself. She sighed deeply, as if helping Todd was a waste of her time. "Ughh. Hold on," she groaned with an attitude so strong it put Todd in a bad mood, too.

The receptionist knocked on a thick wooden door behind her.

"What?!" Todd heard a male shout from behind it.

"We got another one!" she yelled. "A *fresh*man," she added disdainfully. No response. She banged again. Finally, the door opened slowly and out came a middle-aged man and Todd's dad, laughing.

"No problem, John. I'll make sure your son acts right," he said confidently.

Like so many times before, Todd realized he couldn't go anywhere or do anything because someone his parents knew was there. And they told his parents everything. He and Tiffany were regularly approached by strangers who asked if they were related to John Glass.

Looking at Todd, the man extended his hand. "Hi, I'm Leroy, the resident advisor manager. Your dad and I go way back."

"See?" Todd's dad said, "I've got eyes everywhere." This became a recurring theme in Todd's life. Constantly he or Tiffany was approached by strangers asking if he were related to John Glass.

"Let me find your file, Little John," Leroy said. Todd rolled his eyes. He hated that he was always being referred to as Little John by his dad's friends. It was meant as a compliment, but Todd never took it that way.

Opening a file cabinet, Leroy pulled out a manilla folder with Todd's name on it. He set it down on the receptionist's desk. "Sign here and here," he instructed, handing Todd a pen.

Todd leaned over and tried to sign the papers. The table wobbled like crazy. The receptionist shot Todd an annoyed look as she put her hands on the table in an attempt to stabilize it. "Boy, didn't I teach you anything?" his dad asked. "Why would you sign something without reading it first?" He paused, rolling his eyes. Your sister's right, you *can* be dumb sometimes," he finished jokingly.

"It just says I gave you keys to your mailbox and room," Leroy said, laughing. Sensing Todd's annoyance, Leroy leaned in. "I've checked in a lot of students over the years. The majority of the parents who come along couldn't care less what their kid signs, so take joy in your blessings."

Todd didn't view it as a blessing, just a curse.

"Okay," Leroy continued. "You're in room 101 on the ground floor downstairs. The building has five, though," he added. He spoke fast and loud, and his words sounded rehearsed, his tone flat. Todd wondered how many times he'd said them. "Your mailbox number is the same as your room number and entry to it is on the other side of this wall. Large packages are kept in this office. A few guidelines: We are not a 24/7 facility. If you have a guest, they need to leave by 10 during the week, by midnight on weekends. This is not Motel 6; I will not leave the light on for you or your guests to fornicate or party. Also, if you lose your key, don't bang on the door or call me. I will not open up for you. The door you just came through is the only entrance," he continued. "The emergency exits are outside your room and down the hall. You will have people knock on your widows trying to get you to open the door for them. Don't do it. We have security cameras facing both doors. If you get caught letting someone in, both you and they will face consequences. Any questions?"

"No," Todd said. He had tons of questions. Why can't I have company whenever I want? Why can't I let people in? What's the punishment if I do? So much for freedom in college, he thought, let down.

"Oh!" Leroy said, obviously having forgotten something. "There are also no microwaves, hot plates, or mini refrigerators allowed inside your dorm rooms. I'm not going to have someone burn down this dorm because of an appliance. There's a kitchen on this floor if you want to cook, or you can, of course, eat in the dining hall. Let's go see your room."

Leroy escorted Todd and his dad down a flight of steps to a brightly-lit hallway. The fluorescent bulbs were bright and hummed softly. The cinder-block walls were painted white.

"The rec room is to the right," Leroy pointed out. "There's a TV, pool table, ping pong table, chairs, tables, and a couch. There's cable in there but not in your dorm room."

"Good," Todd's dad interjected, "he doesn't need any distractions."

Good? thought Todd How is this good? Other than no barbed wire fence, how are my living conditions any different from a prison? Even the visitation seems similar!

Turning to the left, they walked ten feet to the door to Todd's room. Todd inserted the key, but the door was already unlocked. Inside was a nightmare. The room was far too small for two people. Maybe for even *one* person. His room at home was twice this size. Todd wondered if he could still call it that – 'his' room – or if this closet was now his room and that Other room was a spare room for visitors at his *parents'* house.

As he glanced around, he saw twin beds on both the left and right sides of the room. Both sides also had a four-drawer dresser with a small mirror on top. Above the mirror was a light fixture with two lightbulbs in it. The room was dark, even in the middle of the afternoon; Todd could see the lights weren't going to do much to luminate the space.

Directly in front of him was a heavy wooden desk with two drawers and a cabinet. Behind that was the window with a closed set of miniblinds. On the left side of the room was a dingy yellow wall phone with an extra long cord. On the right side of the room was a small thermostat.

"Wake up, Luther! Your roommate's here!" Leroy yelled.

"Hey," the kid named Luther grumbled, rolling over. He then turned his back to the group and promptly fell back to sleep.

"Don't mind him. He's on a waitlist for an apartment so he'll be moving out soon," Leroy said. "Do you have any questions?"

"I don't think so," Todd responded.

"One more thing," Leroy said. "Outside calls have a long ring. The ring for on-campus calls is probably close to what you're used to at home."

Todd took a deep breath and started for the car to start bringing in his things. Suitcase after suitcase, box after box, Todd made countless trips back and forth from the car to his room. Each drop of his belongings made the room look smaller and more cramped.

"Finally! Last box!" Todd cheered, hopping off the back of the hitch.

"We were just on our way to help you," Tiffany snickered as his family walked around the corner.

"Where'd you go?" Todd asked, annoyed.

"We went to explore the campus," replied their mom. "These hills are going to whip your butt in shape!" she added.

Chapter 14

*T*his is it! Todd thought. College. Years of dreaming about being on his own and he was finally there. Freedom, sweet freedom! I can come and go as I please, clean up when I want to, sleep when I want, get up when I want... So why do I want to be back at my parents' house? His parents just dropped him off and left. He felt like an unwanted puppy, like his parents had driven out to the country and left him alone on the side of a desolate road. This was truly the first time he was on his own without his parents or a relative. Well, the first time besides the two weeks he'd spent at summer camp one year, but this was different. He'd dreamt of this moment. So why wasn't he excited? No parents, more girls around than guys (by 13 to 1!). How could he not be enjoying this?

Todd looked at the stack of textbooks he'd gotten from the bookstore before his family left for home and wondered how much more difficult college courses were going to be compared to high school. He tried calming himself down by rationalizing why he'd struggled in high school. He'd been lazy in high school; it's different now. Now he was a college student.

The pep talk failed. Todd knew he hadn't changed. The only thing that was different was his environment. He still possessed the same bad habits and immaturity that had plagued him in high school. He hadn't gotten his priorities straight over the summer so here he was in a new city, at a new school, and on a new team, but the same lazy Todd. His motivation in high school had been his parents shoving their boots up his ass. But they weren't here. *He*'d have to be the one with the proverbial boot. He was going to have to seek help if he needed it and he already knew that that wasn't going to happen. He knew he was not a networking, reaching-out-for-help type of guy. At times he could be an introvert. Most of his friends were still the same ones he'd had since elementary school, and even they'd been forged by spending a school year with each other. Those friends couldn't help him now, they weren't there. Todd knew no one on campus.

Hearing a commotion outside, Todd walked over to the window. The blinds were shut. He didn't want to appear nosey, so he raised one of the blinds ever so slightly and peered outside. He could hear what sounded like hundreds of students in the parking lot talking and partying. He thought about going out there, too, but that's not the type of person he was. He was the sit-back, wait-until-someone-asks-to-borrow-a-pencil-and-strike-up-a-con versation type of person. Let them approach first. How do adults make friends? he wondered. It's not like you can walk up to someone and say 'Hi, I'm Todd. Let's be friends!' Or can you? he wondered. Sounds creepy, he thought. He knew that wouldn't work in college; it hadn't worked in high school.

Todd began to feel trapped. This place was not for him. He knew he had no real alternative besides being in college, though. He needed to make the best of it. Only thirty minutes since his parents had left and he was already homesick. He missed the safety and security of what he knew and was familiar with. Most of all he missed Amani.

His plan was to visit home every weekend that he could. He didn't know how he was going to do that, though; freshmen weren't allowed to have a car on campus. Not that it mattered. His dad wouldn't have let him bring it, anyway. Too many distractions, h'd say, and he was right. Todd knew he would probably drive all over the city when he was supposed to be in class or studying. Todd knew he needed to go out and make friends, ideally a friend with a car. A car that was headed to St. Louis in two weeks.

Reaching for the door knob, Todd took a deep breath. He couldn't believe he was doing this; he was about to go try to meet some people. As he entered the hallway, several overzealous guys ran past him. Todd opened his mouth to say hi but thought better of it. They were eager to join the festivities in the parking lot but Todd still had to work himself up a bit. Todd exited the side door of the dorm and walked through a small alleyway to the parking lot. The scene was indescribable. The lot was full of cars, each blaring a different song. The cacophony was dizzying to Todd. He could vaguely make out the songs playing as he passed each car, but could only barely make out the conversations everyone was having.

People were discussing their summer, what classes they were going to take, their majors, who was dating whom, and who'd broken up with whom. No one noticed Todd, and he was not about to do anything so that they would. There were hundreds of guys and girls laughing, joking, singing and dancing. Everyone was having a great time. Everyone but Todd. He couldn't wrap his brain around their energy. It was a Sunday night! A school night! He felt like he should be in bed resting for class, even though it was only 8:30 in the evening. The day before the first day of classes, and only Todd appeared anxious.

Finding a friend out here was going to be difficult; everyone seemed to know each other already. Did I miss new friend orientation? Todd asked himself. Oh. Yes I did. I skipped out on all the new student orientation events that weekend he'd come to take his placement tests.

Todd saw a crowd of people to his left and decided to move in that general direction. *I wonder what classes will be like tomorrow.* The only thing he was looking forward to was meeting his new teammates in the morning.

"Heeeeeyyyyyy Quuuuuueeee!" yelled a guy standing next to Todd. Todd turned to see who he was yelling at but was startled by a bunch of guys barking.

What the hell? Todd thought. It reminded him of the Dog Pound from the *Arsenio Hall Show*.

Then, as if someone hit a giant mute button, all the car radios went silent.

"In the beginning," yelled the same guy. "There were two. Eve was a Delta and Adam was a Que!" he shouted. "When they got together, this is what they did. First they made a lamp, and then a pyramid"

"Roooooo-OP!" yelled the dog pound.

Todd had no clue why they were chanting, stomping, and clapping, but the group of guys decked out in purple and gold began yelling, "1-2-3-4-5, Party hard with Que Phi Phi!

6-7-8-9-10, Back it up & say it again! 10-9-8-7-6, all the Ques got real big a!" On 'que,' someone turned on "Atomic Dog" by George Clinton. The group started jumping, stomping, spinning, and marching in Todd's direction.

Desperately trying to get out of the way, Todd bumped into a young woman wearing red and white. She belted out a sound Todd had never heard before and the music stopped. "Get 'em up! Get em up!" she chanted. "Where are all my Soros at?!"

In unison, dozens of women wearing red and white t-shirts with the year 1913 on the front sang in chorus, "Calling all Sorors to the floor! Ahhh, Delta, we got some here but we need some more! Ahhh, Delta!"

The barking men in purple and gold were making noise in support of the women. In the middle of their chant, something that sounded like "Skee-wee" filled the air followed by a group of girls in pink and green outfits emblazoned with the year 1908 chanting, "This is a serious matter! Yes! This is a serious matter! Yes! Yes! Alpha Kappa Alpha! A-K-A! Sororities take note! We paved your way! So if you're not AKA, you went the wrong WAY!"

Todd finally realized he was in some kind of Greek stroll line. He needed to get the hell out of there, and quickly, before everyone labeled him as the freshman that screwed up the Greek strolls.

Avoiding several collisions with the ladies of Delta Sigma Theta and a few more close calls with the ladies of Alpha Kappa Alpha, Todd was boxed in by a group of guys wearing blue and white and holding matching canes. They yelled, "This house, this house, is full, is full, of blue and white! I said this house, this house is full of blue and white! I said this house is full of blue and white! Blue, blue, blue, blue phiiiii! You, you, you, you knoooow!"

If Todd had been anxious before, he *really* was now. It was a labyrinth of Greeks. Everywhere he turned he was surrounded by another group of seething, shouting, singing members of various fraternities and sororities. He turned around, only to be blocked off by yet another fraternity. This one was wearing red and black and also had matching canes. They were chanting and stepping "WE WEAR THE CLOTHES! WE PIMP THE HOES! NUPE NUPE, Mutha Fucka, THAT'S THE WAY IT GOES! DO THIS, YO BABAAAY! I went to England to visit the Queen. She saw I was a NUPE and crowned me King. I threw her the YO, she played the part, now the Queen of England is a KAPPA SWEETHEART!"

Todd had heard of black fraternities and sororities – he had several family members who'd been in one – but had never been this close to active members. He marveled at the clever chants done in unison but didn't feel comfortable in any way. The step routines were really well-choreographed, though, and he could tell the members had worked diligently to time each movement with their line brothers and sisters. The chants were all spoken with confidence and power, too, and it was definitely a moment of pride for each member and their audience. Except for Todd. He'd thought briefly about joining one of these groups once he got to college, but the idea was dashed as he watched them step in unison. He knew he lacked the rhythm to do what they were doing. Really, though, that was a piss poor excuse, as his parents used to say. The real problem was that Todd lacked the work ethic to be as great as the young men and women performing in front of him.

He desperately looked for an opening to make his exit but could only stand in the middle as several of the organizations encircled him as they performed. Finally seeing a chance for escape, he inadvertently smacked into a guy wearing a black shirt with the year 1906 written across the front.

"My bad," Todd apologized. All he got in response was a shove into a group of identically-dressed guys. Apology not accepted,

Todd thought. The group began shoving him back and forth like a rag doll.

"Stop!" he yelled. Cracking his knuckles, Todd stared intently at the group surrounding him. "I'm about to go to jail," he said, loud enough to (hopefully) intimidate his aggressors but not loud enough to incriminate himself.

The group was not intimidated, which didn't surprise Todd. Nothing about him was intimidating. Half the group didn't even pay attention to Todd; they were too busy trying to out-step the other fraternities. But Todd was not about to let the disrespect go. He was mad and ready to start swinging. He knew he couldn't take them all on, but he could give one or two of them something to think about in the morning. He really didn't want to fight; he was just annoyed and embarrassed and wanting to make someone else feel the same way he did.

He knew he had to scale back his aggression. He could see the headlines now: *Freshman gets ass kicked for trying to take on forty members of prominent fraternity*. That would be the easy part, though. Facing his dad after getting kicked out of college before classes had even started would be a whole other beating. He'd rather get his ass kicked by a fraternity.

Deciding to let bygones be bygones – as if he had a choice – Todd could do nothing but listen to the group of guys in black and gold chant "My-y-y old King Tut was the very first Greek. A-a-h, when he clapped his hands, he had the ladies at his feet! A-a-h, Tut, Tut, Tut, a-a-h, Tut, Tut, Tut. I said, when he saw the Sigmas, it made him mad. When he saw the Kappas, it made him mad. A-a-h, when he saw the Ques, it made him sick. When he saw the frat, he had to pledge quick. A-a-h, Tut, Tut, Tut! He had a black and gold whip and a black and gold cane, then he came up a-a-h with this black and gold name. A-a-h! A Phi A!"

Suddenly, a hole opened up in the group and Todd saw his chance to escape. The crowd was getting bigger and bigger and he could not wait to get back inside his dorm room.

Free of his Greek prison, Todd was met with laughter and insults. He had disrupted a show, and the observers weren't happy. Todd ran back toward his dorm as cans of soda and beer were being tossed in his direction.

"Get him!" he could hear members of the crowd shout. He overheard someone accuse him of being a drunk freshman who couldn't hold his liquor.

Safely inside the dormitory, Todd took a deep breath and vowed never to attend another parking lot event. He snuck down the stairs and escaped into his room.

"Fucking freshman," his roommate squawked. "Leave it to a clueless newbie to fuck up a Greek stroll."

Todd jumped in his bed. He didn't want to leave it ever again. He was miserable. His only consolation was seeing Amani in two weeks. That is, if he could find a way to get to her.

Chapter 15

The blaring sound of Todd's alarm clock alerted him that a new day had started. Sunday evening's horrible events had left Todd dreading Monday morning even more than he had before. He hadn't slept well seeing as how he was in an unfamiliar room next to a complete stranger. The noise from the night's parking lot celebration had gone on well past midnight and made it impossible to sleep until he tucked his head between two pillows.

"It's going to be a long four years if I have to sleep like this every night," he moaned. His desk clock read 5:02 AM. He had 58 minutes to get to the baseball diamond for orientation. With zero rest and even less ambition, Todd decided to lay his head back down for a moment. It *had* to be a form of cruel and unusual punishment to have baseball practice this early in the morning. The rest of the campus didn't open until seven, and the season didn't officially start for another six months!

Todd was hungry but didn't have anything to eat in his room. This meant he'd be practicing hungry and rushing to class.

After baseball, Todd had classes at eight, nine, and eleven followed by a gym class at one and practice again at five. He'd have to haul ass if he ever wanted to eat breakfast, lunch, or dinner, with his classes and practices scheduled the way they were.

"Hey Freshman! Wake your ass up!" Todd was startled awake by his roommate kicking his bed aggressively. He opened his eyes to find his roommate staring down at him. "I ain't your pappy," Luther said. "This will be the first and last time I'm gonna wake your ass up to make sure you get to where you have to be on time. Once an apartment unit opens up, you're on your own. Confused, Todd looked at the clock. Oh shit! 5:51! Todd was late.

"Thank you!" Todd exclaimed, jumping out of bed.

Frantic, he shoved everything in his athletic bag. He could hear his father's voice in his head telling him that he should have had everything he needed ready the night before.

"Shit!" he exclaimed. "Where the hell is my sock?"

"Man, shut up!" Luther said. "I don't have class until 10."

Frenetically – but quietly – Todd searched for his socks. He hated admitting that this wouldn't have been a problem if he'd put his clothes away in drawers, instead of leaving them in his suitcases and boxes.

"Found one!" he exclaimed, elated. He searched under his bed, determined to find the other. A glance at the clock told him it was now 5:56. Damn! I'm so screwed, he thought. He stood in the middle of the room, scanning it frantically to see if he could spot his sock. There! He dove nearly halfway across the room to grab it as if it was going to escape his grasp. He wedged his feet inside of two already-tied shoes and hopped toward the door as he tried pulling the tongue out just a bit more. He hurled himself out the door and took off for practice.

As he raced toward the diamond, Todd chided himself for laying back down. He didn't even remember doing it! He was exhausted. He hadn't gotten any good rest for weeks. Being away from Amani worried him, and he couldn't help but think about how he was going to run away with her, take care of her, and protect her from her maniacal family members. And now he'd overslept and would have to spend the morning with nasty breath and eye boogers because there hadn't been enough time for him to brush his teeth or wash his face.

He looked down at his watch and decided to pick up the pace. He could see the field and everyone already gathering in the dugout. It was 6:01. All downhill from here! Todd thought. When he reached the bottom of the hill he broke into a full sprint for the diamond, but he was still a minute or two late.

"Welcome!" Coach Hunter was saying as Todd arrived, breathless. The coach scanned his roster, sizing up the talent, and stopped on Todd. Todd held his breath, desperate not to be called out at his very first practice. "Thank you for taking time out of your busy morning to join us."

Damn, thought Todd. What a lousy way to meet your head coach for the first time. Once again, he could hear his dad's voice in his head: "If you're not 15 minutes early, you're 15 minutes late."

Coach Hunter was a retired professional outfielder with the Montreal Expos' minor league affiliate. His claim to fame was an extra base hit against Roger Clemons during September call-ups. His career ended in the same at bat when, as he was rounding second base, he tore his hamstring muscle off the bone. Thoughts of what might have been had turned Coach Hunter into a grump. His coaching style was built on a cornerstone of discipline, running, and more running.

"Meet your teammates," the coach continued. Todd was greeted with snickering and giggles. He scanned the group looking for Coach Raymond's familiar face. He wasn't there. Hopefully he's just late, too, thought Todd, although his tardiness certainly wouldn't be frowned upon as heavily as Todd's had been. Coach Raymond is an established coach; Todd is an unproven, late-addition freshman.

"We were about to introduce ourselves, but before we begin, I need you to do me a favor." Sheepishly, Todd cleared his throat. "This evening, Mr. Glass, would you do your teammates and me the honor of arriving on time?"

"Definitely, Coach. No problem," Todd answered nervously. "I don't know what happened to my alarm clock," he said.

"I don't want excuses, Son," the coach interrupted. "Ninety-nine percent of failures come from people who have a habit of making excuses. Are you a failure, Mr. Glass?" he asked, sounding more like a drill sergeant than a college baseball coach. "I want results," he added before Todd could tell him he wasn't a failure.

"I will never be late again," Todd promised.

"Good," Coach Hunter said. "And another thing. When you show up to my practices, can you please wear pants?" The entire team, assistant coaches, and medical staff erupted in laughter.

Confused, Todd looked down. "Oh, shit!" he exclaimed. In his rush to get out the door, and in the chaos of trying to find his shoes he'd somehow forgotten to put pants on over his briefs. There was nothing he could do now; he'd already arrived late. He covered his groin and tried not to die of embarrassment as he was heckled by his new teammates and coaches.

"Alright, alright, that's enough," Coach Hunter said. The team quieted instantly. "Mr. Glass is a member of our team, no matter how much of a joke he appears to be based on this morning's events." Todd winced as hearing his new coach call him a joke. "When one of us is being laughed at, we're all being laughed at, and I won't tolerate that," the coach concluded.

Todd admired the coach's interest in the way his team was perceived. His confident baritone voice ricocheted through each of the players there, inspiring respect and awe. They were a team of athletic young men reduced to feeble boys by the words of the man hired to lead them. And yet Todd could sense that each of them would follow Coach Hunter and do everything he could to earn the man's respect.

"This team – *my* team – will not be seen as a joke in this Conference," Coach continued. "Is that understood?" No one said a word; it was obvious that the question was rhetorical, a declaration rather than an actual question.

Coach Hunter stood in silence, making eye contact with each and every player. It was clear he meant business. He was 6' tall with a chiseled physique that suggested he could still play professional baseball, even in his mid-forties. His stare said, "Don't cross me."

"Nice ass!" someone yelled. Todd turned to see a young woman at the head of the girls' track team, who followed her lead by whistling and cheering. Todd wanted to crawl into a hole and die and vowed then and there to never do to another woman what was being done to him. The extra attention seemed to anger Coach even further. He stared silently at Todd, seething.

Todd could feel the heat from the sun as it crept higher in the mid-August sky. The day promised to be another scorchingly humid one, but Todd would have taken that heat ten times over if it meant he could avoid Coach Hunter's soul-piercing frigid stare. Todd didn't dare breathe. Todd looked away several times before coach broke the awkward silence.

Finally, Coach Hunter grumbled, "Coach Raymond leaves the team for greener pastures and I'm stuck with this big fuck you of a freshman recruit. He better hope I never see his ass again." Then, turning to his assistant coaches, he snarled, "From now on I will do the scouting. Now introduce yourself," he ordered Todd.

Knowing he'd already struck out in the first impressions category, Todd searched for a way to introduce himself that might save some face. He was terrified, his confidence decimated. "My name is Todd Glass." he squeaked, attempting – but failing – to match Coach Hunter's masculinity. "I play second base," he said, before sitting down. He had no desire to draw any more attention to himself than he already had.

"What's up, fellow Tigers!" the teammate to Todd's left cried. His voice, too, was deep and quite intimidating. "I'm Eli, the *starting* second baseman," he boasted, turning to sneer at Todd. "Maybe next year, Squirt." Any confidence Todd might have had left was now gone.

Eli did not fit the description of a typical second baseman. They were usually under six feet, but Eli was tall. Very tall. Todd guessed he was close to 6'4", 6'5". He was muscular, too, an adjective no one had ever used to describe Todd. Todd thought

Eli might've been a pitcher or first baseman, but not a second baseman.

"And just so no one's confused, I'll be the one wearing pants," Eli snickered. The team erupted in laughter but stopped abruptly when Coach Hunter shot them a displeased look.

"I'm Elijah," the next person said. He was tall and statuesque, like Eli. "I'm the reigning conference hitting champion and team captain. I will also be wearing pants. Coach is right," Elijah continued. "We made strides the last couple of seasons to be viewed as respectable. We went from two wins my freshman year to two wins away from the cellar of our conference last year." Todd didn't think coming in next-to-last place was respectable. He was used to being on teams that were highly competitive and highly successful.

"This is my senior season," Elijah said, "and I want nothing more than to feel a playoff atmosphere on our home field. Do you feel me?" The team cheered. Even Coach Hunter cracked a slight smile. Todd could see why Elijah was the team captain. He, like Coach Hunter, knew how to motivate. But unlike the coach, Elijah could do it with his words while Coach Hunter did it with fear.

"I'm Javier," said the next young man. "I play third base." Javier had such a thick accent Todd struggled to understand what he was saying. He was able to decipher that Javier was from somewhere in Latin America, or at least somewhere that English was not the primary language. "I wear briefs," he said.

"Better than tighty whities!" Eli said.

"They're the same thing!" Todd said. "Just less stylish. My drawers are supportive but also comfortable," he asserted, attempting to sound conclusive so the jokes about his underwear might stop. He came across as whiny, though, and was met with half-smiles, shrugs, and eye rolls.

Todd stood, stewing over his predicament. So he'd forgotten to put on pants! So what? Surely that didn't mean he should be subjected to this kind of taunting all morning. Not only did he not want to be on the same team with these guys; he didn't really want to be affiliated with them off the field, either.

In high school, Todd had been revered for his speed and defensive skills. He loved it when he overheard other teams' coaches or fans warn players against hitting the ball in his direction. They knew Todd was quick enough to get to and field any ball in his direction. They would tell their defenders not to lollygag because his speed allowed him to turn a single into a double. He'd been an athlete with immense potential. Now he was on a team with others who'd also been high school standouts. He didn't feel respected, and that made him angry.

As the players continued their introductions and listing their mostly college-level achievements, Todd felt he was out of their league. He'd never felt that way before, and he hated it. Todd always aspired to play professional ball and had assumed that college was going to be the springboard to his lofty goals. Sizing up his teammates, Todd realized how far out of reach his goals were. Everyone here appeared to be much more skilled and in much better shape than he was.

Lincoln University, a Division 2 school, was on the second tier athletically-speaking. Todd could only blame himself for not being recruited to play Division 1. Lack of hard work, both on the field and in the classroom, had caused him to fall short of allowing others to see greatness in him. That little nugget of truth was the hardest pill for him to swallow.

"This evening, Coach Hunter started, interrupting Todd's thoughts, "will be the easiest practice of the season. They will get progressively harder. Greatness doesn't come from mediocrity. It comes from pushing yourselves to be better. I will shove you to greatness. Prepare to be pushed to your limits. I hope you all worked out this summer because it'll show if you didn't," he said, looking directly at Todd. "Can you do me and your teammates a favor?"

Todd's sulking kept him from noticing Coach was directing his comments to him. He snapped to attention. "No problem, Coach! Anything! Todd said nervously.

"Be on time?" Once again, the "question" Coach was "asking" was really more of a statement. "Also, please make sure you wear matching shoes." Todd glanced past his once-white drawers which were now a strange grayish brown thanks to the dirt blowing in off the field. He was wearing one cleat and one sneaker. He played back in his mind the difficulty he'd had getting one of his shoes on. Now he knew why. He could slip his tennis shoes on with very little effort, but his cleats took lots of effort.

Each of his teammates laughed.

"Shut the fuck up!" Coach Hunter roared. Todd was amazed that a coach could cuss in college. "You think this is funny?! We only won *twelve* games last year. I told you just ten minutes ago, we will **not** be a joke. Every team in our conference already thinks of us that way. Every team in our *division* thinks of us that way. You are continuing to ignore when I said that making fun of a teammate is like making fun of yourself. Were you laughing last season when our competitors were making fun of us? A team that needed additional players to bail them out of the basement of the standings? We recruit two freshmen to help build our future. One of them is academically ineligible, and the other doesn' know how to put on a fucking pair of pants. What is there to laugh about?"

Once again, the team was silent.

"Since you all want to play around and joke, I'm going to show you how serious I am." He paused. "Hey, Calvin Klein!" he called to Todd. "Pick a number between one and ten." Todd's number in high school had been twenty five, so he added the two numbers and said seven.

"Seven laps up the hill!" Coach Hunter barked. "I want you to run that hill until *I* get tired. And I'm well rested! Now go!" The team moaned. "Go!" Coach hollered again.

The evil looks his teammates shot Todd's way sent chills down his spine. "I should have trained harder over the summer," he thought, starting slowly up the steep, grassy hill. "Train harder," he scoffed at his own thought, "that's a lie. I should have trained, period." The time he should have been practicing or working out he'd spent with Amani. Well, he was paying for it now!

The hill's elevation had to be close to 370 feet high. It was a steady incline for the first three-quarters of the way, then it became steep. As he neared the top for trip #1, Todd's thighs started to burn. With every step, he could feel his quadriceps alight in pain, his hamstrings pulling as if they might detach from his ligaments. His calf muscles tightened with each push off his feet.

The rest of the team was faring no better, continuously slipping on the freshly-cut surface made slick by the morning dew. It was excruciating. Each slip mimicked a mountain climbing exercise, which, by itself, was a high-intensity workout. Every misstep caused him to mimic a pushup off the grass. He looked like he was doing burpees, another high-intensity workout. Todd's core was screaming for him to stop. He finally reached the top but felt no achievement, just the realization that he had to do it six more times.

He saw that Elijah and Eli were already at the bottom of the hill and were about to start their second lap. Todd was ready to pack it in and head home. Less than twelve hours into his college experience, and he already had both fraternity members and teammates ready to beat him up.

The trek down the hill was just as rigorous as the trip up had been. He felt sharp pains in his knees and shins as he regulated his speed down the hill. He longed for the extra adrenalin that he'd had earlier as he was rushing to practice as his core muscles continued to scream for him to stop. Every muscle in his body was working vigorously to keep him from falling over. Falling was the least of his concerns at the moment, though. He was still worried about someone seeing him in his underwear or, worse yet, accidently exposing himself, as the moisture from the morning dew had saturated his underwear, making them transparent in spite of their now grayish-brown hue.

He should've stayed focused. Before he knew it, he was on his butt and sliding down the hill. The relief this brought was short-lived as he saw the majority of his teammates were passing him on their second trip up the hill.

When he reached the bottom, Todd prayed Coach would say they'd done enough, that they could pack it in for the morning. But he didn't. "Move your ass, Glass!" Coach Hunter yelled. "There aren't any participation trophies here! Move it! Move it! Move it!" Todd increased his pace to get away from his screaming coach more quickly. Back up the hill, he thought, bracing for round two of Mount Kilimanjaro. The burning in his thighs was brutal, but were not to be outmatched by the fire in his lungs. On top of everything, he was struggling to breathe as the grass activated his sinuses.

Dripping in sweat, snot, and tears was *not* how Todd wanted to spend his Monday morning. With every step he took, Todd contemplated playing baseball. If this was orientation, what would practice be like? he wondered. Hell, the season doesn't officially start for another six months! He was on a partial scholarship and knew his dad would make him pay the tuition difference if he lost it. "The road to success is filled with indignation," his dad would say. Though Todd did not want to continue, he had to. Almost there, he thought. Just 127 weeks, four days, and 22 hours until graduation. Besides, his parents were going to kill him if he didn't work hard at trying to succeed here. That is if the mountain didn't do it first. If he quit, he wouldn't be able to face the pain in their eyes knowing their son failed them after only one day. Yeah, they're going to kill me. Well, fuck that, he thought. I have a sister; let *Tiffany* make them proud!

As he headed down the hill, Todd could see his teammates were already halfway up for lap number three. He was going to get lapped. It was inevitable. This would be even more disastrous than him showing up without pants on and wearing mismatched shoes. As he neared his coach, Todd could hear his teammates on his heels. He was giving it all he had, but he hadn't worked out since the beginning of May. Now it was the middle of August, and his body just wasn't prepared.

"Lapped, Glass," Coach Hunter yelled. "Your lazy ass better start running at Mach Christ if you plan to stay on this team!" Todd was desperate to stop. He felt like he was running in place. What he was doing hardly even constituted running. He was just swinging his arms and sliding his feet across the grass.

After a few more trips up the hill Todd could see his teammates gathering their stuff to leave. Hallelujah, Todd thought; his legs felt like jello. The prospect of nearing the end of this hellish workout gave Todd a little more pep in his step. Now more energetic, Todd coasted down the hill with speed that had escaped him since his workout began, but as he reached the bottom, he started to cramp up and wanted to collapse. He choked back the vomit that was ready to spew everywhere. He could feel his sodium levels bottoming out and began to stress over how he was going to make it back to the dorms for some pants now that there was more movement on campus. He did *not* want to take that hill again, and he could go the long way around, but that almost guaranteed that someone would see him.

"Glass! What are you doing?" Coach Hunter snapped.

"Breathing," Todd said. That was a lie, he could barely breathe, but he didn't want to let the coach in on his thoughts at the moment.

"I demand a culture of winners," Coach continued, "so the person that comes in last place in any running exercise has to do an extra lap."

Todd thought his eyes were going to pop out of his head. He could barely stand as it was; another lap would kill him! Looking at his watch, Todd saw it was 6:58. He needed to get a move on or he was going to be late to his first class too. Out of breath and in pain,

Todd turned to make his trek back up the hill. As he stood there staring at it, he decided he'd rather quit school on the spot than run this lap. Still, he started, pumping his arms and legs as fast as he could. When he looked back to check his progress, Todd was deflated when he saw he'd only made it a hundred feet.

"Get a move on!" Coach Hunter yelled. Todd was desperate to walk but didn't dare, though his movement probably mimicked it.

"Glass, do you know what the speed of light is?" Coach asked sarcastically. "It's the speed at which you're messing up any chance of staying on my team. Pick up the pace!"

Panting heavily and drenched in sweat, Todd finally made it to the top. His watch read seven fifteen. He ran down the hill.

Faster and faster he went. He couldn't feel his legs. Gravity had taken over, and he couldn't stop, couldn't slow down. He was going too fast and was going to fall flat on his ass. He didn't. He landed on his face.

Todd slid a good five feet before he came to a full stop. His face was covered in freshly-cut grass. He tried to get up, but quickly plopped back down. The only thing he could think of was that he was light years away from achieving his goals. Was he going to have to give up his dreams of playing baseball? He realized it really *does* take hard work and dedication to be successful. Todd was lacking in both.

Todd could hear his dad: "Nothing in this world is given to you. You don't get to the moon riding a bicycle, and you don't achieve goals by half-assing everything." His dad was right. Todd had half-assed *every*thing for the past year. He'd barely graduated from high school because of his lack of effort and had missed out on scholarship opportunities because of his lackadaisical participation in that journalism program his dad had gotten him into. He'd been completely unprepared for practice this morning because he hadn't worked out this summer.

Todd was quickly learning that he wasn't ready for life because he hadn't put any effort into living it. His parents had done everything for him up to this point. "Something's gotta change," he thought. "And it starts now," he declared, still lying face down in the grass.

"Your physical performance is proof that evolution is a lie," Coach Hunter was saying. "Now get up, Chippendales."

Todd struggled to get to one knee, wheezing, coughing, and aching. Finally, he made it to his feet. He didn't dare take a step on his wobbly legs. Glancing at his watch, he saw it was 7:32. He was going to be late to class. His only option was that damn hill again. It was by far the quickest route.

Turning to face it, Todd sighed and took off, but he didn't go anywhere. "Hey, Freshman! Do you want a ride?" Coach Hunter asked. "My truck is right here." Todd couldn't believe the offer. Sore and beginning to cramp, he waddled toward the truck. He opened the passenger door, dreaming of how wonderful it would be to shower.

"What the hell are you doing?" Coach Hunter asked.

"I thought you were going to give me a ride," Todd choked out, confused.

"There's no way I'm going to have a half-naked freshman ride up front with me! Can you imagine the rumors? Get in the bed."

Todd mustered the strength to make the climb. It took him three tries. He could see the disappointment on his coach's face as his new recruit struggled with yet another task.

As they rode across campus, Todd began rifling through his book bag looking for his keys. How he managed to remember his bag but not his pants Todd would never understand. He hadn't even grabbed the books he needed for that morning's classes. Even if he had pants on he wouldn't be able to go straight to class. He smelled. Todd guessed the odor was the *real* reason Coach wouldn't let him ride in the cab. Todd wondered which smelled worse: his breath or his body. He cupped his hand in front of his mouth and breathed in. "My breath," he conceded. "Definitely my breath."

Todd was thankful his dad couldn't see him now. He wondered what he'd say if he could. It probably would be something like, "Todd, "you wouldn't be here with your ass out looking stupid if you were more organized!"

"Why didn't I get today started the night before," he groaned to himself. This was a question his dad had asked him time and time again. He'd also tell him if he couldn't get up with the chickens his ass had better stop hanging out with the owls. Todd still hadn't figured that one out.

Coach pulled in front of the dorm. Todd hopped out. Every muscle and tendon ached when his feet touch the ground. He walked toward the front of the truck to thank the coach for the ride.

"I followed your career all four years you were in high school," Coach began. "A freshman playing varsity; that's an amazing feat. Then you got lazy. Your love for the game can only carry you so far. The rest of the journey is made through hard work."

Todd feigned interest in his words. He'd heard his parents, friends, and coaches tell him he had so much wasted potential so many times he could hardly stand it anymore. He just wanted to go inside so he could shower and stop being seen in his underwear.

"Thanks again, Coach," he said, interrupting what was sure to be a lecture he didn't have the time for. Todd made his way toward the front door of the dorm. Todd regretted walking away from the coach so abruptly, not so much for ending his lecture. It was helpful advice, but the timing was off. Coach was pulling away before Todd's feet even hit the steps leading to the doorway. Then the truck stopped and Coach leaned his head out the window.

"Freshman! You may think you're hot shit. You aren't shit. Just cold diarrhea. Your game and attitude stink." And with that, he then sped off.

Racing into the dorm, Todd quickly gathered his toiletry bag and a towel, but he couldn't wipe Coach's words from his mind. His criticism stung but he didn't have time to think about them. It was 7:41. He had nineteen minutes to shower, dress, and sprint across campus to make it to class on time.

Turning on the water in the showerbay, Todd grabbed his toothbrush and jumped in. The water was freezing, but he didn't have time to wait for it to warm up. He showered, urinated, and brushed his teeth, all at the same time. He still felt dirty as he rushed back to his room. Did he really still smell like grass and sweat? Or was it because the stench was still in his nose after his face plant on the grass?

"There they are!" Todd grabbed the shorts he'd planned to wear to practice. They were resting on the foot of the bed. He threw them into the closet hard, as if they were to blame for not making it onto his body this morning. He searched his suitcase for a shirt and clean underwear. The underwear he practiced in were the same pair he'd worn the day before. He had yet to unpack and began flinging clothes everywhere as he searched for something – anything – to wear. He hadn't folded his clothes when he'd packed, nor had he packed with any organization. "Yes!," he cheered. "A sock! I'm gonna need this. But where's the other one?" He continued his search. "Awesome! A shirt." He sniffed it. He wasn't sure if it was clean. "Clean enough," he thought as he put it on. He jumped up and looked in the mirror. It was horribly wrinkled. "Where is my iron?" he wondered.

"Dude!" his roommate shouted. "Are you going to wake me every morning bare assed and free-balling it? Can't you cover up? I'm not trying to see your buttfro."

"I'm trying," Todd said apologetically. "I can't find anything I need."

He finally located his iron and glanced at the clock on his desk. 7:52. "Shit," he mumbled to himself. "I'm going to be late for class." He couldn't do that. He'd been late for practice; he couldn't also be late to his very first class. He plugged the iron in, anyway, though.

His side of the room looked like a tornado had just blown through it, but Todd managed to find a pair of underwear and a mismatched sock. The iron was hot enough, so he took his shirt off and began to iron it on his bed. But the unstable surface meant any wrinkle he ironed out was replaced by others. The shirt looked worse. He threw it on and ironed it some more.

"Good enough," he thought as he grabbed his bags and ran out the door.

It was 7:58, and for the second time this morning, Todd was sprinting across campus trying to be somewhere in less time than it took to get there. His body still ached from his mornings unexpected workout . Every step was a reminder that he should have spent the past three months exercising.

When he passed the student union, Todd stopped abruptly. He had no clue where he was going. Opening his bookbag, he rifled through his books, folders, and notebook looking for his schedule. Western Civilization. Edwards Hall, room 208. He realized he'd forgotten to switch out the textbooks and still had the wrong ones. "Too late to do anything about it now," he thought.

Scanning the campus Todd spotted a map. He ran toward it. Edwards Hall was the building a hundred yards in front of him. It was eight o'clock on the dot. The bells in the clock tower chimed to remind him he was late.

He opened the door, pausing briefly for a couple of girls to enter. Flashing a smile in their direction, Todd was disappointed when they paid him zero attention. He spotted the stairwell and flew up the stairs two steps at a time, his thighs burning, aching, and cramping. He hobbled toward room 208 like a wrapped mummy and got there just as the professor began closing the door. Todd was out of breath and struggled to wish the professor a good morning.

"You must be a freshman," the professor said, blocking Todd's entry. "Your tardiness is not my emergency. If you can't be here on time, get here early," he finished, shutting the door in Todd's face.

"Please," Todd begged, hoping the professor would take pity on him. The professor shot Todd a cross look from behind the door's glass window. He watched as the professor walked away, noticing a slight limp and his use of a cane. Todd stared in horror, wondering what his Frankenstein walk must have looked like to the professor.

His watch read 8:01. "Shit!" he exclaimed. "I have an hour before my next class, might as well go back and take an *actual* shower."

As he approached the door to his room, he could hear the ringing of an off-campus phone call. Todd quickly unlocked the door and ran inside to answer the phone. His roommate was still sleeping.

"Hello?"

"Shouldn't you be in class?" asked the voice on the other end. Todd gulped hard; he knew instantly who it was.

"Hi, Dad," Todd said. He thought about making up an excuse for why he wasn't in class, but decided not to bother. There *was* no good reason, and his dad would see through it, anyway. "How are you?" he asked instead.

"Let me guess," his dad started. "You somehow managed to oversleep on the first day of class?" Todd was amazed. How was his dad so good at knowing what was going on without him even saying anything?

"My money is a terrible thing to waste," his dad reminded him. "Do not, I repeat, do *not* make your college experience that chapter in life that you're too embarrassed to read aloud." Too late for that, Todd thought to himself as he replayed the last twelve hours.

"I'm walking out the door headed to my nine o'clock class now," he lied, trying to get off the phone quickly.

"Call your mother tonight and let her know how your first day went," his dad said.

"Okay," Todd said.

"And Son?" his dad added. "Don't screw up. This isn't high school." With that, he hung up the phone.

"Hundreds of miles away and he *still* knows when I'm messing up," Todd thought. "Four years of high school, and today proves I'm still an idiot. Maybe four years of college will produce better results."

Before Todd could make it to the door the phone rang again. Again it was an outside call. "Hello?" he answered.

"Get your ass to class," demanded the voice on the other end.

"I'm leaving now, Dad," Todd said, hanging up the phone and heading to the bathroom.

Chapter 16

"Paradise!" Todd exclaimed, looking around the baseball field. Evening practice was already better than this morning's had been. For one, he was fully clothed, but more importantly, he could take in the picturesque view of the stadium.

It wasn't really a stadium, though, but a small playing arena. There was a whitewashed brick backstop behind home plate, and behind that a portable barrier netting system to protect fans from foul balls. The two on deck circles had the initials LU in a bold blue font. The dugouts were painted in navy blue and white. Baseball at the university produced very little fanfare, evidenced by the three portable bleachers. Todd guessed a full house might produce a hundred fans.

The combined smell of dirt and grass was so intoxicating to him. When everything else in his life was going wrong he could always rely on the baseball diamond to make everything right again. This was his Shangri-la.

Todd took his time savoring the field he was going to play on for the next four years. He'd missed the familiarity of the baseball diamond. He almost regretted dismissing her in favor of spending more time with Amani. Baseball had always been the love of his life. Thanks to Amani, it had become his mistress. But that was about to change. He admired her beautiful dimensions and marveled at the curvature and mesmerizing symmetry of its base paths. The bright green of the Kentucky bluegrass in the outfield accompanied with its stimulating aroma sent his heart into a flutter. Todd breathed in his surroundings and felt like he truly belonged. He'd done a complete 180 from the way he'd thought about it that morning and felt a wave of relief wash over him. Now, he was there to play on the field the way it was meant to be played on. He was captivated by the artistically-painted Tiger logo in the heart of its lush green outfield. It was perfectly drawn and made the tiger look as if it was about to leap off the field. He was a Blue Tiger now and it was time to prove that he belonged.

He turned his attention to the infield, enchanted with the contours of her playable surface. He got down on his hands and knees, his face close to the ground, and scrutinized every playable surface at second base. He caressed its surface, feeling for imperfections that may lead to bad hops, or soft spots that may deaden hit balls. Not feeling any, he was elated with anticipation of a time when he would be able to compete on her.

His eyes were drawn to the voluptuous mound of her infield center. He hopped to his feet, guessing the dimensions of the outfield. He calculated how hard he would have to hit the ball to clear the fence. He had yet to do it in a game, but there's always the possibility.

The sound of the clay, sand, and silt moving under his feet made him feel at home, though he was nowhere near it. Baseball can make everything alright in the world, he thought. For the first time since being abandoned by his parents in their quest to make him his own man, Todd was happy. Baseball made him happy, so much so that a tear of joy formed in the corner of his right eye.

"Infielders! Line up for fielding practice!" instructed one of the assistant coaches.

Todd was eager to field some ground balls; it was therapeutic. Lining up behind several of his teammates, Todd waited his turn anxiously. He hopped up and down in place, appearing to get loose. In reality, he just couldn't contain his excitement.

Finally, he was next in line. He observed the effortless fielding of all his teammates before him. Now it was his turn. He crouched in the ready position, awaiting the ball to be hit in play. Todd focused on the tiny white ball with red stitching as the coach tossed it in the air. He waited patiently for the ball to make contact with the bat as it came back down into the path of the coach's swing. Crack! went the bat as it made contact with the ball.

"Oops!" yelled the coach. He'd hit the ball harder than he anticipated. "Leave it!" he yelled, but Todd ignored him and ran hard for the area he thought the ball would travel. He quickly closed the distance from where he started to where he needed to be. When he was just a few feet away, Todd dove for the ball, stretching his glove out.

WHAP! came the satisfying sound the ball makes as it nestles securely in the glove. Todd hit the ground in one fluid, violent motion, ignoring the sting he felt in his lungs. Todd bounced off the ground, rose to his feet, and fired the ball to first base. His actions were effortless, appearing as a single, choreographed motion.

Beaming, Todd ran quickly back into line as if that kind of play was routine. That was fun! he thought to himself, impatiently awaiting another turn. As he made his way to the end of the line, his teammates congratulated him with slaps of their gloves to his back side, the ultimate show of respect.

"Hey, Rook!" yelled Coach Hunter. "Get in the box. Let's see if you're worth keeping."

My time to shine, thought Todd. He'd led his team in hits and runs his senior year and had been fifth in the district in stolen bases. He grabbed his bat bag gleefully and unzipped it gently. He reached into the bag and gingerly pulled out a baby blanket. He unwrapped what it contained as carefully as if he were handling an actual baby. His teammates watched in disbelief as Todd revealed his bat as if it was destined to elevate Todd to greatness.

"What in the hell are you doing?" one of them asked.

"I'm waking Opie up," Todd replied.

"You *named* your **bat**?" asked one of the assistant coaches sarcastically.

"It's not a bat," Todd argued, "it's my baby. I'm getting her acclimated to her new surroundings."

"Why the fuck do all the infielders have to be the most insane players on the field?" yelled the pitcher.

Stepping up to the plate, Todd stared at the pitcher, trying to intimidate him.

"Now take it easy, Butch!" yelled the pitching coach. "He doesn't know you're a pro prospect."

Todd smiled to himself. Facing a pitcher who might go pro meant he had an opportunity to impress the coaches and reap the respect he more than likely lost arriving to practice half naked earlier. Todd, a natural righty, batted from the left side. He wasn't great at it, he just did it because of an urban legend. He'd heard a rumor that batting from the opposite side of the plate helps the batter see the ball differently when hitting again from your normal position. After switching back and forth like this and having eleven hits in a row during his senior season, Todd never went back to batting only from the right. It had been during this streak that the Lincoln scout had seen him play and recruited him. The team was looking for a left-handed hitting second baseman, and Todd was just that, if only with just one week's experience.

Full of confidence that his prowess as a switch hitter had gotten him a partial scholarship and his recruiter a better job with another school, Todd was not about to bat using his natural swing.

"Let's see what you got," Todd snapped at the pitcher. Standing 6'6" and four years Todd's senior, Butch was a man throwing to a boy.

The first pitch Todd took for a strike. He usually did this so he could observe the pitcher's mannerisms and timing. Todd was thoroughly impressed by the sharpness of Butch's curveball and was glad he'd stuck with his habit; he would have looked foolish swinging at that curve.

Todd could tell right away why Butch was being scouted by the pros. He stepped out of the batter's box briefly to try to throw off Butch's rhythm. It didn't work. Butch had probably seen all of Todd's tricks a million times over. His second pitch caught the inside corner of the plate for strike two. Todd was completely fooled by this one, too. He expected it to be on the outside, but it snuck inside, almost hitting Todd as he stepped into it.

"You're out of your league," the catcher sneered.

Todd took a deep breath. "What are you doing?" he asked himself quietly. "This is what we do. Gather yourself and let's make some magic happen, he demanded of his bat. Todd stepped out of the box and took two viscous swings. He was hyped, ready to make contact and fly around the bases. That's what we're here for, he told himself.

Butch started his wind up. Todd clutched his bat, loosened his shoulders, dipped his knees, and dug in with his back foot. He was ready. Butch's high leg kick was unlike anything Todd had ever seen before. Whap! The catcher's glove popped after the ball sizzled through the air.

"What are you doing, Glass?!" yelled Coach Hunter.

"I'm hitting!" Todd replied.

"No, you're hitting the bench," the catcher snickered.

"Hitting is taking the bat off your shoulders!" the coach snapped. "All you've been doing is watching the ball land in the catcher's mitt! That last ball was right down the middle! Why didn't you swing at it?" he demanded.

"Awww, was it too fast for you?" the catcher teased. The entire team erupted in a chorus of laughter.

Todd walked out of the batter's box, his head hanging low. He'd been embarrassed again in front of his new teammates. But in answer to the catcher's comment: yes, it was too fast. He never even saw the ball; he only heard it hiss as it streaked past him.

"Ninety-six!" yelled the pitching coach. Todd was mesmerized that someone could throw an object that fast. He remembered reading that Nolan Ryan could throw a fastball ninety-five miles per hour. It took less than half a second to reach the plate. Todd had never seen it in person before, though. Shoot. He didn't see it this time, either. If you blink you would miss it. Todd blinked.

Chapter 17

Todd sat in the back of the auditorium-style classroom observing the rest of the students as they came in. He was amazed that most of them appeared to have their ducks in a row. No one else appeared nervous. Just Todd. He felt like he didn't belong. He came to college to study television production, yet he was forced to take a Philosophy course. His choices were limited if he didn't want to take extra science and math classes. *I guess that's what happens when you skip out on that portion of new student orientation,* he surmised.

"Welcome," began the professor standing at the front of the class. "I'm Dr. Reed. Welcome to Introductory Philosophy."

Doctor Reed fit the description of what a seasoned college professor was supposed to look like. She was in her early sixties, wiry gray hair, wire-thin glasses, and lots of wrinkles. She wore a lab coat, which was confusing since they weren't in a lab setting, and this was not a science course. Her desk, which was off in the corner, was cluttered with tons of unorganized papers and big books. The podium she stood behind was littered with even more loose papers.

"Let's dive right in," she suggested. "I tend to pick on the quintessential freshmen in the class. You know, the clueless student who sits alone in the back hoping the professor doesn't pick on them." Everyone turned around and stared at Todd. He gulped hard and pretended to be unfazed by the extra attention when, in fact, he was. His feet turned ice cold, and his stomach was churning.

"Stand up young man," Dr. Reed directed. "What are you wearing?"

Todd knew he was being set up for a more difficult question, and he tried to act unbothered by being the center of attention. He cleared his throat as he prepared to be heard by the entire room. "I…," his voice cracked. He cleared his voice again, and tried again, this time speaking from deep in his diaphragm. "I am wearing a shirt, jeans, and tennis shoes."

"A typical freshman answer," the professor snorted. "Tell me more about what you're wearing and why," she said.

"I wanted to look nice for class," Todd explained, "So I wore a Tommy Hilfiger shirt and some Arizona jeans plus a pair of

Reebok tennis shoes." He started to sit down since he was sure he'd answered her questions appropriately.

"Why didn't you just say a red, white, and blue shirt? Or blue jeans? Or whatever color shoes you have on? Why did you try to impress us with name brands? Stand up, and continue standing until I say you may sit down."

Todd felt exposed and put on the spot. He would be judged no matter what answer he gave. He tried to remember what his dad always said about being judged by others, but his mind was blank.

"Are you pretentious?" Dr. Reed asked. Her hand was resting on her chin as she looked Todd up and down as if he was being studied for a social experiment.

"I don't know," he answered with a slight shrug.

"Another typical freshman answer," she replied. Several people chuckled. "Do you think you look cool?" she asked.

"Well, this is what's in style," Todd answered, to a few more scattered chuckles.

"Is he right?" asked Dr. Reed. "Are his clothes stylish? Raise your hand if you believe... Excuse me, young man, what's your name?"

"Todd," he answered. He stopped short of giving his full name because his voice started to crack again.

"Raise your hand if you believe Todd," she mocked, "is stylish." Before she looked for responses, she continued, "Todd, are you famous? "Why the single name? Are you famous? Like Cher, or Prince, or Madonna?"

"No, ma'am," Todd answered.

The professor asked her question again. "Raise your hand if you think the unfamous Todd looks stylish, or if you think the name brands he mentioned are stylish." A majority of the hands in the room went up in the air. Todd breathed a sigh of relief. "What do you think about the class sharing your sense of fashion?"

"Cool," Todd said, a response which was again met with snickers. Todd just wanted to sit down. He didn't like all the attention on him, not in the classroom, anyway. It would be different if he was playing ball. But to have his answers dissected like this was torture.

"So then you're an obsequious individual?" Dr. Reed asked.

"I'm Black," he said, having no idea what *obsequious* meant. The class erupted in laughter.

"I'm asking if you chose this outfit because it pleases you, or because you want to please those around you."

"I guess to please others," Todd answered honestly. "I wanted to make a good impression."

"Thank you for the honest answer," the professor replied. "Round of applause for Todd and his sense of style." The class responded with a few tenuous claps. "So Todd," Dr. Reed continued, "I assume fashionable clothes such as yours don't come cheap."

"Not really," Todd responded bashfully.

"Speak up, young man!" the professor interrupted. "Answer questions with confidence!" she demanded.

"Not really," Todd repeated more loudly.

"Would you agree that it was money well spent since your peers agree with your fashion sense?"

"Yes, ma'am," Todd answered, feigning confidence.

"Thank you for your answers, Mr. Todd. But if you live your life trying to please others, you aren't living for you, but for them. To me, that's the sign of a life wasted. Just one more question before you sit down," she said. "Pick a number between 1 and 10."

Todd couldn't decide between three and seven. He finally settled on seven, the sum of the numbers on the back of his jersey. "Seven," he said.

"You may sit down," Mr. Todd. The professor walked over to the chalkboard. "Your first assignment, due in seven days, thanks to Mr. Todd, will be a seven-page paper, typed and double spaced that answers this question." She began to write on the board. Mumbles and groans filled the room. When she finished writing, the question read: Is it wrong to purchase fast-fashion, rapidly-produced clothing that uses manufacturing methods that has a negative impact on the environment and exploits workers? Todd's heart sank as his classmates shot evil looks in his direction. Hopefully my next class will be better, he thought.

It wasn't.

Chapter 18

"Buenos días. Busca un asiento y escribe en Español lo que esperas aprender en clase este semestre."

A discombobulated Todd looked down at his schedule. He verified the number on the paper and compared it with the number next to the door. He was in the right place. "Introduction to Spanish," he said, sighing. The demure, elderly, Latin woman speaking to him was not practicing intro to anything. She was advanced. Too advanced, at least for Todd. After two years as a C student in high school Spanish, Todd could barely muster enough vocabulary to order at Taco Bell. Time to show her what I know, he guessed.

"¡Buenos días!" he said. "Me llamo Todd."

"Busca un asiento y escribe en Español lo que esperas aprender en clase este semestre," repeated the instructor.

"S.O.C.K.S.," Todd replied. His dad used to joke that he didn't need to know Spanish when he visited Mexico; he just needed to spell socks and he would fit right in. Todd wasn't sure how his Dad's joke fared in Mexico, but it didn't work in Introduction to Spanish at Lincoln University.

The instructor shot Todd an irritated look and turned to greet the student behind Todd. Todd entered the classroom slowly, hoping to hear how the other student responded to what the instructor said.

"¡Buenos días! Busca un asiento y escribe en español lo que esperas aprender en clase este semestre," she repeated.

"¡Buenos días a ti, también! Estoy feliz de estar aquí." The two exchanged a friendly smile.

"Excuse me," Todd said to the student before she could find a seat. " Can I ask what you said to her?"

The girl looked Todd up and down with an expression that said "Why are you here if you don't know basic Spanish?" Todd was asking himself the same question.

"I told her, 'Good morning to you, too. I'm happy to be here.'"

The desks were arranged in a circle. The girl picked a seat directly across from the chalkboard. Todd sat down next to her. "What did the professor say?" he asked. The girl, who'd begun searching her bookbag for a notebook, pen, and folder, stopped in the middle of gathering her things, and shot Todd a look that said she was more than irritated. Todd got lost in her big hazel eyes. They reminded him of Amani. Sadness coursed through him. He missed her.

"Look!" she snapped, interrupting his daydream. "I did not work sixty hours a week in a sweltering hot steel mill this summer so I could afford college, just to be your private tutor. Use the context clues from the words you do know," she said, her tone patronizing, "and figure out the rest using your textbook."

"But she spoke so fast I couldn't even catch all the words," Todd. "It sounded like 'Blah Blah Blah,' but in Spanish. She needs subtitles," he joked.

Todd's humor had broken through. The girl chuckled. "She said good morning," the girl started, softening her tone. "She told us to find a seat and write what we hope to learn this semester in Spanish."

"Man. I didn't get any of that," Todd confessed. "She said it so fast I couldn't have deciphered it if she'd said it in English. Thanks," he said. "I mean ¡Gracias!"

"De nada," she responded.

"By the way, my name is Todd," he said, while extending his hand.

"I'm Mercedes," she replied.

"Nice to meet you," Todd said.

"Oh we've met," Mercedes responded, her annoyance returning.

Todd racked his brain but couldn't remember having met her before. When Mercedes realized he had no clue who she was, she smiled.

"It's okay if you don't remember. It was a brief encounter," she said. Her curly Auburn hair was vibrant as she wrapped it playfully around her finger. She was enjoying watching Todd struggle to remember her. Her deep dimples were prominent as she smiled, and her smooth, caramel complexion was the perfect tone to highlight her mesmerizing eyes. She stood close to five-and-a-half feet. Her physique was one of a woman who'd worked sixty hours a week in a steel mill during the summer. She was fit.

"Give up," she asked.

"Yes," Todd said.

"We ran into each other when you disrupted my Greek stroll."

Now he remembered. "I am *so* sorry," he said, embarrassed.

"It's okay," she replied. "It was actually kinda funny," she said with a chuckle. "You must be a freshman," she concluded.

"Is it that obvious?" Todd asked. "I'd never seen anything like that before," he confessed. "It was all Greek to me." The two laughed as they began their assignment. Todd took Mercedes' advice and used the glossary in the back of the textbook for help.

Having greeted everyone in class the same way she'd greeted Todd and Mercedes, the professor walked to the middle of the circle of desks and began speaking to the whole class, again in Spanish. Todd had no clue what she was saying. He tried listening for keywords and looking up the meaning of others in the back of his book, but she spoke too fast. She walked around the room, collecting the assignment she'd given as people arrived. She stopped to read each one as they were handed to her. When she got to Todd's, she laughed and pointed at him, indicating that she'd be keeping her eyes on him.

"What did yours say?" Mercedes asked, eager to be let in on the joke.

"I wrote, 'Mi objetivo es aprender lo que el maestro está diciendo en Español, sin tener que pedirle a mi compañero de clase que lo traduzca al Inglés para mí.'" Todd did his best to pronounce the words he'd written, but it was clear he was struggling. His pronunciation was so off Mercedes had no clue what he said. When Todd realized it, he said it again, this time in English.

"I said my goal is to learn what the teacher is saying in Spanish without having to ask my classmate to translate it for me."

Mercedes snickered. "By the way," she added. "She's not a teacher."

Puzzled, Todd shrugged. "Then where's our teacher?" he asked, confused.

"Freshmen…," Mercedes sighed, rolling her eyes. Then, whispering so as to not draw too much attention to them, she leaned in close to Todd. "Don't you know the difference between a teacher and a professor?"

"There's a difference?" Todd asked.

"Yes," Mercedes explained. "A teacher is what you had in high school. You're in the big leagues now kid," she joked. "Graduate assistants," she continued, "are at the bottom of the totem pole. If they're late to class you leave immediately. Lecturers come next. You wait five minutes for them. Professors without PhDs get a 15-minute grace period, and PhDs get at least 20 minutes."

"Who makes this stuff up?" Todd asked.

Mercedes continued without answering his question. "If they happen to be a visiting PhD, you have to wait 30- to 45 minutes if they're late."

Todd leaned back in his chair, overwhelmed by all the information Mercedes had just given him. "How long are professors supposed to wait for students?" he joked.

Mercedes looked disappointed. "A student should never be late," she said. "No one is paying *you* to come to class. You're paying *them* to learn a little of what they know. If you can't show up to class on time or even early, you don't deserve to be in college."

Her words stung, but Todd knew she was right. He had a lot to learn. His first lesson? Figure out what the hell his Spanish professor was saying.

Chapter 19

Math had been the bane of Todd's existence since birth. And now it was his next class. He'd tried to avoid it at every juncture in his life. He remembered in one of his high school classes a poster that hung on the wall listing just about every profession ever known and how each used math. Todd made it his goal to find a profession that required zero math. When he finally decided, he would be sure to pursue a Bachelor of Arts – not Science – in an attempt to avoid extra math and science classes.

When he'd taken his placement tests, Todd had tried to bomb the math section. His brilliant idea was to get placed in the easiest math class there was, pass the two semesters he'd need to graduate (regardless of his major), and be done with it. It was a good plan… in theory. The only problem he could think of was if he was being placed in a remedial class that was so low he wouldn't even get credit for it. But he decided he'd even be okay with that since a remedial class could give him the little bit of math skill he might need as an adult. In no scenario could he have been prepared him for what happened next.

He'd *aced* the placement test and had been placed in a 400-level calculus class designed for *graduate level* in college. What are the odds of *that* happening, he wondered. The answer eluded him, of course, because he lacked the mathematical prowess to figure it out. How had randomly shading in various letters on his scantron test lead to this. Damn the luck. And now – thanks to the innate skill both his parents had in the subject – he needed to succeed.

They used to joke that he must have been switched at birth whenever he brought home a failing math grade (which was often). If Todd couldn't find the answer by counting his fingers and toes he felt the problem was too advanced. In Algebra, Todd had always pondered what the big deal was about finding x. Why all the parentheses for a math formula?

As he entered his classroom, Todd was struck by the color scheme. The walls were painted in shades of blue and orange. The school's colors were blue and gray. There was a Lincoln University in Pennsylvania whose colors were blue and orange, so he guessed this room had been painted in an homage to *that* Lincoln University – also a historically Black college – because it had been founded first. However, once he heard the faint sound of classical music playing softly from a stereo in the corner,

Todd surmised it had something to do with stimulating his mind. He knew he was going to need all the help he could get.

In the middle of the classroom was a giant, round table with fancy, plush leather chairs surrounding it. The scene reminded Todd of boardrooms he'd seen on television, not like any of the classrooms he'd been in.

"Good morning, everyone. Please take your seats. My name is Dr. Ezekial Wormley. Welcome to Advanced Calculus."

The small group of students clapped and cheered. Never in his life did Todd think he'd be in a situation where those in attendance for a *math* class would cheer.

"I know it will be boring, but we're going to start by reviewing how to write proofs and completed mathematical notation," Dr. Wormley continued.

"What the hell is that?" Todd thought, looking around at his classmates as they groaned in disappointment.

"I know, I know," Dr. Wormley said. "But then we'll tackle exciting stuff like Dirichlet's Test; the Epsilon-Delta Definition of Limits; how to prove the triangle, reverse triangle, and Bernoulli's Inequality; how to prove pointwise convergence; and how to prove uniform convergence." Again the class erupted in cheers and applause. Todd felt like a fish out of water. He even looked like one as he flopped around in his seat. He was uncomfortable in his current situation and knew he was going to need every bit of luck and prayer not to completely bomb this class.

"Before we get started, are there any questions?" Todd raised his hand, and his classmates chuckled. "You don't have to raise your hand here; this isn't high school," Dr. Wormley said. "What's your question, young man?

"Umm," Todd started. "How do I use this calculator?" he asked, holding it up. The class erupted in laughter. Even Dr. Wormley couldn't contain his amusement. Todd was embarrassed as he, once again, faced ridicule by his classmates. First in Philosophy, now in Calculus.

"That's a good one," Dr. Wormley said. "I'm going to have to keep my eyes on you. Next you'll be asking me how to use an abacus," he joked. The class joined him in a laugh.

"Now that you mention it," Todd replied. "Are you talking about that thing with the sliding balls on it?" he asked. The class burst out in laughter again.

"Oh man!" started Dr. Wormley, laughing and wiping tears from his eyes. "Apparently, we have a class clown with us!" Todd didn't understand what was so funny. He understood the terminology in Spanish class better than here.

"What is your name, young man,?" the professor asked.

"Todd, sir."

"Ahhh... Todd, my sincerest apologies. We don't have a class clown, we have a prodigy." Dr. Wormley paused. "Everyone, this is Mr. Glass. He aced the placement test. He got the highest score in Lincoln University's history. I will be leaning on him to help teach some of this material."

Todd's peers looked at him with amazement and admiration, like he was the eighth wonder of the world.

"Todd. Would you please regale us with some of your mathematical knowledge?" Dr. Wormley asked, obviously excited to hear what Todd had to say.

"I can solve anything using my fingers and toes," Todd replied, wishing he was joking. Once again, everyone in the room laughed uproariously.

"Brilliant. Brilliant!" Dr. Wormly cheered.

That was the only time the rest of the period that Todd felt brilliant in class. The rest of the period was spent struggling to keep up with and understand any of the material. When class was dismissed Todd felt like he'd gone ten rounds against Mike Tyson. His head was pounding. He was overwhelmed. He'd been determined to learn the material, but by halfway through class he'd given up and began formulating a strategy to get out of the class. He'd called his academic advisor as soon as he'd seen his schedule, to no avail. The guy wouldn't budge on allowing Todd to drop it for an easier one. Maybe he could appeal to Dr. Worley. Their talk was going to have to wait for another day, though. The rest of his peers were hanging around him like groupies waiting for the lead singer of a band after a concert. He knew he should join them; maybe he'd learn something. He left. He didn't want anyone catching onto the fact that he knew *nothing* about calculus. He figured they'd learn he was a fraud soon enough. I'll approach him on Thursday or find a math whisperer and try to survive the semester, he thought. Only three classes this morning and Todd was mentally drained.

His head still pounding, he decided to skip lunch and try to rest in his dorm room before practice. It had only been a day, but Todd was finding it hard to sleep away from home, the only place he'd ever known. To make things worse, his roommate snored. Loudly.

As he entered the building, Todd marveled at the sounds of a dorm filled with men. It was loud and rowdy and Todd could hear bits and pieces of conversations about sports, girls, and cars. No one talking about math, though. Not a peep. No mention of classes at all. Todd was starting to realize that the reality of the college experience was nothing like he'd imagined it would be. He'd expected to be in a culture of students with their heads buried in books on their way to and from classes. Not even close. Everything he's seen so far has made it seem like this is all one big social experiment of students running wild as they experience life away from their parents for the first time sprinkled in with the occasional trip to class.

Making his way down the stairs, Todd contemplated turning around and getting a quick snack from the student union. The smell of burnt microwave popcorn quickly changed his mind. I don't think I will *ever* get used to that smell, he thought.

As he entered his room, Todd's roommate nearly knocked him over.

"Move it, freshman!" he yelled. "I've got a girl waiting to study anatomy with me if you catch my meaning."

Luther's declaration made Todd long for Amani. He was lonely. The closest he'd gotten to making a new friend had been the girl in Spanish, and she'd told him to move away from her. Only day two of college and he's already counting the minutes until he can go home for Labor Day weekend. He had eighteen days, 432 hours, 25,920 minutes, or 1,555,200 seconds give or take.

Todd sat down on the edge of his bed, missing Amani and contemplating a trip to the cafeteria. His nervous energy zapped away his hunger, being a stress eater brought it back. He was always stressed. A successful attempt at running away and taking care of Amani depended on his success in college. Still reeling from his stress headache, Todd grabbed a Kudos bar from the care package his parents had left, laid down on his bed, and closed his eyes.

After what felt like just a second, the phone on the wall screamed, startling Todd awake. "What time is it?" he asked, wiping the drool from the corner of his mouth. The clock on his dresser revealed that he'd been sleeping for twenty-two minutes. As the phone continued to ring he realized that it was an outside-of-campus call.

It's probably Dad calling to remind me his money is a terrible thing to waste, Todd thought. Or maybe it's Mom calling to tell me to stop living out of my suitcase and either fold or hang up my clothes. Todd stretched his arm to grab the wall phone that hung just above his head.

"Hello?" he said with a groggy tone, half expecting one of his parents to be on the other end, ready to chastise him.

"There's been a hole in my heart ever since you left. Hearing your voice just filled it." Todd shot straight up in bed. He was cured! His headache was gone, the lonely emptiness filled. No more stress, though he was still hungry. He was full of energy. It was Amani.

Chapter 20

Todd couldn't speak. Every muscle in his face was being overworked with the smile that spread across it when he heard his girlfriend's tender voice.

"Do you miss me yet?" Amani teased, breaking the brief moment of silence. "What have you been doing since you abandoned me, my college man?"

"Since I left you, my hobby has become missing you. My heart is crying out for you," he answered. "You lied to me, Amani. Absence does not make the heart grow fonder. It makes it miserable."

"I know," Amani responded. Todd could hear that she'd started crying. Todd never wanted to cause her hurt or despair, and he knew his honesty had been too brutal. He needed to push his emotions down and lighten the mood.

"Amani," he began, "I miss you like peanut butter misses jelly, like cornflakes miss milk. I want to write 'I miss you' on a stone and throw it at your face so you know how much it hurts to miss you."

Laughter roared on the other end of the line. Amani loved Todd's corny, awkward sense of humor. "I hope it's the smooth type of peanut butter; I don't like the crunchy kind," she said.

"Have you just met me?" he asked. "I'm *both* types. Smooth as silk – the way I captured your heart – and chunky because I am nuts about you."

Amani giggled. Then it dawned on Todd.

"How am I talking to you right now?" he asked. "Aren't you in school?"

"I'm at lunch," she said. "I dumped every silver coin I could find into the pay phone so I could call you. I probably only have thirty seconds left. I just wanted you to know I was thinking about you. I can't wait to see you in eighteen days, or 432 hours…."

"Your time is up. Please deposit additional funds to continue this call," Todd heard a computerized voice say before the line went dead.

Todd jumped up, grabbed a pen and paper, and started writing Amani. He had new life. The brief phone call resurrected his heart and he was aching to tell her how wonderful she was. But writer's block. Todd had so much to say but didn't know how to say it. He ran to one of his many unpacked suitcases and began digging through its contents looking for his music tapes. He finally came across them. TLC? No. Tupac? A *defi*nite no. NWA? Ummm…no. Mariah Carey? Yes. Janet Jackson? Maybe. Luther Vandross? Definitely. Anita Baker? Oh hell yeah.

He grabbed the small pile of cassettes he'd gathered and removed their linings. Opening them up, he began rummaging through the lyrics, looking for anything that said I love you, I miss you. He composed a few paragraphs of excerpts from various songs from various artists on top of what he was feeling. But it wasn't enough. He reached for his literature book. Shakespeare. Reading through a couple of sonnets, he decided to travel down a different avenue. I hope we skip over this crap in class, he thought. Who in the hell can understand this stuff?

He looked through the text, hoping to find something magical that would capture what he wanted to say. This dude's been dead almost 400 years and we still celebrate him. Why?, protested Todd. None of it makes any sense! Maybe I'll try a haiku.

But they were a dead end, too. He decided to end his letter and hope his mixture of R&B slow jams were good enough. He addressed the envelope to Sasha – what he and Amani had agreed they'd do to try and keep their relationship a secret from her parents and Abbas – and attached the stamp. Sasha didn't have the restrictions Amani did when it came to dating outside her religion, so if she got the letter, she could give it to Amani as they walked to school. He knew Amani would destroy it after she read it.

I'll drop this off at the mailroom on my way to grab a bite to eat, he decided, abandoning the thought of taking a nap after Amani's call. He was too full of energy. The cloud above his head had lifted and been replaced by a bluebird on his shoulder.

Rrrrriiiinnnggg! Rrrriiinnng!! the phone hollered from the wall. Another off-campus call.

Yeesss! he thought. She found more change! "Hellllo," he said, donning his most manly voice and then transitioning to his best rendition of the chorus of Jodeci's "Come and Talk to Me."

"Todd!" yelled the voice on the other end. It was his dad, and he wasn't pleased with his son's singing. "Screaming into the receiver is *not* how I taught you to answer the phone. When you're responsible for your own bills you can answer the phone any way you want. For now, act like I raised you with some sense."

"Okay," Todd said, but his tone broadcast his disappointment that it wasn't Amani calling him a second time. Looking at the clock, he realized her lunch break was over and she was in her next class. "Your mom's birthday is next week," his dad said, breaking into Todd's thoughts of Amani. "Make sure you send her a card. Today!" he added. "That way it'll get here on time. Do you understand?"

"Yes, Dad," Todd reassured him.

"What's my number one rule?" his dad asked. Todd rolled his eyes. He'd been hearing rules from his dad since he was in the womb. This rule was the only one that was consistent, and he and Tiffany were reminded of it every time, Todd broke it, which was quite often. "Well?" his dad asked.

"Do not piss Mom off." So far, Todd had broken the rule at least four times a year: every time he got a report card.

"Right!," his dad said. "Happy wife, happy life. Don't make my life unhappy by upsetting my wife." And he hung up.

Todd hung up the receiver. "Sheesh," he said out loud.

The phone rang again. Yet another off-campus call.

"Hello?" Todd said.

"Why aren't you at the store yet?" his dad snapped

"I'm headed out now, Dad," Todd reassured him. "I just want to make sure I have everything I need before I see my academic advisor." He regretted the words as soon as they escaped his lips.

"Academic advisor?" his dad repeated questioningly. "Don't tell me you're already dropping a class. It's the first week of the semester! This has to be a new record."

"I accidentally signed up for the wrong class," Todd said sheepishly. "I want to see if I can switch it before it gets too late in the semester."

"Which class are you trying to switch?" his dad asked curiously.

"Calculus," Todd answered.

"Calculus?" his dad repeated. "How did you accidentally sign up for *that*? The last time I checked, 'remedial' and 'calculus' were not homonyms. You've struggled with math your whole life. How do you now accidentally sign up for calculus? What girl were you trying to impress?" he concluded sarcastically.

"I tried so desperately to fail my placement test so I could get in an easier course, but I somehow guessed the answers so well that I was put in an Einstein level calculus class."

The silence on the line was deafening. Todd could clearly see the folly of his ways. He knew his dad was choosing his words carefully so that they'd echo in Todd's mind for a lifetime.

"I knew I should have packed your bags for you when you threatened to run away as a child," he started. "Okay. Let me get this straight." His father's voice was slow, deep, and deliberate. "Instead of taking your placement test seriously so you could prepare yourself for your future, you decided to try to find an easier way by cheating the system? And it backfired on you?" Hearing it from his dads lips in that way made Todd realize how stupid his plan had been.

"I'll tell you what," his dad continued. "You're going to stay in that class. You're going to bust your ass studying the material.

You will focus on passing it more than you will on baseball, girls, or answering the phone like a damn fool. Because Todd, if you don't, I am selling your car. You can catch the bus to summer school. I can't even tell your mom about this; it'll mean breaking my own rule," he admitted. "It's time to grow up, son. This is your *life*, and you're treating it as if it's a game," he continued. "Baseball is the only game you need to be playing in life. Education is not a game."

"Dad," Todd started, "I *suck* at math."

"So what?!" his dad snapped. "Instead of taking that test seriously so you could figure out what level of math you truly belong to and working hard to get better, you decided to cheat your way into something easier. How do you learn from that?" he asked.

Todd was glad he wasn't in the same room with his dad at this moment; he'd never be able to face the disappointing look he knew was on his face.

"Let me tell you a story, Todd," his father began. "Your grandfather dropped out of school in the 8th grade to get a job to help his family eat. When he got older, he worked hard to provide for me, your uncle, and your grandmother. There was a promotion available at his job but he needed to have algebraic knowledge to be qualified. He did not have that since he dropped out in the eighth grade. But he needed that promotion to better provide for your uncle and me, so he took an algebra class. He worked hard and received an A." There was a pause. "Todd, success is never achieved by avoiding hard work. You can do the work. The only thing holding you back is you're lazy." His words stung. "You have all the potential in the world, but you refuse to work hard," he said. "Todd, it's time to grow up today; tomorrow will be too late. The world will already have passed you by and you'll spend your future fuming over your regrets." He paused again. "At one time, you were the best second baseman in your conference but were too lazy to maintain, or improve your skills. Those beneath you put in the work and surpassed you. Life will do the same thing. Your grandfather truly worked hard. Son, if you had your grandfather's work ethic you could be in the majors or at Harvard right now. When you work hard you can achieve anything you want. I developed my work ethic from your grandfather and it provided me with 20 years of work experience before the age of ten. I worked as many jobs as I could while still going to school and practiced my wrestling moves no matter what the weather was like outside. If my back was up against the wall I could learn calculus by reading the back of a cereal box in the dark while at work, because I am willing to work at being great in everything I do. In all seriousness, Todd, those that have the will to be great find a way to be great. Instead of telling yourself all the reasons why you *can't* do something, tell yourself how you *can*. And then do it." you can achieve anything you want.

The line went dead and Todd was left listening to the melody of the dial tone. Just as he put the receiver back on the cradle the phone rang once more.

"Hello?" Todd answered

"That's better," his dad said on the other end. "Maybe you're not stupid after all. Now go to the store before you forget and wind up breaking my rule." And just like that, the phone went dead again.

Chapter 21

Todd was amazed he wasn't more tired. It had been a long, stressful day, especially after he was tasked with finding a birthday card for his mom. He'd failed at this many times in the past. Last year, for instance, he'd grabbed the first card he saw. He was embarrassed beyond comprehension when his mom read text congratulating her on the birth of her newborn. His dad had promptly pulled him aside and lambasted him.

"**No one** will <u>ever</u> love you longer, deeper, or more unconditionally than your mother," he'd said. "For the first nine months of your life, she alone cared for, nurtured, and supported you, and you have the audacity to disrespect her by picking out a card *blindly*?! You owe her so much more than that, Todd."

With his dad's words echoing in his memory, Todd searched long and hard for a card that might make up for last year's. He knew nothing could really do that, and he found himself grateful for a mother's forgiving, everlasting love.

He finally found a card he thought might work. The front had a picture of a wreath made from $100 bills and asked what you call such a thing. The inside said "Aretha Franklins" and the words "Happy Birthday." The card fit his sense of humor and Todd thought his mom would appreciate that. Todd was proud of the fact that he actually mailed it off. Typically he would sit items that needed to be mailed somewhere until he remembered it should have been mailed out weeks prior. Maybe college would be the catalyst for the start of my maturation process, he told himself. He was still aching from his hellacious baseball practice that morning, and again later that evening. However, Todd was full of energy in spite of it, his classes, and now the errand to get his mom's card. Usually the combination would sap his energy, its only remedy laziness and sleep. Todd would begin winding down and preparing for bed at 7 PM. Even if he *was* in college, why stop a routine that had been his staple for years? Today was different.

Still fueled by Amani's surprise phone call, Todd decided to check out his dorm's rec room instead of laying around hoping to fall asleep. Besides, he was bored with no TV in his room, and falling asleep when he was bored was always difficult. Especially when sharing a dorm room with a stranger. Rec room it is! Todd decided to see what was playing on the television there. Maybe he'd be able to meet some new people and get some of this stressful energy out.

Opening the door, he noticed the room – the size of three dorm rooms put together – was loud and full of excitement. There was a floor model television that was playing the MTV and a young man dancing to the music, attempting to emulate the choreography.

"This is how I be dancing with the girls at the club!" he yelled over his shoulder. No one responded, but he didn't seem to mind and kept dancing.

Todd wished he could do the things he saw in music videos. Even if he could, though, he'd been too shy to go to school dances. Even if he'd gone, though, there'd been no way he'd have asked a girl to dance with him. He was perfectly content being a wallflower.

Sitting in the middle of the Rec Room was yet another outdated orange and brown couch in a paisley pattern. It clearly matched the outdated furniture in the lobby. Unfortunately, this piece was accompanied by a hideous-looking recliner.

Just in front of the outdated furniture sat a decent-looking pool table. There was a slight tear in the table felt, but not in a spot that would impede a novice pool shark's game. A ping pong table sat off in the far corner of the room. Todd could see that its net was slightly crooked and the rubber on several of the paddles were peeling off, but that didn't seem to bother the students who were playing. In the corner nearest him were two card tables, raucous students sitting at each. The whole room was alive.

"Tennis shoe Toddie, all feet and no body," yelled a young man, slamming a domino down. "That's 10 points, bitch!"

"You must not know who I am," replied his opponent.

You're someone who can't play, snapped the first domino player. "Ten on mine," he said. "Ten again on yo ass."

"Twenty five," he blurted again. "Yo' play."

Todd had no clue what was going on. He definitely did not understand the lingo the two players were using. His knowledge of dominos ended at standing them up vertically or in a design and watching them all fall in succession. Or through pizza delivery.

"Hey, Nigga, we need a fourth," said a young man at the next table. Todd ignored the question, still fixated on the domino game. "Ay yo, corny Nigga!" Todd turned his attention to three students sitting at the table.

"Excuse me," Todd replied, irritated that they were talking to him and using the word they'd used.

"I said we need a fourth," the kid repeated. "Do you play?" he asked, not noticing Todd's annoyance.

"Play what?" Todd asked, still miffed. He wasn't sure what irked him most: being called corny, being called a nigga, or being called a combination of both.

The trio were playing Spades, a game he didn't know much about, but knew enough to get by. He remembered a conversation he'd once had with a teammate on a road trip for baseball in high school. They joked about things Black people know how to do without ever having been taught. No one teaches Black people to play Spades, they'd said; they just know how. Their conclusion appeared true when, at lunch the next day, he and his friend asked every black student they could find if they knew how to play and who'd taught them. Everyone knew how to play, but no one knew who taught them. In high school, getting the same answer from the ten people – the number they asked that day – affirmed their hypothesis for all people.

"Yes," he said, his sarcasm obvious, "I know how to play." The question they *should* have asked him was if he was any good, but after watching the spirited, trash-talk-laden domino game, he dared not reveal how much of a novice he really was. Besides, he didn't want to stand around watching everyone else have fun. He damn sure didn't want to watch the kid who was still dancing with himself. A game of spades was definitely better than sitting alone in his room staring at the clock and trying to fall asleep. If he was smart he'd be studying calculus. But he wasn't.

"Good! You can be Rob's partner," said one of the kids at the table. At this point, Todd felt he had no choice but to play. He hadn't made any friends since he arrived on campus. This was an opportunity to change that. He reached across the table and shook his partner's hand as he introduced himself to the group.

"I'm Todd," he said.

"We know who the fuck you are, Nigga," Rob replied, annoyed. "You ruined the Greek stroll."

Was there *any*one on campus who hadn't seen that? Todd wondered. He stayed silent as he was dealt his cards.

"Big J!" Rob introduced a big, dark-skinned student. Though he was sitting down, Todd guessed Big J stood close to 6'3" and weighed no less than 320 pounds. He was intimidating, and Todd could tell he was used to getting his way. Todd watched, shocked, as Big J casually rolled up a blunt, especially since a no smoking sign hung behind him. It was the closest to drugs Todd had ever been. He watched in amazement as Big J focused intently on packing the cigar wrapper with its illegal contents. It sickened him when Big J licked the side of the wrapper to seal it shut. The sight of the guy's slobber was all he needed to continue to say no to drugs.

"This is my boy Ozark," Big J said between licks of his contraband. He pointed to the guy sitting across the table from him. Ozark, who looked to stand just under 6', clearly worked out. His muscular arms were showcased by the wife-beater he wore, though they were nothing in comparison to Big J's. Ozark was medium-complected, bald, and covered with tattoos.

"How many books you got?" asked Rob.

"I have six right now," Todd replied, but I'm going to have to find a calculus book for dummies and Cliff's Notes for my literature class."

Everyone at the table grew silent, blank stares on their faces. After a pause the trio burst into raucous laughter.

"Nigga! Are you serious?" Rob howled. "Books! How many *books* you got?" he asked again, pointing to Todd's cards. "In the game."

"Oh, *booooks*!" Todd responded, realizing Rob was asking how many hands he could win this round. Embarrassed, Todd decided he knew how to play Spades but didn't remember how to win. There was a strategy to the game that he lacked. People take Spades seriously, he remembered. The participants at the table seemed like a serious group.

"I have three," he finally said, guessing. He didn't know what he had, he just knew that his ace of spades was a good card, as were his ace of hearts and king of clubs. *How am I supposed to know how many books I have if I don't know what they all have?* he wondered.

"I miss being at home," Big J admitted.

"Me, too," Todd agreed. He was thrilled someone else was homesick and wasn't afraid to admit it.

Big J stared at Todd blankly and continued with his admission. "I love going to the clubs. I'd especially like to visit three. Every time I'd go I'd leave with about five ladies, which is remarkable since I'm big and don't go iced up. It's dangerous back home, especially since you can't strap up. But I take my knife. I nearly had to cut five people the last time I went."

Todd was mortified, and could only manage to say "Wow!" How was it that someone had to bring a knife with him to have a good time?

"I hear you," Ozark added. "I go to two clubs back home, but as many clubs as I've visited I still haven't found no love."

"I just started dating someone," Todd interjected, but Ozark ignored him. So did the rest of the guys.

"I mean, I have five girls in mind, but I had to cut two of them," Ozark continued.

"Cut this shit out!" Rob yelled. "These mother fuckers are over here cheating!" he declared, slamming his cards down. "Yo' dumb ass is too new to see it!" he shouted, shooting Todd a look of disgust. "Telling these cheaters you have a girlfriend and shit! They don't care! This is a fucking *game*, not some bonding moment!" he yelled.

Completely confused, all Todd could do was shrug his shoulders and stare blankly.

"Man! Fuck you!" Ozark yelled back at Rob. "We don't have to cheat to beat you Busters," he declared.

"How are they cheating?" Todd finally asked.

Rob looked at Todd as if he was blue and wearing a cake on his head.

"How are they cheating? How are they *cheat*ing?" Rob repeated sarcastically. "This nigga!," he announced to the room, pointing at Todd. "Are you deaf?!" he asked. "Have you not been listening to da bullshit about going to clubs back home?!"

All Todd could pay attention to was Rob's lack of enunciation. It irritated him that a guy seeking higher education had such a lazy tongue.

"The mention of *clubs*," Rob said. "They're talking about their *cards*, not some hangout spot, you idiot. J has three, Ozark has two." It was clear Todd still didn't get it, so Rob kept going, "Big J has five hearts, Ozark has none."

Todd looked at Rob in amazement. How could he break down his opponents' story to figure out what cards they held? "Ladies are hearts," Rob continued, noticing that Todd was still lost. "Big J isn't iced up, so he doesn't have any diamonds. You *do* know ice is another word for diamonds, right?" Rob asked Todd, mocking him. "Ozark has five. Big J has five spades, and Ozark has two. Cut!"

Todd guessed his face was still blank because Rob explained that cut meant spades.

Finally it all clicked. Todd was impressed by the length Big J and Ozark went to to communicate the cards the other possessed. "Man, you buggin'! We were just reminiscing about what we do at home!" Big J argued.

"I want a reshuffle," Rob barked. "You do it," he demanded of Todd.

Todd had never been accused of being a card shark, and his shuffling skills were proof that he wasn't one. He'd seen it done plenty of times, so it should've been simple enough. A man who needs good hand-eye coordination on the baseball diamond should be more than capable of shuffling fifty-two little cards, but he wasn't. Todd was all thumbs.

"What the hell are you doing?" Ozark cried, laughing hysterically as the deck of cards flew out of Todd's hands. Todd gathered them and tried again. This attempt was even more disastrous as a few cards escaped onto the domino table. The only thing his shuffle accomplished was momentarily silencing the domino players.

"Dude!" Rob sighed. "I got you," he said, annoyingly snatching the remaining cards out of Todd's hand.

"I guess I'm a little rusty," Todd chuckled nervously.

After thirty minutes of card playing, Todd was ready for bed. He contemplated the repercussions of ending the game early. For the past half hour, he'd watched Rob, Big J, and Ozark slamming down each card they played. Their back and forth banter made Todd wonder how much they'd wagered on the game.

"Give me this book, Nigga," Rob yelled as he and Todd won another hand.

"You said you had five!" Big J yelled, verbally attacking his partner.

"DON'T BRING THAT SHIT HERE!" Ozark yelled. "If you didn't cut me two hands ago we'd be winning," he continued.

"I can't believe we're losing to these two scrubs," Big J snapped.

"We only need five more books," Rob declared. "If you have three, bet three. If you have two, bet two," he cautioned. "No more, no less than what you have."

"Alright," Todd snapped, rolling his eyes and sighing.

"White wash is going to lose it for you," Big J declared.

"Whitewash?" Todd asked.

"Yes, Whitewash<" Big J replied.

"What's 'Whitewash,'" Todd asked, though he had an inkling as to who they were referring to and why. He didn't like it.

"*YOU*, Nigga!" Big J responded angrily, looking intently at Todd. His glare said he was challenging Todd to argue.

Man, Todd thought. Talk about a bunch of sore losers. He broke eye contact with Big J, hoping that would quell any animosity brewing inside him from a silly little card game.

"How am I whitewashed?" he asked, his tone casual. He kept his eyes on his cards.

"Man, *look* at you!" Big J snapped. "The way you talk, dress, play Spades. I bet you're from the county. You ain't from the hood like us. You ain't a *real* Nigga!"

"Where you from?" Rob asked, in a way that suggested he was about to join in Big J's ridicule of him.

"Okay, okay," Todd relented. "Yes, I'm from the county. But that doesn't mean I'm whitewashed."

"I bet you hang around white people," Rob declared.

"Yeah. So?" Todd answered mockingly.

"I bet you went to a white school," Ozark added.

"Yes, my school was predominantly white, but so is this university," Todd replied. Todd was amazed that Historically Black College or University didn't mean predominantly black.

"You assimilate to your surroundings," Rob answered, irritated that he once again had to explain something he thought was apparent. "If it acts like a duck…" he continued. Todd was surprised. Rob sounded educated. It was the first time he'd said something coherent and had pronounced every syllable clearly.

"That doesn't mean I'm less Black than any of the rest of you," Todd argued. Everyone in the room laughed.

"I'm from an affluent neighborhood, but even *I* know there's a difference between Black people from the hood and blacks from the county," interjected the kid who'd been dancing to the music videos.

"It doesn't matter where someone's from; we're all the same," Todd replied.

"I bet you don't even have a hood name," Rob said.

"No!" Todd answered, twisting his lips in disgust at the thought of there even being such a thing as 'hood names.' "Do you?"

"Mother fucker, my name's not Rob," Rob said. "Robbing is what I *do*," he clarified matter-of-factly.

Todd shifted in his seat, casually trying to feel if his wallet was still in his back pocket.

"His name is Ozark," Rob continued, "because his biceps are like the Ozark mountains. Big! He's Big J not because of his size but because he's known for jacking you up if you mess with him."

Todd was incredulous at the hood roll call happening before him. Does everyone here have an alias?

"Having a nickname doesn't make you more Black than someone who doesn't have one," he said, still annoyed that he'd been labeled 'Whitewash.' *This has to be the dumbest argument I've ever been in.* He now understood what his dad meant when he said to never argue with a fool because onlookers may not be able to tell the difference.

"You're in college," Big J started, "let's take a quiz," he suggested. Todd was intrigued by the idiocracy of an 'How Black are you?' test. Intrigued in spite of the fact that he was fairly sure he looked as foolish as the rest of them, Todd asked, "You're going to test how accurately I fit some Black stereotype? I used to fear not being smart enough to make it in college, but after listening to you, I'm confident I'm going to graduate *summa cum laude*," he declared.

"Name a flavor of Kool-Aid," Big J directed, ignoring Todd's criticism.

"Tropical fruit punch," he answered. Everyone laughed.

"Everyone one knows it's called 'red,'" declared Music Video Boy.

Todd rolled his eyes. "You all *do* realize red is a color, not a flavor, right?" he said. "Do you call grape-flavored Kool-Aid 'purple'?" he asked, trying to poke holes in their logic. Everyone there waved off his argument.

"What do you store in a tub of margarine?" Ozark asked.

"Is this a trick question?" Todd asked. "Margarine, of course."

"Mrrh!" Rob screeched, making the sound of a buzzer. "The correct answer is leftovers."

"Don't you have tupperware for that?" Todd asked.

The room once again erupted in laughter. "What's so funny?" But his question was, again, ignored.

"What three types of seasoning do you have on your table?" asked one of the domino players.

"Umm…" Todd hesitated. He didn't want to get another question wrong. "Salt, pepper, and, umm… well we *do* keep a sugar dish on the table."

"Mrrh!" Rob said. "Wrong again!" he laughed. "The correct answer is salt, pepper, and hot sauce." More laughter. The domino players began debating which hot sauce was better: Crystal Louisiana or Frank's Red Hot sauce. The debate got rather *heated*.

"What do you need hot sauce for?" Todd asked. The room got quiet. The TV got muted.

"Are you joking right now?" Big J asked. Todd kept his mouth closed and shrugged his shoulders.

"I can't believe he asked that!" Rob cried. "I put that shit on everything!" he declared.

"Does the pizza man deliver to your neighborhood?" asked Big J.

"Of course he does," Todd replied. "What does that have to do with anything?"

"It means you may be black in color, but you aren't really Black," Ozark replied. "Pizza guys don't deliver to the hood, where *real* Black people live."

"How does living in a safe area mean I'm not Black?" Todd asked. "All that means is you should be mad at the pizza company for not delivering in your area, or mad at those who create an unsafe environment. But that doesn't mean I'm not Black," he concluded.

"If you lived where we do you'd understand our argument, Todd," Rob snapped. "Being Black is about the struggle," he continued. "Blacks struggled when they were brought over on slave ships. Blacks struggled as slaves. Blacks struggled during the Jim Crow era. And Blacks struggled during the civil rights era. We may be free now, and we're supposed to have equal rights, but the Rodney King verdict proves Blacks are still struggling. But you don't get that, Todd, because you come from a good area. You don't struggle, so you aren't really Black."

Todd opened his mouth to protest but was quickly silenced as Rob continued. "Sure your skin is brown, but on the inside you're white. That's why I see you as a Hostess cupcake: white on the inside, black on the outside. Where we live, book smarts can get you killed. You need to have *street* smarts. Where we live, wearing the wrong colors, the wrong shoes, or greeting someone the wrong way could be a death sentence. Where we live, we *al*ways fit the description of someone who did something sinister. The only job opportunities where we live are on street corners selling drugs, sex, or something stolen. Case in point. If you were in the hood, how would you say hello to a man on the corner?" Rob asked.

"I'd say 'What's up?'" Todd replied

"Are you *crazy*?" Big J interrupted. "That's a death sentence on some streets."

"Why?" Todd asked. "It's just a greeting."

"If you get asked where you from, or 'What's up?' isn't acceptable," Rob said. "On the streets it's a challenge. So is 'What's happening.'"

"Stop it!" Todd cried. "Being from the 'hood,'" he said, using air quotes, "doesn't mean you're Blacker or struggle more than someone from where I live. Hell, the struggle is *deeper* where I'm from," he continued. The guys laughed, but the look on Todd's face said he wasn't joking. He looked Rob in the eyes, ready to challenge his argument. "Being Black where *I*'m from is just as great a struggle. I'm *constantly* having to prove I belong. That I'm not there because I can run fast or jump high. I have to prove I belong because I'm intelligent and articulate and not because I check some box off on an Affirmative Action checklist. Then I have to struggle because people like you want to question my authenticity because I enunciate when I speak and use proper English. Or I'm cast out by my own people because I don't follow disrespectful stereotypes. Come on, man, how far do you expect to get in life when you choose a nickname that's a verb?"

Rob appeared dumbfounded.

Todd continued. "For you all to single me out because of where I'm from proves that *you*'re the true sellouts. You should accept other Blacks because they're running the same race, avoiding the same obstacles as you."

"Man, I spent the weekend with a girl from the county," Rob said. "Worst experience I ever had," he continued, once again ignoring every argument Todd had presented. "Everybody stares at you with hate in their eyes," he concluded.

"People in the hood stare you down with just as much hate," Todd interjected.

"Hey Rob, tell us more about your night in the county," Ozark said. The county and the country are the real scary places, Ozark continued.

"How do you figure?" Todd asked. "The hood is just as scary a place," he added, trying to head off Rob's story before it got going. "Every time I go into the hood I hear gunshots and worry about stray bullets."

Everyone laughed again.

"What's so funny about gunshots?" Todd asked, confused.

"Most of those gunshots are warning shots," Big J offered.

"It's the ones from a slowly-approaching car that you have to worry about," Rob added.

"Drivebys," Ozark and Big J said in unison.

Todd couldn't believe how dismissive they all were about bullets. *Am I in some sort of twilight zone? Or is this a prank?*

"Every horror movie happens in the suburbs or in the country," Ozark continued. "Freddy, Michael Meyers, The Exorcist, and the Stepford wives were in the 'burbs. Even the movie *The 'Burbs* was in the burbs. What scary movie happened in the projects?" he asked.

Todd scratched his head at Ozark turning fictional characters into fact.

"Besides," said Rob, ignoring Ozark's change of subject, "you can tell where a gunshot is coming from. When I was in the county all these sinister bugs were lurking in the dark. You couldn't see them, just hear them. You hear a chirping cricket in one corner, you go investigate, and nothing's there. It's like a ventriloquist bug! You hear bugs screaming in the distance, but they never reveal themselves. Scared me shitless," he added.

Todd chuckled. "They were probably just June bugs," he said. His statement was met with blank stares. "They make noises to attract a mate," he continued in explanation. "They're completely harmless."

"If they're completely harmless, how come they only come out at night?" Big J asked. Todd didn't have an answer.

"Only freaks and creepy crawlies come out at night," Rob added. "June bugs my ass," he snapped. "It was August."

"This conversation is the most idiotic thing I've ever been a part of," Todd said. "Are we really at an HBCU, labeling each other's value based on where we're from? I'm not who I am because of where I live," he said. "Neither are any of you. If we were, we wouldn't be here. I don't sound white; I sound educated. I take enough pride in my vocabulary and my ability to speak that I would never purposely try to sound less educated just to fit in," he declared, looking pointedly at Rob. "I don't use the "n" word out of respect for the ancestors who gave their lives so none of us would have to be labeled so deplorably."

"We use the word 'Nigga' because we're reclaiming the word," Big J declared.

Todd chose to ignore his explanation because it would lead to a discussion Todd didn't have the patience to tolerate.

Looking at the table behind him, he continued, "I don't know how to play Dominos. I don't like watermelon. If I have to eat pie I prefer pumpkin over sweet potato. I don't know how to do the electric slide. Hell, I don't have rhythm so I can't dance. I can't handle spicy foods, and I play baseball, not basketball. None of these things make me look more or less Black, because no matter what, no one is going to ignore my skin color whether I live in the city, hood, county, country, or Mars." Todd took a deep breath. His declaration was a weight off his shoulders.

The guys in the room were quiet, clearly stunned by Todd's monologue.

"Is no one going to say anything?" Todd asked, breaking the silence. He felt he led a normal existence. Everything he liked was liked by those he grew up with. The awkward silence and the feeling that he still held the room's attention inspired him to continue. "We're all the same," he said, pointing to everyone in the room. "We reached a major milestone when we turned eighteen. Lots of African Americans don't live that long. We're free," he continued. "Lots of our peers are in jail unjustly or because they had no other option but to do something that got them locked up. We're all going to be judged in life because of the color of our skin, so why are we judging each other rather than giving each other a hand? We're lucky to have the opportunity to go to college. Many people who look like us aren't afforded the same opportunity."

Todd had reached a breaking point. Blacks and whites alike persecuted him because he didn't fit the stereotype they thought he should. He was pissed that he allowed society to dictate the places he could visit, the girls he could date, and the music he could listen to. He was tired of people asking him how he should be labeled: Black, Afro-American, African American… He wanted them to stop labeling him and just refer to him as Todd. What bothered him most was the fact that here in college, educated students the same race he was were basing who he was on a stereotype. College is about learning. Todd hoped he'd just given them a lesson in humility.

Chapter 22

"What in the heck did he say?" Todd asked, leaning over to the person seated next to him.

Annoyed, the student got up and changed seats before answering. Embarrassed, Todd made a mental note to stop asking his peers to explain the things their professors said. He understood not being able to decipher what his Spanish professor said, but this was English. The professor, a short, bald, dark-skinned man in his mid-thirties appeared to be of African descent. His heavy accent and deep voice made Todd have to strain to hear each word he said.

"Blah Mr. Abdullahu blah blah" was all Todd heard now. Then silence, and an angry expression on the professor's face. He was clearly both agitated and annoyed, probably, Todd thought, from constantly having to repeat himself."

Todd took comfort in gazing around the room and realizing his wasn't the only face staring blankly at the professor.

Slowly, the professor repeated his request that everyone open their books to page 11 to learn about prose.

"YOU!" snapped Professor Abdullahi, staring at Todd. "Tell me what prose is."

Todd froze. *Is there a target on my forehead that tells professors I don't know the answer so they should pick on me?* he wondered. He began to sweat as he thought about the answer to the question.

"Hurry, hurry," prompted the professor. "Why are you in college if you can't have a discussion?" The comment was bitter. Todd was angry at himself for not knowing the answer but irritated at the tone with which the professor spoke to him.

"I'm in college to *learn*," he retorted. "How can you be a professor if you can't teach the material? You can barely *speak* the material."

Everyone gasped. Todd, himself, was surprised by what he'd said. He was falling apart, and that response felt like he'd hit rock bottom.

"This is a college Literature course, young man," the professor began. He spoke deliberately and slowly, wanting to make sure Todd understood everything he was saying. "My purpose in asking you this question is to gauge how simple or how complex our discussions need to be," he finished." Obviously, with you, I must use the most simplistic terms."

Todd realized how deliberate the professor's words had become as he walked the room slowly, making uncomfortable eye contact with each student. He was speaking as if the class was a remedial reading class. This infuriated Todd. English was the one area in which he felt competent. He loved to read and to discuss what he read.

"Ladies and gentlemen, you're in college now. This is not high school," he added, as if he'd read Todd's mind. He stopped directly in front of Todd's desk before continuing. "To be successful in college, you need to use every tool afforded you. The library," he said, "the computer lab, and the resource center, if need be. It's up to you. You and only you are responsible for how successful you will be in my class. You and only you are responsible for how successful you will be in this world." The lecture was starting to sound like one of Todd's dad's, but Professor Abdullahi wasn't done.

"You need to use common sense in life. Know when to talk, and when to be quiet. If you know the answer to a question in class, speak clearly and answer it. If you don't know the answer, say so. Don't waste people's time trying to come up with some b.s. answer, because people can see through it. I cannot speak for other educators at this institution," he said, "but in my classroom, wasting my time is a cardinal sin, and the quickest path to failing." Tapping the book on Todd's desk, Professor Abdullah continued. "Sometimes the answers you seek are right before your eyes."

Todd looked down to see where the professor was tapping. Just as he'd said, the answer was right in front of him. Touché, Todd thought, filled with embarrassment. Professor Abdullah shot Todd a glance as if to say, "don't fuck with me, kid, you're out of your league."

Turning his attention to the class, the professor began outlining the course of the semester. "The syllabus says we're going to be reading and discussing *1984* by George Orwell. However, in light of today's revelation that I do not know how to teach," – his eyes darted in Todd's direction – we will now be reading *The Sound and the Fury*" by William Faulkner." The class groaned in disappointment, making sure to direct their reactions at Todd, whose outburst caused the change.

"I want a ten page report every week. This needs to be typed and double spaced, and focused on the subtleties of the passages I select. In addition to the paper, you each will speak for three minutes about what you wrote in your paper." The professor paused. "On Friday, we will discuss "The Chaos" by Gerard Nolst Trenité. This poem has about 800 spelling irregularities and pronunciation differences. It will be up to you to find them all."

Todd sat in stunned silence. He knew he had to get his shit together, but he was completely overwhelmed. His stress turned his thoughts away from class and toward Amani. He knew he wanted to spend his life with her, but he didn't have a clue as to how to make that a reality.

When Professor Abdullah dismissed the class, Todd left as quickly as he could, before the other students could pounce on him. His first time on his own and he was failing. He understood now why institutions such as prison, the armed services, and high schools were so structured; they were built to think for those who either hadn't developed the skill to think for themselves or, as in Todd's case, tried to but failed miserably.

Todd walked the campus slowly. He liked people watching, but he was beginning to feel like a social misfit. It appeared as if everyone was paired with someone else. There was no way he was going to make Greek friends after ruining their pre-semester soiree. His upperclassman roommate was, so far, anyway, either always gone or sleeping; and he knew he wasn't going to be best friends with him. How do you even *make* friends? he thought. It had been years since he'd done that with someone new. In elementary and high school he just gravitated toward those who were in his classes and they assimilated into friendships. Honestly, though, they really just became associates. Todd was never one to have or go to sleepovers. He rarely had anyone come into his house. Friends would ring his doorbell, and Todd would just run out and play with them. Those who called the house weren't really friends, they were just people Todd would call when he was bored. Whenever he needed to talk to someone he didn't; he buried whatever he needed to talk about. Buried the rage, buried the pain, buried the hurt. Or he would go to the batting cages and take his frustrations out on a couple of fastballs.

Todd headed for his dorm room. He was lonely. He finally had someone in his life that he could talk to but couldn't. He'd already fallen in love with her, but now he felt like he should end the relationship before they fell deeper in love. The heartbreak of only being able to share life with someone sporadically was overwhelming. Every fiber in his being was saying, "Todd, there are so many more fish in the sea. *Safer* fish." But he couldn't help himself; he ignored his mind, intending to follow his heart.

No matter the pitfalls and bouts of loneliness, Todd was determined to choose – to always choose – the girl who first stole his heart.

Chapter 23

The loud knock on the door startled Todd. He was obsessively scanning his room for anything he might need for his trip back home.

"Let's go!" yelled a voice from behind the door. It was Rob.

Todd shoved every piece of dirty laundry he had into a trash bag and grabbed his toothbrush and his wallet. He was grateful he'd overheard a conversation with Rob and Big J about heading to St. Louis for the holiday weekend, even though they were leaving earlier than Todd had planned to and he was having to miss two classes in order to ride with them. Rob wasn't planning on heading back until early Tuesday morning. Todd planned to maximize all the time he could with Amani.

As he approached Rob's 1982 yellow Dodge Omni, he noticed a crowd around the car. "No one gets in until I have my money," Rob said. Todd pulled out his last ten dollars and handed it to Rob. Though Rob was only charging $5 per person, Todd felt he should pay an extra $5 – a kind of convenience tax – since he and Rob lived so far from each other. Todd knew he could make the money back working his old job over the weekend. This was an added bonus since his boss paid him in cash. It also kept his parents from taking him to the Lake of the Ozarks for their annual family trip. That trip would've meant not seeing Amani. Plus, Todd knew his dad was not going to block any opportunity for Todd to earn money.

"Okay. I got ten from Todd," Rob said. "He's the only one guaranteed a seat to and from."

Annoyed, the other potential passengers dug through their possessions looking for money. Some tried to barter with Rob, or to negotiate future payments.

"Hop in, Todd," Rob said. Todd opened the door to the passenger's seat but Rob quickly blocked him. "That seat's for Big J," he explained. "He has to sit in the front. I don't think my rear axle can handle his weight," he added. Todd picked the seat directly behind the passenger's seat and set his trash bag full of clothes on the floor between his legs.

Big J was the next person to take a seat. "What up, Nigga?" he said to Todd.

"Good morning," Todd replied.

"I get to see where this county Nigga lives!" Big J shouted.

The rear driver's side door opened, and in stepped a girl Todd didn't know. She was short and plump, with a darker complexion. Todd guessed she was a little older than he was. She appeared confident, with a smidge of arrogance in the way she presented herself. Her long hair flowed in a rough locs style, and she was clearly proud of that.

"I hope I don't get carsick," she said to Todd. That was his cue to roll down the window as far as it would go. Her perfume was thick, but still didn't mask the smell of weed emanating from her. Todd thought he might get car sick, too, from having to smell her…aroma…for the couple of hours it would take to get to St. Louis.

One more occupant – a quiet young man Todd had seen around campus but didn't know – squeezed into the rear of the car. The trio were crammed in tight. There was very little leg room and even less elbow room.

"Where am *I* going to sit?" asked another potential passenger Todd didn't recognize. Inspecting the situation in the back seat, Rob suggested that he lay across the trio who were already seated. A fury of protest arose, mostly from the young lady seated next to Todd. No one wanted a six-foot-tall man laying across their lap in an already-cramped car, especially not in the August heat.

"By the way, my A/C doesn't work," laughed Rob as he started the engine. They were off. Todd tried to lose himself planning how he was going to make his weekend with Amani special. He didn't care what they did this weekend; he just wanted to hold her in his arms again.

His thoughts were interrupted as Rob made a sharp right turn. The weight of the other two passengers pinned Todd painfully against the door, and the kid on top of them, whom Todd referred to as slim, had to bend his legs to keep his feet from sticking out further through the window. The girl's braids scraped Todd's cheek with every turn. Todd tried to make the best out of a bad situation, but it was hard. What should have been a two-hour trip would be lucky to be made in three. The weighed-down Dodge Omni struggled to reach fifty miles per hour, its top speed, on a straight away, thirty five miles per hour on an incline, and needed the emergency hand brake's assistance to slow down going down a hill.

Todd wondered what time it was. The clock on the car's dashboard died at 4:30. The strong scent of the cucumber melon scented body lotion the girl next to him was wearing tickled his nose. It was tortuous not being able to scratch it. He tried in vain to free either arm but all four of his limbs were pinned down.

"Hey. Diamond," Rob called out. Diamond. Todd could finally put a name to the person pinned to his left side. Though she was named after a precious gem, she was anything but. Every minute or so, Diamond snorted in an attempt to clear the mucous in her throat. It interrupted any chance Todd had to nap, and the sickening sound of each snort made him cringe. He was in hell. Diamond reminded him of that fact by making incessant comments about the heat and complaining about her comfort level as she struggled to adjust in the seat. But no matter how hard any of them tried to move, they were stuck in place until they reached their destination.

"Ay! Dee, pull out something to ease our travel woes," suggested Rob.

"Mutha fucka," Diamond began. Maybe she was a diamond in the rough, thought Todd. "Does it look like I can pull anything out?," she continued. "I got this smelly nigga on my left side, a corny nigga on my right side, and this long nigga on top of me while you two niggas up front there have ya'll mutha fuckin seats all the way back."

"I'm just trying to make the trip more comfortable," Rob responded. Todd wondered if Rob regretted getting her riled up.

"Can't this mutha fucka go any faster?" she complained. "Got me cramped in this mutha fucka; I should ride for free." Todd wondered what Diamond's major was. Whatever her course of study, Todd hoped it would expand her vocabulary, and not something where she would be working with people. It seemed like "nigga" and "mutha fucka" were her primary means of communication. Each final syllable in every phrase she spoke was cut off, and she was unnecessarily loud.

Todd wondered if Diamond had practiced not enunciating when she spoke. If she was *trying* to speak so freely and so poorly. Todd often spoke in a relaxed vernacular around his friends, too, but his parents always stopped him when they would catch him.

"We're not raising you to sound like a fool," his mom would tell him. His dad would tell him "No matter what you do, someone is always watching you and judging you. Always present the best version of yourself because it will either come back to reward you or haunt you."

"Turn on some mutha fuckin music in this bish," Diamond suddenly demanded.

"I got you," Big J said, merrily popping a tape into the tape deck. "This is my partna's mixtape," he bragged. "This shit is bangin' in the streets." As the music began, the speakers behind Todd's head reverberated the distorted base. The rapper on the tape sounded like he was mad at the microphone as he yelled out his lyrics. Todd could barely understand him, but what he could make out sounded either like threats or confessions over a loud beat. Either way, the organized noise added to his discomfort.

"Who *is* this?" yelled Diamond over the music.

"This my nigga MC Hold-up," Big J said.

"Let me see the tape," Diamond said, struggling mightily to free her arms. Big J popped the tape out of the cassette player and handed it to Diamond. The static from an out-of-range radio station echoed throughout the car. Todd definitely preferred the static to MC Hold-up. Being held up at gunpoint was the only other way Todd would want to hear his music again. He wondered if it was the rotted speaker cone or the cracked dust cap on the speaker that distorted the sound. In his mind, Todd was trying to give the musician any excuse for the horrible sound that had played off the cassette tape. Maybe it was just a horrible musical arrangement on Big J's homie's mixtape. Todd wondered if the musician got his name from holding up a recording studio and forcing the engineer to give him time in the recording booth. Either way, Todd was relieved that the noise had stopped. He'd started to wonder how much hearing loss might result if the tape had continued to play.

"You said this mutha fucka bangin in the streets of St. Louis?" Diamond asked.

"This shits hittin' hard in the streets," Big J confirmed.

"Let's see how hard it's hittin' in the streets out here," Diamond said. Todd instantly knew what was about to happen. He moved his head back just in time to avoid being hit by the cassette tape as it flew from Diamond's hand out the window.

"Bitch, what the fuck?!" Big J shouted. "Oh shit!" he shouted, quickly turning back around in his seat. "5- 0," he said to Rob. Rob instantly straightened up in his seat, too.

"What's going on?" the kid behind Rob asked.

"It's one time," Rob responded. "Don't look," he warned. Todd didn't listen to the direction, turning around to take a glance. What did "one time" and "5-0" mean?

Just then, the siren from a police squad car blared.

"Nigga!" Rob started, glaring at Todd. "I told your dumb ass not to look!"

"It's just the police," Todd said. "They'll probably give us a ticket for littering and let us go."

"Nigga," shouted Diamond, "Do you not know what happens when a car full of black people get pulled over and one of 'em ain't even in a mutha fuckin seat?!"

"Everybody stay quiet," Rob said. "Don't say a damn thing. I got this."

Todd was furious at Diamond. Her throwing that tape out the window caused them to get pulled over. This was definitely going to delay him getting back home. Getting back to Amani.

As Rob pulled the car onto the shoulder, Todd could feel the energy in the car change. It grew tense. Everyone but Todd was nervous. Two officers slowly approached the car. One of them stopped right outside Todd's window, his hand hovering close to his holster. Todd couldn't understand why the officer was so apprehensive, but he made Todd feel nervous, too. Todd tried brushing off the officer's actions..

The other officer approached the driver's side door. "What the hell is going on here? Driver! Step out of the car," he ordered. Rob, whose demeanor went from aggressive to customer service friendly, did exactly what the officer asked.

"Yes, sir," he replied in as chipper a voice as he could. "And how are you?" he added. Rob's behavior reminded Todd of Eddie Haskill from *Leave it to Beaver*. His current temperament was not befitting a person named after an illegal action.

"What is this?," asked the officer, pointing to the crowd in the back seat.

"I apologize, sir," Rob replied sheepishly. "I was trying to be a good samaritan and get my fellow classmates back home safely to their families for the holiday." Todd chuckled out loud at Rob's over-the-top performance.

"What's so funny back there?" the officer demanded.

"Pardon me, sir. It was a cough sneeze hiccup," Todd lied.

"Nigga, seriously, what the fuck is going on in your pants?! Mutha fucka, do you have a boner?" Diamond yelled, ignoring the officers and the seriousness of the situation.

"I get excited when I get nervous," confessed Slim, laying across their laps.

"Everybody out of the car. Now!" ordered the officer.

The passengers struggled to exit. Slim, laying on top, punched and kicked the others on his way out. Todd fell to the ground as soon as he attempted to stand; his legs had fallen asleep thanks to the position he'd been in. As he struggled to his feet, he heard Big J laughing.

"Hahaha! You look like you're giving him head!" he cackled. From where he was on his knees, Todd looked up and straight at the "excited" Slim's bulging groin. He jumped up quickly, but his legs were still stiff so he lost his balance and fell backwards.

Tumbling a small distance into a patch of thistle, he looked like one of the Three Stooges. Probably looked like one, too. He jumped up, the painful sting from the weed helping him ignore the absence of feeling in his legs. Everyone was laughing, including the two officers. What happened to protect and serve? Shouldn't they be helping him climb back up the small embankment instead of chuckling about his less-than-graceful fall?

"This was the funniest thing I've ever seen," said one of the officers. "You all take it easy, and be careful," he added, "especially since you have an unbuckled passenger."

"Of course, sir," Rob replied. The two officers walked away, still laughing.

"Ya mutha fuckas shouldn't have stopped us in the first place," Diamond shouted. "Fuckin' pigs. Keep on walking! I ain't Rodney King; I'll take one of *you* out!"

The policemen stopped dead in their tracks and turned around to face the passengers, all traces of happiness erased. Todd watched as they went from good cop, past bad cop, to make-my-day cop. As much as Todd was not ready to get back into the car, he knew it would be better than what they were about to experience.

"10-38," radioed one of the officers. "We're going to need back up." Todd gulped hard. This can't be good.

"Everyone on the ground! Now!" yelled the second officer. Todd threw himself to the hot pavement, but couldn't help but realize that even this was better than the situation in the back seat of the car. "Legs crossed! Hands on top of your head!" the officer demanded.

Todd was furious. We would've been almost home, he said to himself, but Diamond just had to open her big, stupid mouth. He was desperate to get home to Amani, even though she'd still be in school and unable to see him until after it was dismissed. Todd felt comfort thinking of them being in the same city.

"Driver! Open your trunk," the cop ordered. Rob popped off the ground and did what he was told.

"Y'all can't do that!" Diamond screamed.

"Bitch, you have the *right* to be **silent**!" Big J snapped. Todd couldn't help but snicker; he'd been wanting to say the same thing to her since she started complaining in the car.

"What are you laughing at, corny mutha fucka?" Diamond asked Todd, her eyes burning right through him. Todd exercised his own right to remain silent. He was pissed. And while he didn't know what he'd say to her, he knew it wouldn't be respectful. He also knew as mean-spirited as Diamond was, the situation might turn physical. He would never hit a girl, though. The repercussions of that would definitely lead to bigger issues. The last thing Todd needed was a boyfriend, relative, or friend coming after him if he caused her to get arrested.

Back at the trunk, Todd heard one of the officers ask if Rob had any weapons or drugs inside. "No, sir," Rob said. "As I said before, sir, we're college students trying to get home. We say no to drugs and yes to education."

Todd couldn't decide if he wanted to laugh or barf at Rob's clean cut American kid act, especially since no one was buying it. Barf, Todd thought as his father's words came to mind. "Never get into a car with someone if there's a chance they have drugs or a weapon with them, and don't ride in a car full of passengers."

Todd suddenly felt lightheaded as he remembered Rob asking Diamond for something to make the trip better. Todd knew then and feared now it was drugs. He worried about himself since he'd been sitting next to her. What if the smell from her clothes permeated through his?

Todd held his breath as the officers looked meticulously through the car. He was too nervous to move, and didn't even dare to blink.

"Partner?" called one officer to the other. Todd's stomach began doing flips. Had they found something? The first officer approached the second one and the two talked in low tones.

"IDs! Let's see them!" demanded one of the officers. After collecting everyone's drivers license, he headed for the squad car. Todd was amazed by how quiet Diamond had become. She was even pale, her demeanor one of a defeated fighter.

"They got weed!" shouted a passenger from a passing vehicle, laughing and honking as he drove by.

"Have a seat down there," instructed the remaining officer. Time ticked by, as the group waited for the first officer to return. Another squad car appeared. The officer inside was a woman, and she clearly meant business.

"Everyone stand up," the first officer ordered. "Hands on the car. Miss?" he said to Diamond, "You go with her," he added, gesturing to the female officer. "Does anyone have any weapons or drugs on them? If you do and you don't tell me I'm going to be very pissed off and it will not be a good thing for you," he warned.

"What is going on here?" asked the female officer, looking at Slim's erect penis still poking through his pants.

"Yeah he gets aroused when he gets nervous," the first officer explained, laughing. "I think he likes how I look in my uniform," he joked. "That thing has been at full attention the whole time we've been here."

Laughing, the female officer said, "They're gonna love his nervous energy in lock up."

The area around the kid's midsection darkened and it was suddenly clear that he'd wet himself. The strong stench alerted everyone that he may have shit himself, too. Todd thought he might join that party. He couldn't get past the officer's words about lock-up. Had they found something? Todd knew he should be concerned with how a possession charge would look on his record; his life could be over before it began! But his only thoughts were how he was going to let Amani know that he was in jail.

"Well what do we have here?" asked the female officer, interrupting Todd's panicked thoughts. She reached into Diamond's shirt and pulled out a small baggie of weed. Everyone gasped, but then groaned. Todd couldn't believe himself. In the middle of this dire situation, all he could think of was where drug dealers get the little baggies.

Now, the group turned on Diamond.

"Where did you get that?" asked Rob.

"Bitch, how could you?" Big J asked.

Through sobs, the kid who'd been sitting behind Rob pleaded with the officer. "I just needed a ride home. I didn't know she was a drug mule! Just lock her up," he pleaded. "I honestly just want to go home."

The look on Diamond's face made Todd actually feel bad for her. Everyone had turned on her to save their own butts. His feelings of sorrow were short-lived, replaced quickly by concern for his own well being. The second officer threw Todd onto the hood of the car. "Hands on the hood!" the officer demanded, shoving Todd in the back. The car's warm hood startled Todd and he flinched. The officer shoved him in the back again, only this time Todd failed to catch himself, and his face slammed against the hood of the car. The smell of antifreeze and transmission fluid tickled his nose. It was torture, but he didn't dare move. TV had not prepared Todd for being frisked. On television it seemed like just a series of smooth, gentle pat downs. In reality, now, it was anything but. The officer forcefully moved his hands up and down Todd's body, slapping his pockets hard before shoving his hands into each. He groped Todd's buttocks and tried pulling his cheeks apart through his jeans. Todd struggled to keep from farting out of nervousness. He was nauseous. His mind began to wander as the officer felt around his inseam, trying to focus on the cars whizzing past them on the highway rather than on what was happening to him. He wondered if he knew anyone driving past this display and how it looked to passersby. He wanted nothing more than to be in one of those cars. A car with plenty of legroom that had no drugs in it and was finely-tuned.

The heat from the hood snapped Todd back to reality. He breathed in the scent of the car's leaking oil as it mixed with the grass just off the shoulder. He wondered if his parents would get him out of jail or if this would be a lesson in tough love. This was about to be the most trouble he'd ever been in. This was adults breaking the law. He was no longer a minor. A few weeks on my own and I'm about to be arrested, he thought. There goes my perfect record.

Todd had avoided many house parties in high school just to stay out of trouble. He knew people his age were drinking and doing drugs there (illegally, of course). The one party he'd gone to turned into a melee of inebriated teens tearing up a fellow student's home while their parents were away. Todd never saw any appeal in sneaking around and raiding his or anyone else's liquor cabinet. He'd tried beer once before, but it didn't suit him. Not even a little. He was told it was an acquired taste, but he had no desire to try to acquire it.

After that, his exposure to alcohol was slim, his exposure to drugs nonexistent. He hadn't ever smelled pot until he moved into the dorms. He could smell the faintest hint of weed there as it mixed with the constant scent of burnt popcorn. Today, however, was the first time he'd seen weed up close. It looks like the mulched grass he pulls from the lawnmower. He wondered if this was why they called it grass. He'd heard the drug terminology dime bag, an ounce, gram, a pound, an eighth ounce, but he'd never known how that pertained to the law. He definitely didn't want a first-hand lesson now.

"This one's clean," declared the officer, pulling Todd off the hood of the car by his shirt collar. Todd looked around and noticed another officer had joined them. All their belongings had also been strewn about on the ground. Todd wished he'd packed his stuff more responsibly; his makeshift travel bag was falling apart at the seams.

"What do you want to do with them, Sergeant?" Todd heard an officer ask. He hated the thought of his fate being in the hands of another person, but here he was.

"If we take them in they won't see the judge until Tuesday," the Sergeant informed his deputy. Todd felt his legs wobble and his knees weaken. Tuesday?! he thought. Those couple of days might as well be a life sentence. He wouldn't be able to see

Amani, and that's all that had been keeping him going the last few weeks. He could feel last night's dinner making its way back up. He was at the mercy of the law. He had a ton of questions running through his head, yet he couldn't think straight. Was he going to be held responsible for another person's drugs? Drugs he didn't even know they were carrying? That was a lie. He knew Diamond had had some type of drug on her. He *knew* he should have gotten out of the car. *Don't let someone else's problem become your problem* Todd could hear his dad saying. Why do I always remember his advice *after* I need it, Todd wondered. I can't go to jail. Or, at least, my parents can't know I went to jail. His dad would be disappointed in him, but his mom would kill him. Maybe jail would be the safest place for him if his parents found out about the predicament he was in.

"Take her in for possession of a controlled substance," the Sergeant decided. "Write the others up for a warning of constructive possession."

A warning. I can handle a warning, Todd thought, his demeanor beginning to brighten.

"Give the piggyback rider and the driver a seat belt violation."

"Am I the only one going to jail?" Diamond snapped. Her eyes turned red as tears reached the surface of her eyes. Todd couldn't tell if the tears were of sadness or anger.

"Yes, you are," the officer answered as she guided Diamond toward her squad car.

Diamond planted her feet. "Fuck you, Rob!" she shouted.

Anger. Definitely anger, Todd thought as he watched Diamond try to wiggle free of her cuffs and move toward Rob. He was definitely looking at a woman scorned. As small as she was, she was giving the officers all they could handle, putting up quite a fight.

"You gave me the money for these drugs, you low life!" she screamed. She continued to curse and kick and scream, drowning out the sounds of the highway in an effort not to escape but to attack Rob. Rob hurriedly moved toward his car before the officers changed their minds and took him in for questioning, too. Diamond's legs flailed wildly in the air as if she was going to magically free herself from the officers' grasp. "Wait wait wait," she pleaded, but the arresting officer ignored her.

Diamond next tried escaping by stomping on the officer's foot. She was free for a few seconds before the officers caught up to her. Before being tackled to the ground she hocked a loogie in Rob's direction. It missed its mark, hitting Todd directly on the side of the face. Disgusted, Todd wiped the slimy mucus off. For a split second, he considered throwing it back at her but thought better of it given the presence of the angry officers.

Once on the ground, Diamond continued screaming vile threats against Rob. Todd was beyond ready to get home, far, *far* away from this nightmare of a road trip. He had places he needed to be. He mapped out every stop he planned to make when he got home: haircut, his old job, and his alma mater's pep rally.

"Sir, would you like to file a formal complaint?" an officer asked him. Todd was confused. A complaint against who? Was he being asked to take a survey on the conduct of the officers? Was this something new that police officers were doing after the Rodney King incident? "For Ms. Brown assaulting you with her bodily fluid. It's a fourth degree assault in Missouri," the officer said. As mad as Todd was for being spit on, he did *not* want to waste any more time on the side of the road. He also didn't want to be the target of Diamond's wrath whenever she got out of jail. As loud and brash as she was, Todd had a sinking suspicion she would actually do everything she was threatening to do. If she was crazy enough to assault an officer, he could only imagine what she would do to him. Todd already anticipated Amani's family coming after him if they ever ran off together; the last thing he needed was another person with a vendetta against him. Diamond was also already facing a growing mountain of charges; he didn't want to add to them.

"No thank you, Officer," Todd said.

Just before Diamond was placed in the back of the patrol car, she stopped. All her fight was gone. She turned around calmly to face everyone who'd been in the car. The calm before the storm, Todd thought. "Watch yourselves," she cautioned. "People like me don't have people, we're the people that people have." And she calmly ducked her head as she got in the back of the squad car. She had a sinister look on her face, as if she knew something no one else knew. Todd's feeling of caution around her now became fear.

"I'd hate to be on her bad side," said an officer as he handed Todd his citation. Then they were free to go. The rest of the ride home was peaceful. Crowded, but peaceful. The only sound was the wind blowing through the open car windows. It calmed Todd and was much needed, even though their ordeal could have been much worse.

His father's words echoed in his ears yet again. *Walk with the wise and you, too, will become wise. Walk with fools…* Todd was a fool. He'd known from his first interaction with these guys that he needed to distance himself from them. They were in college – an institution of higher learning – but chose to be lazy, uneducated, and foolish. He should have taken the train like his parents suggested; his nerves would be much calmer. But he was also worried about how he was going to meet up with Amani. There was no guarantee he would see her at the pep rally, and it wasn't like he could call her after school.

Todd tried napping; but the vibration from the car's four bald, uneven tires along with the oppressive heat and humidity made that impossible. Excitement built up as businesses he knew were featured on the billboards they passed. That actually made miles pass more slowly. The half hour ordeal with Diamond and the police on top of the fact that Rob's car struggled to cruise the minimum posted highway speed limit of 45 mph made what should have been a two-hour trip more than two-and-a-half. Dripping with sweat, Todd fantasized about taking a refreshing shower at his parents' house – one that didn't require flip flops – and in a bathroom that didn't reek of urine from unflushed toilets. Knowing he'd be able to sit down to do his business with ample toilet paper was a dream come true.

"Oh shit!" Rob exclaimed. The car sputtered, and smoke poured out from underneath the hood. Rob quickly turned on his hazards and let the car coast to the shoulder.

"So close yet so far away," Todd grumbled under his breath. "What's going on?" he asked more loudly. He knew it had to be something with the radiator but was hoping it was something less pressing.

"Mother fucker, look!" Big J yelled. "The car's on fire!"

Annoyed at being spoken to so disrespectfully, Todd got out of the car once it hit the shoulder. He didn't even wait for it to come to a full stop. He tried to remind himself that they were all irritable from the stifling heat and unyielding humidity, but he needed air and space. Also, burning alive in a car was not on the agenda for the holiday weekend.

"Calm your scary ass down!" Rob yelled at Big J. "It's not on fire. The radiator just needs some water."

"Where are we going to get water?" whined Slim. "I think I saw a sign that said the nearest exit with a gas station was close to two miles away."

"Are you sure?" Rob asked.

"I'm pretty sure. I was looking because I have to pee."

"Just pee into the radiator," Todd said sarcastically. "There's no way this hunk of junk is going to limp two miles down the road. I'm surprised it made it this far." His irritability was showing. He didn't care. He was tired, hot, and wanted this ride from hell to be over with.

"Will that work?" Rob asked curiously, hoping Todd's suggestion might provide an easy fix.

"I have no clue," Todd replied, "But I don't see why it wouldn't."

Rob took off his shirt and wrapped it around the radiator cap. Pushing down, he twisted it to release the pressure and hot steam. Everyone jumped back at the hiss.

"Go ahead," Rob invited his passenger.

"Don't look at me!" Slim exclaimed. "On second thought, I can't hold it any longer. Turn around and shield me so none of these passing cars can see me. I don't need no more interactions with the police," he added.

He jumped on the car's bumper straddling the engine and squatted, but recklessly peed all over the car.

"Mutha Fucka, can't you pee straight?!" Rob yelled. Slim altered his aim, and a sizzle could be heard as the stream came in contact with the car's hot radiator.

Todd started to wonder again when this dreadful journey would be over. Before he could think further, he heard a blood-curdling scream come from Slim. "Arrggghhhh!"

Steaming hot radiator fluid was erupting from the car and cascading in a reverse waterfall. A few splatters landed on Todd, stinging his arm.

Slim's screams drowned out the sounds from the highway and he began jumping up and down before dropping to his knees. His penis had been burned by the escaping radiator fluid and he was crying in anguish as he tried to manage the pain. Each man grabbed his own crotch at the thought of the agony Slim was enduring.

Slim blew hard on his injured penis, trying to cool the scalding. Todd was amazed that a dark-complected man could develop bright red blisters.

"Dude! Your dick's on fire!" yelled Big J. "My prom date did the same thing to me," he teased, trying unsuccessfully to lighten the mood.

Todd used to do the same thing when he caused his sister an injury. He'd always heard laughter is the best medicine, but he knew it was going to take more than a joke to relieve Slim of this pain.

Slim looked down at his injury and promptly threw up. Todd couldn't imagine how much pain he was in.

"I guess the radiator wasn't empty, just blocked," Rob shouted. "Let's get you home so you can put some ointment on your dick."

He needs a hospital, Todd thought, pretty sure that Slim had second and third degree burns. Selfishly, he kept quiet. He was too close to St. Louis to suggest they spend several hours in the emergency room. Slim would just have to wait until after Todd got dropped off.

Cautiously, Slim pulled his pants back up and waddled toward the car. Todd was thrilled they were back on the road, but the rest of the way home he felt sick as Slim let out a tiny squeal with every bump or sharp turn.

When they were less than two miles from his home, Todd felt a feeling he'd only experienced with baseball and at Christmas time as a kid. Every tree, every house, every store he recognized gave him butterflies in his stomach.

"Turn left here," Todd directed Rob when they got to his street. He couldn't have cared less what happened to the car or the other passengers at this point. He was home.

"It's the fifth house on the right," he said.

"Damn, Nigga!" started Big J. "Is your pops a doctor and your mom a lawyer?" he asked mockingly.

Todd brushed his question off, but he couldn't help feeling insulted. People had compared Todd and his family to TV's Huxtables forever because they were a Black family with both parents in the home, both of whom were successful professionally, as if working hard and raising children who spoke proper English turned them into the family off *The Cosby Show*. Todd didn't spend too much thought on it, though; he was too focused on how thrilled he was to be home.

Todd's dad was there. That was surprising. Todd couldn't remember a time his dad had ever taken off work to welcome him home. He was packing the car for the trip to the lake. Todd usually loved spending this holiday at the lake, but not this year. This year was different. This year he was thrilled to be home, and stay home. It was a chance to recharge after three torrid weeks in college. More importantly, it was an opportunity to be with Amani.

Todd experienced an indescribable feeling of relief as he hopped out of the car. He was free from Rob's compact prison on wheels.

"Welcome home, Son!," his dad called. "Who's this?"

Todd was in no mood to be cordial and introduce anyone to his dad, especially since he didn't know any of their real names. Everyone in the car helped create the worst trip he'd ever experienced, and he was pissed. But his dad had expectations, so…

"Dad, this is Rob, and that's Big J," he started, his tone mopy, but he was quickly interrupted by Slim.

"Sir? Do you happen to have some aspirin and burn cream?" He eased himself out of the car, waddled around to the passenger's side, dropped his pants, and showed Todd's dad his injury.

"What happened to you?" Todd's dad exclaimed. This was the first time in Todd's life that he'd heard his dad sound horrified and perplexed. When he was growing up, Todd thought his dad knew the answer to everything, but now his dad was at a loss for words.

Todd glanced quickly at Slim's penis. It had gotten worse. The puss-filled blisters were more prevalent now and the penis had begun to swell.

"Todd, go get some aloe vera ointment to treat that burn," his father instructed him.

Todd went inside and rummaged through the medicine cabinet looking for some ointment. He took a deep breath and reveled at how wonderful it was to be home. He'd never noticed before, but his home had a specific scent to it. He'd missed it.

As he returned to the garage with the aloe vera he heard everyone recounting the details of their trip to his dad, including the incident with the police. Todd stole a quick glance at his dad and knew exactly what he was thinking. It wasn't good.

Todd gulped hard. He'd ignored the rules his dad expected him to follow to keep him safe. "Todd, he would say, you will not be viewed the same as others because you're a Black youth in

America. No matter where you go, your mom and I need to know where you are; who you're going with; who will be there; and when you get there, check in with us so we know you arrived safely." He would also tell him not to ride in a crowded car, or in a car blasting loud music. Todd was not allowed to leave the house wearing a wife-beater or a du-rag on his head.

"Your appearance shapes people's perception of you," he'd say. "If you dress like a thug, people will treat you like one."

Todd was to carry his ID at all times – especially essential if a high-profile crime had been committed in the area since, no matter what, he was always going to fit the description of whichever Black person had done it (even if they looked nothing alike) – but Todd often failed to do this since he couldn't keep up with his wallet.

"I thought I told you not to get in a car with lots of people," his dad said. "But did you listen? No! And what happened? You almost got hauled off to jail." Todd's dad spoke firmly, but without anger. It still shook Todd to his core, though.

"You draw unwanted attention," his dad continued. "Do not get in a car with drugs or weapons because you could be held accountable if something goes wrong." He paused. "What happened?" his dad asked rhetorically. "You all knew there were drugs in the car but when the officer asked you developed amnesia? And *please* tell me how four college students devised a plan of urinating inside a hot radiator. What idiot thought *that* was a good idea?"

The group looked at Todd, but his dad wasn't done. "Why not just pee into a cup or a can?" he asked. "It would have been easier to pour," he added, "and I'm pretty sure you could have found either littered on the side of the highway." Todd's dad was growing angrier by the moment. Todd could tell it wasn't so much over the stupidity of fixing the overheating car's radiator by peeing in it, but because Todd hadn't followed the rules.

Inspecting the car through a closed hood, he sniffed around where the engine could be. "Let me guess," he said, "it was a blocked line; you weren't empty."

The group was astonished. "How did you know?" Rob asked. Todd's father ignored him. Todd could tell from the look on his face that his dad was definitely angry.

"Hey!" his dad yelled in Slim's direction. "Go into the garage or into the house to put the ointment on." Slim still had his pants around his ankles with the aloe vera in one hand and his penis in the other.

Mr. Andrews, the neighbor across the street, happened to be outside to grab the newspaper from his driveway. He glanced at the group of boys with a flabbergasted expression. "I see your son's experiencing a lot in college. I guess you can't learn everything from a book," he snickered as he retreated back into his house.

Todd wanted to hide. Not from the neighbor, but from his dad who was, at that moment, staring him down, even angrier than before because he was embarrassed.

Returning to the question Rob had asked him, Todd's dad said, "There's not enough urine in your body to fill the radiator to an acceptable level to fix your car." His tone showed his disdain for the idiots Todd had chosen to ride home with. "I guess that's why your car smells like piss," he deduced. "But to answer your question completely," Todd's dad said, turning to Rob, "you wouldn't be able to get the radiator cap off without burning yourself. The contents under pressure is over 200 degrees. I'm guessing the blockage coincidentally dislodged when what's-his-name started urinating in it. Take him to the doctor and get this thing out of my driveway," he finished, turning angrily and marching back into the house.

"Nigga, your dad is a gangsta!" Rob said. "Let me get out of here before he comes back with that 357."

Todd had never heard his dad referred to as a gangsta before. And he'd never even considered the possibility that he would have a gun.

Todd watched the crew drive off before turning hesitantly toward the house. He dreaded the lecture he was sure to endure.

Opening the door, he was met with his dad on the phone. "Remember he's your kid," his dad said to whoever was on the other end. Todd assumed it was his mom.

Hanging up the phone, his dad took a long, deep breath. "You rode home in that piece of crap?" he asked.

"Unfortunately," Todd answered quietly. Here it comes, he thought. A lecture. Just one more in a long line of 'you-never-listen-what-the-hell-is-wrong-with-you lectures.' Instead, his dad held out a $10 bill. "When you get back to school, I want you to give this to someone who isn't a freshman. Have them go to the registrar's office and get you a parking pass so you don't have to rely on drug-transporting, urine-filled cars to get you around."

Todd was dumbstruck. Was his dad high? Was Todd having a stroke? Was *Todd* high? He could not believe his dad was allowing him to take the car to college. Todd was ecstatic. He grabbed the key and ran out the door. He couldn't care less that he needed to take a shower or change his clothes. He just wanted to leave before his dad changed his mind. He heard the phone ringing and worried that it was his mom calling, that she'd change his dad's mind for him. His dad may be the head of the house, but his mom was the neck. And the head can't go anywhere without the neck. Todd was certain the neck had made the decision to allow him to take his car to college.

Chapter 24

It was 1:00 when Todd arrived at the barber shop. He had just enough time to get a haircut, rush back home, change clothes, and be at his old school for the pep rally at 2:15.

"Little Toby!" Ms. Rose greeted Todd as he entered. Toby was the nickname his father had been given when a relative who wore surprisingly-loose dentures first laid eyes on him. She tried to say he looked like a teddy bear, but the loose dentures made it sound like Toby bear. The nickname stuck all the way until the next generation, and Todd was affectionately called "Little Toby" by relatives or his dad's friends.

"Have a seat here," Ms. Rose instructed Todd. "And not a minute too soon," she said, looking at Todd's hair. In high school, Todd got his haircut weekly. He liked feeling fresh and clean. It gave him confidence. He knew his clothes might not match, and his shoes weren't the most stylish but his hair was always exceptional.

"How's college?" Ms. Rose asked. Before Todd could answer, the four regular patrons stopped their conversation about the Clinton/Bush presidential race and started talking to Todd about college.

"You know you don't have to go to class and still pass with all A's," one of them said. "What's your minor? It's not about your major, Son, it's about your minor. Everyone knows that. Let me give you advice about college," he continued. "Choose a major you love and you'll never work a day in your life. Because that field probably ain't hiring." The room exploded with laughter. Todd began to wonder if any of them had even been to college.

"You ain't in college," said another of the men, "You don't look fat!" he exclaimed. "Don't all college kids gain fifteen pounds their freshman year?"

"The semester just started," noted one of the barbers. "He'll be fat in a couple more months.

"He should have joined the service," said an old man wearing a camouflage shirt. "We would have put fifteen pounds of muscle on him by now."

"How are the parties?" another one chimed in. "Everyone knows college parties are the best ones."

Todd had yet to go to a college party. Is that something I should be doing? he asked himself. He'd always heard how legendary university parties were, especially Homecoming, which was rapidly approaching.

"College is a waste of time," said a customer wearing a United States Postal uniform. "It's like looking both ways before you cross the street and then getting hit by an airplane; it doesn't prepare you for life," he added. "You need a government job."

"I bet you have a lot of girls swarming around you," hypothesized one of the men. Todd was eager to brag about Amani, but the conversation quickly turned toward the men's own reputations as ladies men. Todd's stomach churned as the group reminisced about both their past and present partners.

"You all need to be quiet," Ms. Rose snapped. "You know none of you have the working equipment to do what you used to or want to do. I doubt your old wrinkled parts will work without Spanish fly and ginseng anyway. Besides, what woman wants your old asses bouncing and sweating on top of them," she teased.

"My Johnson might not work all the time," retorted one man, "but my tongue does!"

"I don't doubt that!" Ms. Rose laughed goodnaturedly. "Judging by the fat around your belly it works very well."

"I'll take you in the back room and show you," he offered.

"Don't make me throw up," she said, making a puking sound. Then, turning to Todd, Ms. Rose said, "Don't listen to that old fart. He'll teach you all the wrong ways to handle a woman. A real man doesn't have to spit in it to get her wet," she joked. "A real man turns a woman on by the things he does when they *aren't* naked. By checking in on her during the day, letting her know what she means to him. By filling up her gas tank without her asking. By holding her hand in public and saying 'I love you' in front of his friends. A real man helps clean up and helps with the laundry. A real man," she began.

"Your 'real man' sounds like a soft man," joked one of the men. "Don't listen to her, young buck. What does she know about what a woman wants? Take it from me," he instructed. "If you want to knock a woman off her feet, sometimes you have to go down on her and eat." The group chuckled and went back to discussing their past relationship conquests.

As Todd left the barbershop he could hear one of the men accuse him of being a virgin. He'll understand what we're talking about when he stops being wet behind the ears and gets some from a girl for the first time. Todd prayed he was right. He didn't know half of what the men were talking about. He only heard half of it from locker room banter after baseball games, and tried to picture some of what his teammates were describing.

For the first time since he graduated high school, he felt good about being in college. There's direction and promise of a bright future, he told himself. He couldn't imagine spending his life sitting in a barber shop reminiscing about the glory of his past or arguing about politics but not doing anything to make the world a better place.

Todd walked toward his car and began to have second thoughts about going to the pep rally. As a college student, going to a high school pep rally wouldn't be any better than what the guys at the barber shop were doing. He'd just be going back to the place he'd worked to escape the past four years. He'd be trying to recapture a time in his life he could never go back to. The phrase *you can never go back home again* actually began to make sense to him now. Then again, if there was even a slight chance of seeing Amani, he had to take it.

After a quick shower and a change of clothes, Todd headed out.

"Todd! Come here!" his dad shouted from upstairs. Todd could tell from the tone in his father's voice that he was in trouble. He headed up the steps.

"Yes, Dad?" he asked. His dad was in his parents' closet. In his hands were a bunch of business shirts he'd had pressed by the cleaners.

"Todd," he started, "I work hard for everything I own. I take care of everything I own," he added. "One day, after years of hard work, I hope you will own nice things. I hope you sacrifice your time and energy and that you reward yourself by buying yourself something nice." He paused for what Todd could tell was dramatic effect. "I pray that when you try to enjoy the fruits of your labor," he continued, "that your son funks up your expensive clothes and tries to hide it in the back of the closet."

How'd he know it was me? Todd wondered, throwing up his hands to catch the purple shirt his father chucked at him. Todd remembered repairing the shirt carefully and returning it without his dad knowing. The perfect crime, or so Todd had thought. Just then, he remembered having gym class that day, and though he changed out of his dad's shirt, he'd put it back without washing it.

"I want this taken to the cleaners, laundered, and returned before you leave to go back to school," his dad said.

"Yes, sir," Todd replied. He stood there for a moment waiting for his dad to…

"Oh are you waiting for me to give you money to clean the expensive shirt you funked up without permission? Not happening." Todd realized he'd be paying for that himself.

Heading down the stairs, Todd contemplated washing and ironing the shirt himself to save a few bucks. Nah, he thought; with my luck I'd either shrink the shirt in the wash or burn it with the iron.

Todd could hear students cheering as he entered the athletic wing of his alma mater. The cheerleaders were amping up the crowd as the band played. A crowd at the door was keeping Todd from getting inside.

"You can't get in there," he heard someone say. Todd recognized him as a football player, though Todd couldn't remember his name.

"Heyyy!" Todd greeted him with a tone meant to suggest they were the best of friends. "How have you been?"

"Ehh," the kid replied, "I went to State to play football but got cut."

Todd vaguely remembered him being a decent ball player as well as a ladies man, but at their school, even the kicker was treated as a celebrity. He felt bad for the kid; he couldn't imagine what he'd do if *his* college told him he was no longer good enough to do the thing he loved most. How would he handle transitioning from being **the** man to being just another man? I'd better get to work, he told himself. He was already considered second string. Lincoln was always recruiting; he might be just one recruit away from being replaced, one who'd be willing to out-work him, who'd be willing to improve constantly rather than resting on his laurels.

The gym's mezzanine was full of graduates. There were old football players, honor students, and cheerleaders. Most of them donned their generation's uniforms or worn out letterman jackets. The school was celebrating its current students and players, not realizing its past was lingering in the halls, watching, wanting to be the celebrated center of attention again.

"Enjoy it, Todd said softly. "Once you graduate you'll become nothing more than the past to future players." Again, he found himself thinking you can never go home again. His past couldn't be re-lived. I'm going to start making a way toward my future, he told himself.

As he watched former cheerleaders perform routines in the shadow of the current generation – albeit slower and with less rhythm – Todd had seen enough. He abandoned his plan to stick around driving his car to impress current students. He was coming to the realization that he was on the verge of being thought of as an old head. He and his friends made fun of old heads who came back to school flashing their material possessions to garner the attention of younger girls because women their age ignored them. They'd joke that the old heads would retreat to their parents' basement after hitting on naive little girls who didn't know any better.

"You guys take care," Todd told the group. No one was listening. The football players were too busy comparing their teams to the current one. They bragged about how much faster and bigger their competition had been compared to what today's players faced. The cheerleaders continued to search for the fountain of youth, cheering in outfits that barely fit and trying to move to steps they were obviously too old for.

Walking to the door, Todd heard a group of former graduates discuss how much easier the curriculum is now that the current students have newer textbooks. Pathetic, he thought. This visit had been a wake up call. As he drove off campus he vowed never to come back again unless Tiffany was competing or performing there. You can't come home again if you move, he told himself. And that's what I'm doing. Moving. Moving on.

Chapter 25

Fifteen minutes later, Todd hadn't moved far toward his future. He dropped his dad's shirt off at the cleaners, and headed toward the Plaza. It was time to revisit another blast from his past so he could pay to have the shirt laundered. Green Leaf Kitchen was his plan. His overconfidence that they would put him on the schedule, last minute turned to unfounded arrogance. *I should have called a week ago and told them I'd be in town. That's something the new Todd will do,* he thought. *Plan ahead.*

Just like always, the restaurant was full of empty tables. There were a couple mall employees standing near the entrance waiting for their to-go order to be filled. There was a new hostess who gave Todd a nasty look as he walked past the wait-to-be-seated sign.

"Excuuuse me!" she barked. Todd shot her an arrogant smile and a wave as if she should know who he was.

"Todd! You're back!" Marla cheered, running toward him and giving him a big hug.

"How have you been?" he asked, happy to see someone who was happy he was back in town.

"Oh. Hey, Todd," Tim said. He was, as usual, gone before Todd could respond. "Oh!" Tim stopped dead in his tracks. "Did I forget to pay you?" he asked, a concerned look on his face. Todd chuckled to himself. *One day I'm going to say yes and see if he* does *pay me for time I didn't even work.* He was irritated that Tim hadn't realized he'd been gone for a couple of weeks.

"No, Tim," he said. "I'm in town for the holiday and wanted to know if you needed any help this weekend.

"You want to pick up some extra hours?" Tim asked, curious. "Here?" He paused, seemingly surprised that Todd was asking to work *there*. "When can you start?"

Before Todd could answer, Tim grabbed his arm. "Look, we're desperate. Everyone's been calling in sick because it's a holiday weekend. I'll pay you double if you can work tonight, tomorrow, and Sunday, and I'll pay you triple for Monday."

Wow, he *must* be desperate, Todd thought. Easy money, but did he really want to spend his time home working? Why not? His family was going to be gone, anyway. "You got a deal," Todd said, shaking Tim's hand.

"Great," Tim said. "You can start at five. I'll tell Rick," he said, walking away.

Looking at his watch, Todd saw that he only had ninety minutes before he had to be back. Just enough time to see my mom and sister before they head out of town. Hopefully I'll hear from Amani during that time, too.

His mom greeted him as soon as he walked in. "Welcome home!" she sang. "Are you sure you don't want to come to the lake with us?" she asked.

"I'd really love to, Mom," Todd lied, "but I got asked to work for double pay the next few days and triple pay on the holiday. I could really use the money."

That was enough for his mom. She gave him a huge hug and a big kiss on his cheek. Todd immediately wiped it away. "I bet you don't wipe away these kisses from your little girlfriends," Mom teased.

"Todd's too ugly to have a girlfriend," Tiffany joked. Both parents chuckled.

"I bet my handsome man here has all the girls at college swooning over him," Mom replied.

"Him *who*?" asked Tiffany. "Your child is a loser, Mom. Capital L. Capital O."

"Don't strain your brain trying to spell it," Todd interrupted.

"Stop it!" Mom barked. "This is the first time in three weeks I've had both my kids home. Don't make me kick you both out," she threatened.

"Sorry, Mom." Tiffany apologized. "I just don't know how your son, who wears more makeup than you, is anything but a loser," she said. "Over the past four years, you," she continued, pointing at Todd, "have put more make-up on than Boy George and Prince combined."

Both parents stopped dead in their tracks. Looking at Tiffany, their faces begged for her to continue. Snickering, Tiffany sauntered out of the room.

"Get back in here now, young lady," Dad demanded. "Tell us about your brother wearing make-up." Both parents turned toward Todd, confused. Todd had been gesturing for Tiffany to keep her mouth shut when their attention wasn't focused on him.

"Twisted sister over there," Tiffany teased, "would take your mascara, Mom, and paint his upper lip to try to make that peach fuzz of a mustache look like a full-grown one. He even used your mascara to paint little curly cues on his chest to make it look like he had chest hair." Dad covered his eyes and shook his head in disbelief.

"When he went to parties, he and his friends would dab lipstick on their collars and a little on their necks to make it look like they had some girl making out with them," Tiffany continued.

"Why?" Mom asked. "Sounds like a girl *repellent* to me," she added.

"He and his loser friends think girls find boys more attractive if other girls want them," Tiffany added.

"How do you know what me and my friends talk about?" Todd asked, angry.

"Because I eavesdropped on your phone calls," Tiffany confessed. "I find your stupidity quite entertaining," she teased. "It still baffles me that after some of the dumb things you've done in your life someone thought you were qualified enough to attend college. They probably got fired right after they signed your acceptance letter."

Todd was about to retaliate but stopped when Tiffany put her hand up to silence him. She turned back to their parents. "Then he puts a mixture of almond and walnut liquid foundation on his neck to cover up his hickies."

"Talk to your son," Mom said to his dad.

"Don't blame me for raising Little Richard!" Dad joked. "I don't care what idiocracy he uses to get girls," he continued, "as long as he doesn't bring home any babies or any failing grades." He paused. "Speaking of grades," he started, but the phone rang.

Saved by the bell, thought Todd. He'd felt a lecture coming on. "Hello?" he answered.

"That's another thing," he heard Tiffany say, "this fool drinks Listerine before he answers phone calls because he thinks it makes his voice sound deeper."

Todd was irritated at his sister exposing his secrets. Though they hardly ever worked, he still thought they were a great plan, just poorly executed.

"Hi," said the voice on the other end. Todd immediately recognized Amani's voice.

"Hold on," he said. Handing the phone to his dad, Todd asked, "can you hang up when I get upstairs? And *please* keep the phone away from Tiffany?"

"Why can't you talk in front of us?" his dad asked. Todd just gave him an annoyed look. "Hurry up," Dad responded, setting the phone on the table.

Todd ran upstairs to his bedroom to pick up the phone. "I got it!" he yelled.

"Bye, Loverboy!" Tiffany giggled into the receiver as she hung up. Amused, Amani chuckled.

"Siblings," Todd grumbled.

"I know," Amani said. "I have five, remember? How's school?" she asked. Todd ran down the gauntlet of his three weeks of hell, including signing up for the wrong class and showing up to practice in his underwear. He marveled at the concern Amani showed for his mishaps.

"Don't worry," she said. "I'll help you in any way I can. I'm in Honors Calculus right now. It might not be like *College Calculus*, but I can teach you the basics so you can understand better."

"You can start by teaching me how to use a calculator," Todd joked.

"I also speak three languages," she said. "I'm not fluent in Spanish, but I am in Catalan, which is very similar to Spanish."

"You'll really help me out?" Todd asked.

"Sempre estaré al costat del meu home i l'ajudaré a tenir èxit a la vida," Amani replied.

"I don't know what you said," Todd said, "but the way you said it was sexy as hell. The two giggled.

"I told you I'll always stand by my man and help him succeed!"

"Oh, yes," Todd said. "Say I'm your man again." Amani laughed.

Todd glanced at the clock and realized he was going to be late for work. "Shit. I have to go. I love you!" he said, hanging up quickly.

"Son," Todd's dad began, standing in the doorway.

"Hey, Dad, what's up? I gotta get ready for work," he said, embarrassed that his dad may have overheard some of his conversation.

"Your mom wanted me to talk to you," his dad said, sitting down on Todd's bed and looking around the room. The walls were covered with baseball memorabilia, mostly featuring the Cardinals. And there were a few cutouts from Kathy Ireland's *Sports Illustrated* swimsuit issue, too. "I hope all your plots and tricks to get girls are behind you," Dad continued. Then, quoting the bible, he said, "When I was a child, I spoke as a child, I understood as a child, I thought as a child: but when I became a man, I put away childish things. It's time to be a man, Todd," his dad said. "If you plan to continue playing baseball, you need to stop *playing* it and start *working on* it. All these guys on your wall stopped playing the sport at some point and began working at being the best at it. As a man, it's time to stop chasing after girls and find a woman. A woman who will support you but also have ambitions and goals of her own. Goals you can work on and achieve together. I heard you tell the young lady you love her," he said, "but does she love you, too? You're an adult now. It's time to mature from puppy love and find a woman who is in love with you." He paused. "Do you even know the difference, Son?"

Todd thought about it. He honestly *didn't* know the difference. Amani was the first girl he'd actually had feelings for. He'd had crushes, but he was pretty sure what he has with Amani is love. "No, I don't," he told his dad.

"So, when you like someone," his dad said, "you try to impress them. When you *love* someone you can be yourself around them. No more painting your face with your mom's makeup," he said, shaking his head in disappointment. "When you're in love you want that person to love you back equally. It takes time to be in love with someone; it doesn't happen overnight. That's why being in love with someone means growing with that person. You'll know when you have the right person when she doesn't use her love to make you weak but uses it to make you strong." With that, he got up to leave, then, turning around, he stopped. "You have plenty of time to figure it out. You're transitioning from childhood to adulthood. Don't preoccupy yourself trying to make someone like, love, or fall in love with you if you don't yet know who you are or who you're becoming. The most important part is to become the man you want to become and to love that man. Girls will come after that."

Chapter 26

It was another slow night at Green Leaf Kitchen. It had only been three weeks since Todd last worked a shift, but so much had changed yet somehow also stayed the same. Like every year, a new batch of first-time job seekers had applied and started, including the cook who took Todd's place. "You'll like him, he's nice," is what everybody kept telling Todd, but Todd knew he wouldn't like him. He wasn't even going to even give him a chance. Todd took it personally that this kid was hired to replace him. I'm irreplaceable, he told himself.

The one bright spot in all the newer employees was that Dave had been hired as a dishwasher and was scheduled to work tonight. Lucky thing, Todd thought. I'll have someone to talk to. He didn't really want to interact with the new employees; by the time he got to know them, either he or they would be forgotten by the time he came back for Christmas. And by then there wouldn't be time to socialize, anyway, because Christmas was the only time every store at the mall – Green Leaf Kitchen included – was busy. Todd intended to use his time this weekend to work hard, clean, and to show Rick it would be a great idea to allow him to work during Winter Break.

An hour into his shift, Todd had already begun prepping the kitchen for the next day and cleaning up the half he could, to close for the night.

"Looking good in here!" Rick said to Todd as he walked by. Rule number one when working with Rick: get caught working. As he scrubbed the counters, Todd started thinking about what his dad had said earlier. What kind of man did he want to be? His dad's words echoed in his head. Of course I want to be like my father, he thought: a hardworking family man who was well-liked but mostly well-respected in the community. He gave back by mentoring at-risk youth and helping at church. The problem with being like his dad was that Todd didn't have his work ethic or his analytical thinking skills. When his dad saw a problem, he could formulate multiple solutions instantly. When Todd saw the same problem, it would take him a while to understand it, much less solve it. He'd use the most basic one, and if that didn't work he'd try it again the same way, not because he's stupid, he would tell himself, but because he's stubborn. But maybe that *did* make him stupid.

Two hours into his shift, Todd was bored out of his mind. He'd only had two orders, both from mall employees. The kitchen had been deep cleaned, a chore he'd done to leave a lasting impression on Tim and Rick. Dave had just been hanging out while Todd cleaned and filled him in on everything that had been happening while he was away. This might have interested Todd earlier in the day, but now that he'd told himself he's a new man who's not living in the past he couldn't care less. Todd began to see Dave as a kid, even though they were only a year apart. Todd found this ironic considering Amani was the same age as Dave.

As Dave talked about his teachers and who was dating who, Todd began to wonder about school. The old him would wait until the last minute to get assignments done. The new him began to formulate a plan of attack. Dave's presence was suddenly irritating as Todd considered how to get organized, a task he'd never accomplished before. His droning on about high school matters irritated him like the buzzing of a mosquito in his ear.

"Hey, Dave! Who the heck is Todd?" he heard one of the new waitresses ask.

Todd popped up from the spot on the floor where he'd been cleaning a grease spill that had probably been there since he last worked. "That's me," he said.

"Oh!" she exclaimed, startled by his appearing out of nowhere. "You have someone here to see you."

Todd could see it was Amani through the open window area in the kitchen. As he made his way toward her, Todd could hear Dave ask him to ask her if Sasha was with her. Todd rolled his eyes. He didn't even say hello once he was close enough to touch her, he just wrapped his arms tightly around her. A world of stress melted away in her arms; he never wanted to let her go. He felt comfortable and safe in her embrace. His heart fluttered as he breathed her in. Amani rubbed his back gently, whispering "I love you" into his ear. Her words coursed through every corner of Todd's body, filling it with joy. He sent up a prayer to the heavens: don't ever let this moment…

"Hey, is Sasha with you?" Dave interrupted. Moment ruined, thought Todd.

"Umm," Amani started, "she came to the mall with me, but I don't know where she went." She looked at Todd as if to say that Sasha had come to see someone else.

"Okay," Dave replied, defeated.

"I'm so happy to see you," Todd finally said. He was disappointed that he couldn't find words that would accurately convey how it felt to see her.

"I don't have long," she said. "I told my parents I was running to the store with Sasha to get feminine products. They know Sasha takes her time doing everything, so I have maybe a half hour."

"I'll take every second I can get," Todd said.

"Good. Go get your Calculus book," she replied.

"My what?" Todd couldn't believe that she wanted to spend the little time they had doing homework.

"I made a promise to make my man successful, remember?" she giggled. "How are you going to whisk me away if you're stuck in college because you can't pass Calculus?" she teased.

Todd excused himself to run to his car to get his book. He had planned to study at work, but had the book in his car. He ran as fast as he could; he didn't want to waste any of the precious moments he had with Amani.

"I don't care about her; I was just curious if she was here. I don't need her; I'm going to be alright." Todd could hear Dave complaining to Amani as he returned with his book. No doubt he was referring to Sasha. Todd remembered how well they got along and was surprised they weren't a couple, but a little thing like prejudice can throw a monkey wrench into a relationship, he thought.

"Let's get started," Amani said, grateful to have something to get her away from Dave. "Now," she began. "There are four main concepts of calculus: limits, differential calculus (or differentiation), integral calculus (or integration), and multivariable calculus (or function theory)."

Todd found it difficult to concentrate on the material. Her hand brushing softly against his gave him goosebumps. Her soft breath tantalized his senses as she described how sequences, series, and derivatives are used to analyze functions. When she accidentally bumped her leg against his, she apologized and sensuously rubbed her his knee.

Remembering what Ms. Rose had told him earlier, Todd tried to make the same kinds of sweet gestures of affection, from offering her something to drink to removing a strand of hair after it fell in her face. With every answer he got right on the impromptu quiz she gave him, he would take her hand in his, softly caressing it.

Todd learned a lot during his 30-minute tutoring session, more than he had in three weeks of college. Another 30 minutes and he'd be a math scholar, he joked to himself, but another ten minutes of this kind of sexual tension and he might explode.

"You ready, girl?" Sasha asked, running into the restaurant. Todd hated to see Amani go. He wanted to come up with an excuse to make her stay but knew she had to go. Her being there with him now was dangerous for the both of them. Thankfully, Green Leaf Kitchen was dimly lit and rarely frequented.

Todd waited as long as he could to get up to tell Amani goodbye, partly because he didn't want her to go, but mostly because he was waiting for an annoying body part to settle down. He tried to focus on baseball, but that didn't calm the arousal. First base, he imagined making out with Amani. Second base, he imagined caressing her breasts. Third base, he fantasized touching her juice box.

"Hi, Dave," he heard Sasha say.

"Hey," Dave responded nonchalantly, collecting the only used dish and glassware in the restaurant. Sasha's eyes followed his every move.

"How have you been?" she asked as he walked past her.

"Good," he replied coldly. The look of hurt in Sasha's eyes was comical. She didn't want him when he wanted her, and now that he's acting like he's moved on, she wants him. Highschoolers, Todd said to himself, rolling his eyes. He knew what Dave was doing, and it was one big ploy.

"Are you going to give me a hug goodbye?" Amani asked. The coast is clear, Todd thought, his midsection crisis averted. "I love you," she whispered as they embraced. Her words set his heart on fire. Just as he was about to release her, she held him tighter. Placing her hand on the back of his head, she drew him in closer. She softly placed her lips on his ear and whispered, "I'm ready to give you all of me."

Todd pulled back a little and looked into her eyes. "I love you, Amani. And I'm not going anywhere," he assured her. "We can wait if you want. You're the one my soul has been longing for; I want to be with you and only you." He gulped hard. I should be excited, he thought, but all he felt was anxiety. He'd never had sex. Hell, he'd never even seen it done before. Sure he'd seen a *Playboy*, or occasionally if he closed one eye, cocked his head to the side while upside down he could partially make out an image on the scrambled pay-per-view, but that was it.

"Are you alright?" Amani asked, wiping the sweat from his brow. He nodded, too nervous to speak. He knew any attempt would result in a stutter.

"Tell your boy I said 'bye,'" Sasha snorted, interrupting the couple's moment. "He thinks I'm stupid," she continued. "Us girls know what you, umm, little boys are up to."

Todd didn't like her generalization. Sure, he'd done some dumb things to get girls' attention, but that was different.

"If he really thinks being cold to me is going to make me fall in love with him, I have a game to play, too," Sasha said. "It's called pretending like I'm falling for it until he buys me a pair of these gorgeous white denim-washed Guess! jean shorts that I've had my eyes on for a while."

Amani and Todd re-engaged with each other, ignoring everything around them, including Sasha's plan for retaliation against Dave. "Meet me at the park at midnight," Amani said. "I may be a little late, depending on my brother, but wait for me. I'll be there."

"I'd wait an eternity for you," Todd said, kissing her forehead softly.

The rest of the night was a blur; Todd was on a mission to make their first time memorable.

***

It was 1:45 by the time Amani popped out from behind some bushes and made her way through the park into Todd's car. Todd killed the dome light when his door opened so no one would see her. He leaned over and gave her a quick kiss, but she grabbed the back of his head to extend it. After a long moment, they looked adoringly into each other's eyes. They both knew tonight was going to be special. Butterflies danced in their stomachs. Todd reached for Amani's hand, interlocking his fingers with hers, and they were off.

They rode to Todd's house in silence. Todd feared Amani could hear his stomach rumbling. Doubt started to creep its way into his thoughts. He knew he wanted to make love to Amani, but he worried about how he'd perform, if he would live up to whatever expectations she might have. How long should sex last? Where did all the parts go? And while he hoped Amani was wondering the same thing, he was fairly sure she was focusing on the fact that she'd be killed if anyone found out what she was about to do.

The house was quiet. Todd's family had left for the lake while he was at work.

"Let's go to the basement," he suggested, guiding her down the stairs. Amani froze mid-way, amazed at the setting Todd had created. The unfinished space came to life as the shadows of dozens of lit candles danced along the walls. Rose petals were scattered about, and soft jazz played in the background. Todd had dreamt of this moment for most of his teenage years. He was finally going to lose his virginity. More importantly, he was going to lose it to the woman he loved. He was thrilled by the look on Amani's face as she scanned the room. The pull-out couch was opened and dressed with his parents' cream-colored satin sheets, and the sweet aroma of his sister's Bath and Body Works Rose water and Ivy mist had been spritzed about to add to the ambiance. Amani's dimples deepened as she blushed. The familiar scent tantalized her; it was something her little sisters also wore. Todd could tell she was pleased. If all else failed, he knew she was happy that he'd worked so hard to please her.

The two stood in silence in front of the pull-out couch. Each giggled in an attempt to break the awkward silence, as each waited for the other to make the first move. Inhaling deeply as if to say here goes nothing, Todd took a step closer to Amani, kissing her forehead gently. He placed his arms on her hips, guiding her into him. She responded freely and tilted her head slightly as Todd caressed it with his lips down the left side of her neck and back up the right side. He kissed her neck softly and slowly, savoring every part of her that he touched. Amani moaned faintly with every kiss.

Todd next moved on to her lips, kissing her deeply. His hands rubbed her from her hips to the small of her back as he drew her further into him. She moaned harder and seemed to be turned on by the way he took control. She was giving herself to him completely. Todd slowly moved his hands toward the front of her body, gingerly explored her as he began to undress her. That was easier said than done. He fumbled as he tried to remove her pants, lost focus, and decided to just move back to kissing her.

A few moments later, he tried – again unsuccessfully – to remove Amani's shirt the way he'd seen it done in movies. "Let me," she said, taking it off quickly and throwing it to the side.

Todd switched his focus to removing her jeans while she tried to get his shirt off. The whole situation was clumsy and awkward and threatened to extinguish the fiery passion they'd built up during foreplay, but eventually they stood before each other in just their undergarments.

Todd was captivated. Amani's bra and panties were plain white, unassuming and modest, yet they stood out beautifully against her naturally tan skin. She was angelic, pure, and Todd was suddenly too nervous to touch her. He knew she was a virgin based on their conversations, but now he could both feel and see it. She reminded him of the scene after a blizzard: the pure untouched snow, a picturesque work of art.

He inhaled deeply. It's now or never he thought as he encircled her waist, drawing her body into his firmly. Slowly, he moved his arms from her waist to her bra, kissing her neck as he tried awkwardly to unhook the clasp. The attempt began erotically and romantically but quickly disintegrated to aggravation and frustration.

Amused by his efforts, Amani took matters into her own hands. Literally. She removed her bra and panties while he removed his underwear. The two gazed at each other, each feeling more than a little insecure. This was the first time Todd had ever seen a naked woman without the staples from the magazine spread getting in the way. And no one except his doctor had seen him nude since he'd developed a man's body. He watched Amani as she fixed her gaze on his midsection. Todd was nervous that he wasn't measuring up.

A shiver coursed through his body, though he couldn't be sure if it was caused by nervous anticipation or the cold basement floor. Attempting to break the awkwardness of the situation, Todd guided Amani to sit next to him on the pull-out. It was old. Older than him, in fact. The springs poked them uncomfortably as they went from a seated position to a horizontal one. They hurriedly covered themselves with the satin sheets.

They were mere inches from each other now, and Todd took Amani's hand gently. "Amani," he began. He knew intimacy was a huge step in both their relationship and in their lives. Although she'd never said anything about it and he tried to ignore it, the simple fact remained that what they were about to do was forbidden. Todd knew that in some parts of the world their interfaith relationship meant death, and as desperately as he wanted to lose his virginity to her, he wanted her to be safe even more. Even if that meant waiting.

"I love you," he continued, "but we don't have to…"

Amani cut him off by softly placing her index finger on his lips. "You gave me your heart," she said. "Now I am giving you my body, even if it means my life." The words frightened Todd to his core. But before he could reply she brushed her lips against his sensuously. As quick as the kiss was, Todd knew it was going to linger in his heart for the rest of his life. Their impending intimacy was proof of her love for him. The pressure to perform was greater now than ever before. Amani was giving her heart and possibly her life for him. He had to get this right.

He moved to kiss her again, but bumped his nose against hers. His eyes were closed as he tried to maneuver his mouth into position. Amani's head snapped back as his incisor poked her lip. They giggled. "Take two," Todd said, leaning in for another attempt. Their lips touched, and Todd felt her breath tickle his nose each time she exhaled. He giggled again, but this time Amani didn't giggle with him. This time *she* took charge, grasping his head and softly stroking it with her fingers. The feeling electrified him and he became even more aroused. The taste of her lips on his was intoxicating. The heat between them rose. Their breathing, their heartbeats were in unison. They were becoming one. Their tongues danced slowly around each other, quick, electric, and delicious.

As the passion escalated, their kisses became firmer, more determined. Amani continued to caress the back of Todd's neck and head while Todd moved his hand down her thigh, caressing her inner leg, chasing down the elusive liquid nectar. Amani released a deep purr, arching her back and allowing Todd's fingers to enter her. His fingers continued to explore between her legs. Moving into position, Todd tore open a condom he stole from his dad's dresser drawer.

Todd had collected many condoms over the years. His parents had given him several, convinced he was already sexually active.

However, this particular condom had caught his eye. Because of his naivety, Todd failed to realize it was just a novelty. The packaging read "French Tickler" and featured an artist's rendering of devil horns underneath the wording that promised to give her sinful pleasure. It also said something he glossed over: something about how it wasn't to be used during intercourse.

As Todd slipped the condom over his penis he felt an increasing confidence that this was going to be a moment Amani would never forget. He tried entering Amani's warmth, but his penis met a roadblock.

"Ummm," she said, "we're not going in there today."

Backing up, Todd realized he was at the wrong hole. Resting on his knees, he turned his head, perplexed. "Where the hell is it?" he blurted out. Amani pulled him in close, guiding him to where he needed to be. He tried again, pushing harder this time. He didn't understand why this was so difficult. Suddenly, he heard Amani wince in pain and snapped back into consciousness.

"This isn't bumper cars," she cried. "Take it easy!"

"I'm sorry," Todd said, trying to unsuccessfully recapture the mood that had led to this moment.

"Take it slow, be gentle," she said, grabbing his penis and guiding it cautiously inside her. "Be careful," she said, fearing there would be pain as he eased himself into her.

When Todd felt Amani grimacing in pain, he retreated, regrouped, and tried again. What seemed like a frustrating eternity melted away; he was finally inside. He moved his hips in a counterclockwise motion, timing his kisses on Amani's lips to when his hips reached twelve o'clock. His initial disinterest in sex faded quickly. After three gyrations, a euphoric shiver coursed through body. The pleasure he felt was indescribable. The smooth rhythm he's established disintegrated into a chaotic crescendo of.

Feeling a sensation he'd never felt before, Todd exited Amani, fully paralyzed with pleasure. What felt like minutes had been a mere twenty seconds. Todd could feel his heartbeat echoing in his ears as he gently laid his head on Amani's soft belly. Every movement felt like an intense tickle. His toes curled, his eyes crossed, and his hair stood on end. He took some deep breaths in an attempt to regain his composure. Amani stroked his head softly, wondering if sex gets better the more you do it.

"I love you," she whispered. The words made Todd melt.

"I can hear my heart echoing off your tummy," he replied. He instantly regretted it. Amani had just spoken sincerely from her heart after they'd shared a tender moment and he'd gone and made a silly observation.

"Do you hear my heart beating?" she asked. "No matter what happens in life, my heart will beat only for you. Our souls are intertwined now." Todd's heart smiled, but finding the right words to say in response proved elusive. All he could do was embrace the love of his life, his soulmate in every sense of the word. Nothing could ever ruin this moment, he thought.

"I have to go to the bathroom," Amani announced. Except that, Todd thought.

Chapter 27

Watching Amani's naked body run up the basement stairs made Todd smile. He had admired her front, now he could fawn over her backside.

She'd only been gone for twenty seconds but Todd felt empty in her absence. He missed her warmth and longed for the heat she produced when she held him close. She was right: they now shared a soul tie and he felt lost without her near. She was the catalyst to him wanting to be a better man, and he felt so blessed that she was his. He wanted to be able to take care of her. That's what I should have said when she was here, he thought, rather than making that stupid heartbeat comment. I'll tell her when she gets back from the bathroom.

Still basking in their euphoric adventure, Todd was eager for round two, but his mind began focusing on more important things. Being intimate with Amani was more than just pleasure; it was the start of a lifetime of responsibility. What if she got pregnant? How would he take care of her and the baby while running away from those who believed their interfaith relationship was an abomination? An education is a good option, but waiting four years to finish his degree might be too long, especially since Amani was less than a year away from her parents considering her for an arranged marriage. Plus, with the stress he'd endured in school so far, graduating might be a pipe dream.

And what about baseball? he wondered. As much as he hated to admit it, his father might be right. Todd hadn't worked hard enough for his dream of being a professional ball player a reality. He wasn't being scouted; he wasn't even close to being on any professional team's radar. There was still time for that to happen, but therein lay the issue: it was going to take time.

Todd had heard his dad say many times that the elevator to success was out of order. There is no get rich quick scheme that will magically erase all your financial problems.

There's always the military, Todd thought. He could enlist, marry Amani in a year when she turned eighteen, have a place for them to live, and possibly even protection from those who would wish to do them harm. Let's put a pin on that, Todd thought. The United States was currently in a skirmish in the

Middle East, and getting shot at by going to work wasn't a career path Todd wanted to explore.

Todd was so deep in thought that he hadn't noticed that Amani had returned from the bathroom. It wasn't until she placed her hand on his shoulder that he realized he wasn't alone.

"Are you alright?" she asked.

"I didn't know you were back," he confessed as he tried to regulate his breathing.

"I called your name but I guess you didn't hear me," she said. Leaning in close, Amani kissed Todd's forehead softly. Something was wrong. The same lips that had kissed him just ten minutes before felt different now.

"What's wrong?" he asked. He could tell Amani could feel his stress and didn't want to add to it.

Todd stood up. Her silence meant it couldn't be anything good and he'd never handled bad news well sitting down. His mind raced as he paced the basement floor. Worrying made his still-erect penis flaccid.

"I don't know how to tell you this," she began. Todd saw a tear fall from her eye and stopped pacing. Amani's skin had gone pale and Todd could feel his heart beating out of his chest. Amani stretched out her hand. Her fist was closed. Todd held his hand out to receive whatever it was she was giving him. He immediately recognized the red object when it dropped from her hand to his. It was a horn from his French Tickler condom.

"I found this and lots of blood inside me. I think your condom broke."

***

"Todd! Todd! Are you alright?"

Todd opened his eyes, confused as to why he was on the floor, why Amani was kneeling next to him. He shivered, then realized he must have passed out. What had happened? Oh. Yeah. Amani said the condom had broken.

He sat up too quickly, his head spinning. Staring into Amani's light brown eyes, he asked, "Are we having a baby?"

Amani chuckled. "You're so cute," she said, but Todd didn't understand what was so amusing. He heard his parents in his head again: don't start having sex until you can handle the responsibilities that might result from it. Todd realized at that moment that he was nowhere near being able to handle kids. Having a child at their age would be difficult enough, but having one given, what would almost certainly happen if her family found out, was a whole other thing.

"Habibi," she said, obviously trying to pacify his fears. It worked. "I was just telling you your condom broke because that, pointing at the horn, fell off. By the way, umm, are condoms *supposed* to have spikes?"

"They aren't spikes, they're horns," Todd said. "They're supposed to tickle your insides."

"Tickle my insides?" she asked. "It kind of hurts," she added. "I didn't say anything at first because I wasn't sure if this is how sex was supposed to feel. Can I see the package?" Before Todd could react, Amani grabbed the condom wrapper and began reading. "Tickle her insides," Todd could hear Amani say softly. "Not to be used for sexual intercourse," she continued. "May cause injury to the cervix which may lead to an infection," she concluded. The pitch of her voice had risen with each line she'd read, and now she exhaled hard and fast. She was infuriated. Todd leaned in to kiss her, but she moved away quickly, gesturing for him to leave her alone. She looked ready to erupt.

Suddenly, her hands dropped to her sides and she let out a heavy sigh. Todd was trying hard to read her emotions but was at a complete loss.

Through clenched teeth, Amani spat the final words written on the wrapper, "You, me, and the devil makes three?" Then came several phrases in her native tongue that Todd didn't understand, though he suspected they weren't words you'd find in a Hallmark card.

Seeing the confusion on his face, Amani reverted back to English. "Giving myself to a man that is not of my faith is a **huge** sin in my world," she said angrily. Her face was now a deep red. "I did it because I love you. I told you I would <u>**DIE**</u> for you!" she shouted. "Giving my body to you was me sacrificing my life for you. Was I just a conquest to you?" she asked, the tears starting to flow. "A notch on your bedpost? You're evil," she sobbed.

Todd remained silent. He knew he needed to say something but he was at a complete loss for words. He put his arms around her.

"Don't you *dare* touch me," she exploded, raising her hands to a defensive position in case he tried to touch her again. Todd's synapses began firing, contemplating what Amani was going to say next and how he could escape the situation. Todd could see the hurt, frustration, and pain on her face, but he could feel it all, as well. It crushed him to his core. He'd let her down.

Todd knew that in every relationship, a single incident could change a person's feelings from unconditional love to "I will continue to love you under certain conditions." He wondered if this was that incident for Amani, or if it would be the end.

"I can't believe I chose you over my faith and you had the nerve to enter my body with a condom that has the slogan "you, me, and the devil makes three" she said. She sounded weary. Devastated. "You insensitive prick. Take me home. NOW. I never want to see you again," she cried. Tears streamed down her face and she began trembling.

Todd was paralyzed by the pain he'd caused her. He tried to think but couldn't. The fear of losing her crippled him. How could he have done this? How could he have hurt her? He felt the tears streaming down his face, too, and was shocked. He was crying. He never cried.

"I only wanted you to experience the indescribable joy you've brought into my life," he said softly. "I wanted nothing more than to both tell you and show you how deeply in love with you I am. I will never be able to explain how honored and privileged I feel that you allowed me – one of the billions of men on this earth – to become one with you," he continued. "I was so afraid I wouldn't live up to the pleasure you bless me with every day. Just to know you fills me with bliss. You are my soulmate, Amani. I saw the word 'pleasure' on the condom and focused only on how I wanted to provide you with that."

Todd was afraid of what his words sounded like to her, but they worked. Something he'd said must've warmed her heart because she smiled; placed her hand on his cheek; wiped away his tears; and leaned in for the deepest, most passionate kiss Todd had ever experienced. All was right with the world again. He held her close, determined to remember how close he'd come to losing her. He never wanted it to happen again. Nothing else in the world mattered. Not school, not baseball, not her family or their future, and not his dad looking right at him.

"What in the *hell* is going on here?!" he yelled.

Chapter 28

"Why are you home?" Todd asked, embarrassed…and naked.

"I'm the parent," his dad snapped. "I *own* this house. Take her home. Now. And get back here immediately," he ordered, marching back up the steps.

Todd had hoped his father's reaction would be more like what he'd seen in movies where his dad would give him a high five, offer Amani a Zima, and laugh at the awkwardness of the situation.

Todd heard his dad muttering under his breath, complaining about how someone who has to be reminded to wash his ass was trying to get some ass. Then there was something about responsibilities. He got dressed and he and Amani headed out.

***

The ride back to Amani's neighborhood was blissful. They held hands, their fingers interlocked. Amani's head nestled comfortably on Todd's arm. Neither had regrets about what they'd just done. Todd took solace in the way they breathed in a rhythm that resonated in his heart and spirit. They really were one. At this moment he felt their love could overcome any obstacle in their path.

When Todd pulled into Amani's neighborhood, their breathing quickened, as if the fantasy was over and they were back to their everyday lives.

So as not to be seen by any neighbors or Amani's family, Todd parked the car a block from her house. He cut the headlights and the engine. The two sat quietly, neither wanting the moment to end since they didn't know when they'd next see each other.

"Do you want me to walk you to your house?" Todd asked, attempting to be chivalrous. He knew Amani being seen with a mysterious man in the middle of the night would certainly get back to her parents, but he was trying to be a gentleman. He was also concerned for her well-being. If she got caught sneaking back into her home, Todd was certain he'd never know and that he'd never see her again. That would kill him.

"I'll be fine," she said, failing to convince either of them.

Amani took a deep breath and got out of the car. She raced through one of her neighbor's backyards. Frozen with anxiety, Todd rolled down his windows, straining to hear anything that might come from her house. He waited for what felt like an eternity and then, feeling helpless, started his car up to head back home where he knew his dad was waiting to unleash hell.

The ride home was extremely short, even though he tried desperately to take his time. It was 3 AM, so there was no traffic, and it must have rained in the time he and Amani had been together because the streets were wet. Todd was usually comforted by the sound of tires cascading across dampened pavement, but this time he could only hear his heart pounding, from worried thoughts. Had Amani gotten back inside successfully? Had anyone noticed she wasn't home? He knew she wouldn't call to let him know she was safe since he didn't have a private line. She wasn't going to disturb his entire household, especially after the way his dad had reacted when he'd seen them. She also couldn't chance her parents or siblings picking up the phone line and hearing her on it. Any word of her well-being was going to have to wait until sometime after the sun had risen.

Todd could see lightning in the distance. He guessed that the storm was the reason his family's trip to the lake didn't happen.

As he pulled into the driveway, Todd could feel his anxiety skyrocket. The lights were still on. In an instant, his exhaustion hit full force. He had zero energy for the certain interrogation that awaited him. He was half hoping his parents were asleep and had just left the light on.

Todd entered through the garage and wasn't shocked to see both of his parents waiting for him at the kitchen table. Each held a cup of coffee, obviously settled in for a long conversation with him, and both were clearly agitated.

"Who was that girl?" his dad asked. His voice was calm and steady. He was usually the calm one, though, something that always concerned Todd since he never knew what his dad was thinking. When Todd was younger, his dad's silence either meant there was something to be learned and he was formulating the perfect anecdotes, or he was so pissed off he needed to calm himself down in silence before he put a belt to Todd's backside. Either way, Todd suffered. And now that Todd was considered an adult – too old to be hit with a belt – he knew his parents would hit him with something far worse. Tough love.

Chapter 29

"Was this the proverbial final straw? Was Todd going to be put out on his own to make his own way? Was he going to pay for room and board in college, car notes, car insurance, and everything else responsible adults pay for? He was beginning to realize all the things his parents actually did for him, things he just took for granted. Amazing how getting caught bare-bottomed in your parents home could paint a clearer picture in your life.

Todd had grown accustomed to his parents' routine for scolding him. How could he not? It was almost a weekly occurrence. He never learned his lesson enough to avoid getting into these situations, though. He knew he couldn't win in these discussions, so maybe that was the problem. Maybe he was trying to win instead of trying to learn and grow. In the past – meaning before tonight's incident – he knew that if he told his parents what they wanted to hear he'd come off as blatantly disregarding their rules and simple common sense in order to be selfish, both of which deserve punishment. No matter what they asked, Todd's parents knew the answers beforehand. They were just waiting for their clueless son to see the light. They were playing chess, thinking three moves ahead whereas Todd never knew what the hell he was doing. Their goal in asking Todd anything was to help him arrive at their thought process, or to, at least, figure out what the hell he was thinking when he did the dumb shit he did.

Todd knew he'd done what he'd done this time for love. He also knew his parents would think he'd done it just to get laid. Either way, he knew trying to get his parents to see things the way he saw them was a losing battle.

History had prepared Todd for his parents' good cop/bad cop routine. His mom was always the bad cop. She never sugarcoated *any*thing. She said what was on her mind, sparing no feelings. If the lesson warranted tanning his backside, his mom played by her own rules. Where Todd's dad would spank him no more than five times, his mom would yank arms, push, pull, yell, and spank him until he pleaded for divine intervention. By the time it was over Todd would forget why he was being punished.

At the moment, Todd was still praying his dad would high-five him for losing his virginity or, if not, that he'd at least hide the fact that Todd had used his mom's good linens. In Todd's opinion, it was a shame for the satin sheets to go to waste. The thought of his parents ever using them was disgusting. No matter what age his parents were he thought of them as too old to have sex. He could only bring himself to think of them doing it twice: both times to have him and then Tiffany.

"That girl is my girlfriend," Todd said, finally answering his father's question.

"I don't care *who* she is," his mom snapped, seething with anger. "Tell me why you thought it was appropriate to bring her into my home when I'm not here to ruin my honeymoon sheets?"

"Our sheets," his dad interjected. Todd took comfort when his mother shot his dad the same look she'd given Todd.

Not wanting to draw his mother's ire, Todd just stood there quiet, a tactic he'd learned over the years was best since anything he said was going to be used against him.

"Son, you need to get your shit together," his dad said, calmly sipping his coffee. Todd could hear Tiffany snickering around the corner.

"I thought I told you to take your ass to bed," their mom said, not looking at her. Tiffany turned and ran up the stairs toward her bedroom; she knew when their mom meant business.

Todd's dad waited to continue until he knew Tiffany was gone. "Don't bring any more of your scallywags into my home," he said.

"She's not a scallywag," Todd interrupted, meaning to defend Amani's honor but instantly regretting it.

"Have you introduced us to her?" his mom snapped. "No," she said, answering her own question. "Have we met her parents?" she continued. "No," she said, answering her own question again. "This is the first time I've even heard that you *had* a girlfriend. Did you know your son had a girlfriend?" directing her rhetorical question to his dad and referring to Todd as only his dad's, the way she did when Todd did something wrong.

"If you can't walk her through my front door instead of sneaking her in through the back she is a scallywag," his mom continued, fully in bad cop mode now.

"Furthermore, if you continue treating my home as if it's your personal love shack, you are no longer welcome here." She paused. "Tiffany!" she shouted. In the silence that followed,

Tiffany could be heard retreating to her room from where she'd been eavesdropping. This time, though, their mom left to deal with her.

His dad took over with Todd. "I assume," he said, "that you finished all your assignments and aced all your exams before turning my basement into a brothel?"

"Ummm…no," Todd replied, confused.

"Your mom and I sent you to school to get an education. But an education just gets your foot in the door somewhere. We want to allow you the chance to learn to fend for yourself, to prepare yourself for the future. We **did not** send you to college so you could make plans to run back here and prioritize getting a piece of ass over focusing on your education. Girls are always going to be there."

"But I love this one," Todd interrupted. "I don't see what the big deal is," he continued.

His dad took a deep breath and looked at Todd. He wore an I-can't-believe-I'm-failing-at-raising-my-son look on his face.

"We used a condom," Todd offered. He knew he should've kept his mouth shut and listened to whatever his parents were going to say, but he didn't. Because he's an idiot. He could feel that his dad was about to throw a haymaker of facts to knock Todd back into reality.

"You used a condom?" his dad chuckled. "Todd, tell me how effective condoms are at preventing pregnancy." Todd didn't know.

"95%?" he guessed.

"Are you asking me or telling me?" his dad asked.

"Telling you?" Todd said, his response again sounding more like a question than a statement.

"So you're saying it's not 100% effective?" his dad asked rhetorically. "So have you thought about what you plan to do if you and this young lady are one of the 5% that become pregnant?" Todd stayed silent. He knew he hadn't considered anything logically the whole night. "Where are you going to live? Because you aren't going to be staying here, I'll tell you that right now. How are you going to support your new family?" He paused. "Todd, how old is your girlfriend?"

"Seventeen," Todd answered proudly.

"You're eighteen," his dad replied. Todd stared at him blankly. His dad paused, waiting for Todd to catch what he was saying, but he didn't. Rolling his eyes, his dad continued, "What if she gets mad and wants to hurt you?" he began. "She could say you had sex, but because she's underage and you're not it'd be considered statutory rape."

"But she loves me!" Todd exclaimed.

"Boy, people fall in and out of love all the time. You kids are always trying to rush to do adult things while you're still thinking like children! You don't need to be worrying about sex until you're ready to handle the lifelong effects that can come with it. When you're ready to take care of yourself, a baby, *and* a woman, then – and only then – should you start thinking about sex. Then make sure your other half will be your better half. Otherwise she'll make you half of what you could be and take half of what you own. As you mature and success is upon you, your taste in women will change. What you desire today will not fulfill you tomorrow. You're still figuring out who you are, Todd. How can you decide what you want in a woman now, five years from now, or for the rest of your life? Just a few weeks ago you weren't sure where you wanted to go to college. You didn't know what you wanted to study. But now all of a sudden you know who you love and want to spend the rest of your life with? Please," he said sarcastically. "I can only assume you want to marry this one because you ignored your parents' rules in order to be with her. If I'm going to have a grown man disobey and disrespect my rules in my own home, I have to assume this is your form of leave to cleave."

Todd had no clue what his father was talking about and his dad knew it.

"Read the Bible sometime," he snapped, seeing Todd's confusion. Take this opportunity to buckle down and figure out your five-year plan. Work hard to make it a reality, to establish yourself in a career. *Then* worry about getting a woman." He paused. "Right now you have a wish, but no plan. You don't own anything. You don't have a pot to piss in or a window to throw it out of. If she got pregnant, how would you take care of her and the baby?"

"I used protection," Todd repeated.

"You actually had protection?" his dad asked. "You can't remember to bring your wallet with you when you go to the store, but all of a sudden you remember to bring a condom?"

Todd began to respond but was cut off. "Don't tell me you went to the store to buy one because I know you're cheap."

Silence filled the room. Todd's dad stared at him, waiting for him to answer a question he hadn't asked. Usually this meant he already knew the answer. Todd decided to be forthcoming. "I grabbed one from your dresser drawer," he confessed. Todd's dad looked at him, puzzled.

"Todd," he started, "your mom and I have been married for ages. We don't use condoms anymore, so I know you didn't get one from my drawer."

"It was your devil condom," Todd said, "the one at the back of your drawer."

The sip of coffee his dad had just taken was suddenly all over Todd's face. "Are you on drugs?" he asked Todd. "That was a novelty condom I got at a truck stop when I was *your* age," he said. "I'm surprised it didn't turn to dust when you tried to put it on. This is proof that you have no business having sex." He paused and ran his hands down his face in exasperation.

"Do you remember when I taught you to play chess?" he continued. At that moment, Todd's mom reappeared. Todd was thankful she'd missed his revelation about the condom. "At this moment, you are a pawn. However, your current situation does not limit your future. Align yourself with those who will make a positive impact. Carve your own path. Become the king of your *own* castle. Then and only then should you find your queen." He looked up at Todd's mom, then said, "Your first priority is replacing my – I mean *our* – sheets and candles."

"And I want the whole basement swept and mopped," his mom added. "Then take your black ass back to school and hit those books. Stop running back home to see your little girlfriend. This chapter of your life is over."

And with that, his parents headed upstairs to bed while Todd mulled the conversation over. He heard his mom ask what she missed. His dad answered confidently, "Your son is a buffoon."

Todd had heard everything his parents said, and he knew his dad was partly correct. He also knew that they didn't understand what was going on. Not really. They wouldn't understand the danger he and Amani were in and wouldn't support them if they did. Trying to explain it to them would just cause more trouble. My best bet, he thought to himself, is to handle this on my own.

Still wide awake, Todd grabbed a broom and headed to the basement to start cleaning up.

Chapter 30

The next day at work was a blur. Todd snuck out of the house earlier than he normally would on a weekend morning, mostly to escape another lecture from his parents and teasing from Tiffany. He arrived at work almost an hour before he had to be there. 59 minutes early to be exact, 60 minutes earlier than he would normally show up. The morning rush of mall walkers kept the staff at Green Leaf Kitchen busy.

Todd was tired. Mentally drained. His father's lecture echoed through his mind while worry for Amani's safety tore at his heart. He was going through the motions on autopilot. Keeping his mind clear of any thoughts was easier said than done. He felt like he was treading water as a tsunami of emotions was about to overtake him.

"Hey, Todd," asked Kenny, the line cook who was working the morning shift. "Could you do me a favor?" He continued without waiting for a response. "Go in the back and ask Ms.

Savannah to slice up some roast beef? We're almost out, and I want to be prepared for the lunch crowd."

"Why don't *you* ask?" he asked, but he knew it was because Ms. Savannah wouldn't yell at him. Kenny should have prepped his area before the restaurant opened, Todd thought angrily, instead of waiting until the last minute.

"Come on man, please?" Kenny whined.

"Talk to the hand," Todd said, throwing up a palm as he walked off.

Heading into the prep area, Todd moved like a zombie. He was so heavy in his thoughts and so tired from cleaning up last night that he forgot why he was back there.

"You got laid for the first time last night, didn't you?" asked Ms. Savannah. Her question snapped Todd back to reality. He wondered if something changes about a person's demeanor when they become sexually active. Was his voice deeper? Did he stand taller? Were his pheromones stronger? More manly?

"All my lovers had the same lost look on their faces after I was done with them," she joked. Todd was disgusted by the thought of Ms. Savannah having sex. He must've made a face that she thought meant he didn't understand because she continued, " All the blood from a man's brain and feet go to their midsections, Todd. That's why men can't think straight before sex or run away after it."

This made complete sense to Todd.

"That's why I usually get on top," Anne said, joining the conversation from behind Todd as she entered the prep area. "I want to make sure they can't run away," she snickered. Ms. Savannah huffed at Anne's intrusion, but Anne wasn't done. "Then I feed them. It's hard to run on a full belly."

"Is that after the drugs you use to get them in your bed wear off?" Ms. Savannah said venomously.

Wow. She *really* doesn't like her, Todd thought. He could feel Anne's pain as she added somberly, "In the end all you can do is move on to the next guy." Giggling in an attempt to get back to her normal self, she said, "The best way to get over a man is to get under a new one."

"Are you actually *bragging* about being a hoe?" Ms. Savannah asked incredulously. Todd's eyes widened. He tried making eye contact with Ms. Savannah to let her know she'd gone too far, but it was too late.

"Fuck you!" Anne said, her tone fierce as she approached Ms. Savannah. Todd knew he needed to get in between the two women, but he didn't want to become collateral damage. Anne was several inches shorter and weighed a hundred pounds less than Ms. Savannah.

"I'm not a hoe, you bitch," Anne snarled.

"Then you must be a volunteer prostitute," Ms. Savannah spat back.

Todd glanced around the corner, hoping someone would be walking by who could assist him in breaking up the impending fight.

"You wouldn't call me that if I was a man," Anne said. "I'd be revered. I'd be called a ladies' man and congratulated. But because I'm a woman I get called a hoe. There're lots of reasons people have sex. I happen to do it because I'm lonely, and you shouldn't make assumptions about people and their motives when you don't know anything about them. I'm not heartless; I've just learned to use my heart less. Todd!" she said, turning her attention away from Ms. Savannah, "I came back here to tell you you have a phone call." She turned and began to walk out of the prep area, but Ms. Savannah stopped her.

"Hey!" the older woman yelled. Anne stopped but didn't turn around. "You're alright with me." It was clear to Todd that Ms. Savannah respected Anne for standing up for herself. Anne nodded and kept walking.

"Todd, remember this," Ms. Savannah began. "Sex is fun, but don't have it unless you're completely sure you're doing it with the right person. Sex is a momentary physical act that your body craves, but making love is when your heart won't let go. When you don't know the difference between the two is when life gets messy."

"Huh?" Todd responded, completely confused.

"Boy!" she began. "I see the blood that's supposed to flow to your brain is still in your dick. Just know this. When you lay with a woman you develop soul ties. Those don't just go away." Todd didn't know how to respond. Maybe it was the exhaustion he felt after last night's activity and subsequent ordeal with his parents. His face must've shown it because Ms. Savannah said, "I honestly believe sex turns members of your gender into imbeciles." She took a deep breath, obviously frustrated and trying to decide if continuing this discussion with Todd was worth her time.

Todd waited impatiently. He wanted to attend to his phone call, especially if it was Amani, but he knew better than to walk away from Ms. Savannah. Such a decision would make her his enemy for life. Plus, he was interested in what Miss Savannah was about to say because she'd guided him wisely in the past.

Finally, she said, "These other boys here carelessly stick their dicks in any hole they can find, not realizing the person they have sex with becomes part of them, hence the phrase 'two become one.' Sex isn't ever just sex; after the deed is done and the person is gone their thoughts, their vibrations, their soul becomes intertwined with yours. If you're intimate with several people at the same time, you're taking in several energies. There's a reason you randomly feel confused, depressed, drained, angry, happy, or stressed. Remember that all the people your partner sleeps with become part of you, too." She paused, hoping her message was sinking in. "Now take your phone call and this damn roast beef and tell Kenny the next time he forgets to set up his area and cowers like a little bitch and sends someone else to do what he should have, I'm going to shove my foot up his ass."

Todd sighed wearily and headed for the phone. He was amazed how eerily similar Ms. Savannah's message was to his dad's.

"Hello?" he said, picking up the phone. As much as he wanted it to be Amani, he assumed it was one of his parents reminding him to do something he'd forgotten to or to chastise him for leaving without saying goodbye, a huge no-no in his household.

"What's wrong?" asked the voice on the other end. It was Amani. Todd perked up.

"Nothing now," he replied.

"Please tell me," she said. Todd perked up even more. The fact that she could sense something was wrong and cared about what it was was all the proof he needed that he'd found the right person."

"Hello?" Someone else had joined the call, someone older and gruff. Todd could tell he wasn't nice. "Who's on the phone?" he asked, annoyed. Todd knew not to say anything.

"It's me," Amani replied.

"Who are you talking to?" Todd heard him ask. He grabbed the first waitress who walked by.

"$5 if you just say hello," Todd offered. He had no clue who she was. She looked a little familiar, but she must have been hired in the three weeks he'd been at school.

"Money first," she demanded. Todd pulled a $10 bill from his pocket and handed it over. She put the bill in her pocket and grabbed the receiver.

Todd thought about asking for change but didn't want to take the time. This was a life or death situation. Or was it, he wondered. He wasn't sure how dire the situation really was. This was all new to him.

"Hel…" the waitress started, then paused.

"What's going on?" Todd whispered. She waved at him to be quiet. "Because you're yelling at me!" she snapped into the phone. Another pause.

"What is going *on*?" Todd whispered again, more impatient this time. The waitress brushed him away again.

"Okay," she said, handing the phone back to Todd. "Whoever that was is incredibly rude."

"What did he say?" Todd asked.

The waitress set her tray down and took a deep breath. "He was yelling at some girl in two languages, demanding she tell him who she was talking to. Then they were both talking in a foreign language. I said hello and he asked me why I hadn't spoken earlier. I told him he was yelling on the phone so I couldn't. He demanded I respond to him immediately in the future when he asked a question, and I said okay, not for your benefit, but for mine. He was so intimidating. I don't know who the hell he is, but I never want to meet him in real life. Next time you ask me to talk on the phone for you, make it $20," she said.

"I appreciate you so much," Todd told her.

"Little advice," she continued, "whoever this chick is you're sneaking around trying to talk to, make sure she's worth the headache, because the baggage she appears to come with is *not* healthy. He spoke *horribly* to her. I don't know what you're mixed up in, but it sounds dangerous."

"I have it all under control," Todd replied, but his tone and demeanor weren't fooling anyone. He had no clue what he was doing or how he was going to do anything.

"You still don't know my name, do you?" the waitress asked. The question took Todd by surprise. Why would she say that, he wondered; I just met her. He looked at her lapel, searching for her name tag, but she wisely covered it.

Todd took a long look at her. The waitress sighed and shot him an evil look. "Helllooo," she said sarcastically, and then she offered what Todd guessed was supposed to be a hint. "I used to be a brunette."

"Emily?" he guessed cautiously. The angry look she gave him as she stalked off was all the answer he needed. "I meant Erica!" he called after her, realizing his mistake.

Embarrassed, Todd's first instinct was to find her and apologize, but his priority was to Amani, who'd he been keeping on hold during the episode of Who am I. He cautiously placed the phone up to his ear and hummed softly into the receiver.

"It's okay," Amani answered.

"That was a close one," Todd said.

"*Now* are you going to tell me what's wrong?" she asked. Amani completely ignored her interaction with her father as if it was a common occurrence.

"Is everything okay?" Todd asked.

"That's what I'm trying to get *you* to tell **me**," she answered. Todd loved how attuned she was to his feelings.

"Last night was just a lot," he said. "I'm just a little tired."

"We'll get some rest when you get off work," she said. "I want to see you again tonight."

"Tonight, tonight?" he asked. "Later tonight?" Todd knew his question made no sense to anyone outside his head. He was shocked when Amani not only understood but responded, "Later tonight."

"How?" he asked. "My parents are in town and Tiffany is nosey. There's zero chance of me sneaking you in."

"I figured that, silly," Amani giggled. "I thought you would come over here." Todd almost dropped the phone. Had she lost her ever loving mind? Him going to her house was not an option he was willing to explore. His previous encounters with Abbas and Akilah was enough to suggest that any version of *Guess who's coming to dinner* might turn out as if it were being hosted by *Rambo*.

After a long, awkward silence, Amani cleared her throat. "Are you still there?"

"I'm here," Todd said, "but are you all there?" he asked, questioning her mental state. "I don't really want to die before I have a chance at a life with you."

"Akilah is with her new husband," Amani said, "and my other sisters and my parents will all be asleep. My brother's never home, and we have a motor home in the driveway we can hang out in," she added.

This plan didn't make Todd feel any more comfortable. His first visit to her house had cost him blood loss and a footprint on his back, just for saying hello. A second trip might result in cerebral hemorrhaging from the bullet her father or brother would surely fire into him if either found him on their property.

"Wait," Todd said. "When did your sister get married?" Todd couldn't believe Amani hadn't shared any details of her sister's nuptials before now.

"Since she wasn't going anywhere in life, my parents arranged her with one of my dad's business partners."

This is insane, Todd thought. And how could Amani be so nonchalant about the whole thing? Wasn't getting married a big deal? Something to have strong emotion about?

"Will *you* be 'arranged?'" Todd asked, mockingly.

"No, because I'll be with you," she answered simply.

"Amani!" Todd said sharply, frustrated by the direction the conversation had taken.

"I also plan to go to college," she added, "so that buys us a little time."

"Todd! Get back in the kitchen," Rick snapped, "we have orders backing up."

Todd glanced over at the order wheel on the counter. It was ticketless, the morning rush clearly over. Rick saw where Todd was looking and, realizing he'd been foiled, said, "Well, I'm paying you to work in the kitchen, not to run up my phone bill."

"I'll be there in a second," Todd said. He still didn't think visiting Amani was a good idea, but he'd run out of time to debate it.

"Habibi, can you meet me around the corner from my house at midnight?" That pet name again, Todd thought. She got me with that damn pet name. "I love you," she said, hanging up the phone.

"I love you, too," Todd said to the dial tone. For the rest of his shift he played in his head all the ways tonight was going to go terribly wrong.

***

After work, Todd went home to rest, but his nerves prevented it. Might as well be productive, he told himself, cracking open his literature book. That didn't work, either. As hard as he tried to study, he just couldn't focus enough on the words in front of him.

"Todd! Todd!" A gentle shake of his shoulder woke Todd from his slumber. He was so stressed and tired he didn't realize he'd fallen asleep on top of his textbook.

"Burning the midnight oil?" his dad asked.

Midnight? Todd started to panic, then realized it was just an expression.

"Oh shoot! You already woke him?" his mom said, disappointed. "I ran to get the camera for nothing!"

"Camera?" Todd asked, still trying to get his bearings. The clock on his dresser showed it was 9:32 pm. He'd apparently been sleeping for a couple hours.

"Do you know how long your dad and I have prayed that you would finally do your homework?" his mom asked. "It's like finally seeing Bigfoot," she joked. "I had to get photographic proof."

"We're proud of you, Son. Keep up the good work," his dad said.

As they walked off, Todd heard his dad say, "See? My talk with him worked. And you wanted to kill him."

Todd beamed at the admiration. Too bad it wasn't for what they believed it was for. Rather than continue trying to actually study, he decided to take a shower and get ready for his date. A long hot shower did little to calm his nerves, though.

It was just after 10 pm. He had two hours, plenty of time to figure out how to sneak out of the house. When he was at school, Todd was able to come and go as he pleased. This wasn't the case at his parents' house. They still expected him to tell them when he was leaving, when he was coming back, and who was going to be wherever he was going, all answers Todd could not provide in this particular case.

Todd was a master at sneaking out of the house. He was willing to play the long game to achieve his goal of exiting undetected. He tied his tennis shoes together and carried them in his mouth by their shoelaces. He carefully walked on his tiptoes, emulating the countless movie ninjas he'd admired when he was younger and more impressionable. He took a step and waited. He paused at any hint of the floor creaking, recalculated his route, tested a new part of the floor, and stepped again.

By 10:52 PM he'd made it the twenty feet from his bedroom to the stairs. His parents' bedroom door was outside the top of the staircase. Todd put his ear up against it, listening intently for any sign that his parents were awake. The sound of their snoring was all the reassurance he needed that both were sleeping.

Rather than waste any more time avoiding creaks in the floor, Todd reached out for the banister, using his left hand for balance and stretching his right hand toward the middle of the banister on the opposite side. He lifted his feet, balanced himself just above the steps, and slowly inched his hands along the banister, propelling his body down the thirteen stairs without stepping on any of them. Landing graciously and, more importantly, silently,

Todd threw his hands up in triumph as if he was an Olympic gymnast completing his routine. He often wondered when he did this if his parents could hear him or if they cared whether he walked down the stairs like a normal person. Who cares, he thought. Where's the excitement in being normal? The *Mission: Impossible* theme played in his head.

He crept slowly to the family room. Unlocking the patio door, he stopped and listened. The house was still quiet and dark. He tiptoed into the kitchen; he was now under his parents' bedroom. He grabbed his car keys and crept back into the family room. Slowly opening the sliding glass door, Todd escaped into the night. The calm call of nature was annoyingly loud. The distant hoot of an owl accompanied by the soft chirps of cicadas seemed deafening. He tiptoed through the grass that appeared to crunch loudly with each step.

Almost free! Todd thought as he unlocked his car door. Placing his hand on the handle, he took a deep breath, counted down from three, opened the door, and threw himself in quickly and quietly, closing the door behind him. He looked around frantically to see if the door's chime had alerted anyone that the door had been opened but he didn't see any movement outside the car.

Todd put the key into the ignition, released the emergency brake, and put the car in neutral. The car coasted down the hill away from his house. He waited until he was a safe distance before he came to a complete stop; he didn't want to trigger the brake lights within sight of his house. When he thought he was far enough away, he put the car in park, stepped on the brake, and turned the engine over. With his headlights still off, Todd circled the cul de sac, drove back past his house, and headed for his rendezvous with Amani. Anything that might happen at home would have to be dealt with when he got back.

Chapter 31

The drive to Amani's went quickly. And though he longed to spend as much time with her as possible, there was a nervous pit in his stomach that gave him pause. Todd was a stranger to nervous energy. He'd only really experienced it when report cards came out. This was different. He felt a sense of impending doom. He tried to ignore it but couldn't. He wasn't a kid anymore; he was an adult now playing adult games, and he was out of his league.

When he parked at the rendezvous spot he prayed that Amani had been unable to get out of the house. His heart sank just a little when he saw her waving him over to where she was waiting. He ran to her quickly and she greeted him with a sensuous kiss and a tight hug. It was enough to melt all his worries away.

"Shh!" Amani said, her finger up to her lips. Todd was reminded that they weren't out of the woods yet.

They crept cautiously onto her driveway, using the shadows to cloak their movements. Amani opened the door to her family's motor home. It took a while for Todd's eyes to adjust to the complete darkness inside. Not even light from the street lights made its way inside the motor home due to the trees that blocked the light. Todd felt around, trying not to bump into anything.

Amani felt for his hand and guided him toward a large Murphy bed/sofa combo.

"This is nice," he started, but before he could finish his sentence Amani grabbed his head and kissed him. Hard. They undressed themselves, quickly this time. It was a complete reversal of yesterday.

Todd barely had the condom on before Amani fell back onto the couch and guided him inside her. Their breathing became more rapid with each stroke, the moans deeper. Amani caressed his backside, urging him deeper inside her. He explored her bosom with his tongue.

"Don't stop," she pleaded as his strokes became faster.

"Yes! Right there," she directed. She spoke softly and erotically in her native tongue. Todd had no clue what she was saying, but he liked hearing it.

"Stop," she urged softly. Todd stroked as hard and deep as he could. "Stop." she repeated, this time tapping him on the head. Todd froze like a deer in headlights.

Amani slithered from underneath him and began gathering her clothes. Before Todd knew what was happening, she was crouched down behind the passenger side's captain's chair. "Hide," she mouthed to him. Then Todd heard it. Abbas was just outside the door, steps away from entering the motor home.

Todd had two options: fight or flight. He briefly thought about combining the two, to bumrush Abbas as he entered, pushing him out of the way and running for dear life. He figured he could make it ninety feet in about four seconds. That's the distance between first and second base. Well, maybe in just over three seconds with all the adrenaline coursing through his veins with his life in danger. Then he remembered at Boy Scouts he learned that a bullet could travel 2500 plus feet per second. And Abbas was known to carry a gun.

Todd could also hear a second voice. Make that two guns firing at him at several thousand feet per second. No matter how many bases he's stolen in baseball he wasn't safe all the time so out-running a bullet was definitely an impossibility. Todd chose option three. He froze.

"Go!" Amani mouthed to Todd, urging him to hide immediately. The fear in her eyes was debilitating. He scanned the vehicle. There was nowhere to hide, so Todd headed to the back of the motor home just as the door swung open. He ducked inside the cramped shower just as Abbas entered. He stood still. Frozen with fear. Beads of sweat trickled down his face as he held his breath and closed his eyes. He strained to hear what was going on but could only hear the heavy thumping of his heart. He was afraid it was loud enough for others to hear, too.

The moon was the only light that shone inside the vehicle. An overcast sky cast an eerie glow inside the cabin when the moon peeked out from behind the clouds. Although the cabin was still dark, Todd couldn't help thinking that the moonlight beamed a spotlight just outside of the small shower. He prayed Abbas didn't decide to use the restroom. The giggling and moaning helped Todd realize that Abbas was there to do what he and Amani had been doing.

"What is this? The love shack?" he whispered sarcastically. He wondered if he could sneak out the back. Or maybe he could sneak past them, as distracted as they were.

"Ouch!" Todd heard Abbas whisper harshly. "What is your *deal*, bitch?!" Todd waited for the sound of a smack.

"My *deal* is something is poking me and it hurts," the girl said, annoyed. Todd was surprised that she allowed him to refer to her that way. *I guess some women truly are attracted to the bad boy,* he reasoned.

"If you stop screaming, I'll poke you myself," Abbas said drily. "It'll only hurt if you want it to."

The room went eerily silent. This freightened Todd even more. He couldn't see or hear what was going on.

"Stop it," he heard the girl demand. "What *is* that?" she asked, "And don't tell me it's your dick." Todd was curious, too. He secretly hoped it was Abbas' dick, but feared it was probably a weapon.

"Hold on," he heard Abbas say. The sickening sound of metal thudding on the table nearly dropped Todd to his knees. He gulped hard.

"Why are you carrying that around?" the girl asked.

"For protection," Abbas answered quickly. *So it* is *a gun,* Todd thought. He pressed himself tighter against the wall as if doing so would hide him more.

"Protection from what?" she asked.

"From Americans," he said. There was a long pause.

"You're *in* America," she informed him.

Todd waited impatiently for this ordeal to be over. His legs felt like jello, and he thought he might pass out, throw up, or piss himself. Maybe all three.

"I'm not American," Abbas said. "When people look at me, they see a foreigner. They see I'm not white, black, Mexican, or Asian and they wonder what I am. People ask me what I am as if I'm some sort of mutt. They assume I'm not Christian. I get ridiculed constantly for practicing a religion different from theirs. I get persecuted because I won't change beliefs, or I get called a terrorist when I try to tell them their way isn't the only way, when I try to shed light on my beliefs and teach them about my way of life."

Abbas' volume had gradually increased throughout his monologue. The more he spoke, the more passionate he became. He was so loud now that Todd was afraid they'd all get caught by the parents just inside the house.

"The entire country ignores the possibility that not everyone celebrates Christmas and Easter and says 'Merry Christmas' and 'Happy Easter,' anyway," Abbas continued. "Do you know how awkward that is? What am I supposed to say back? I don't celebrate Christmas and Easter, but I don't ridicule anyone for worshiping a fat man or a rabbit. But rather than respect my beliefs, accept my practices, or honor the freedom to practice religion bullshit that this country was supposedly built upon, I have their religion forced upon me and I get ostracized. Did you know there are over twenty holidays observed by seven major religions between November and January?" he asked the girl. "But all we ever hear about is Christmas."

"I like Christmas and Easter," his guest replied.

Todd flinched at Abbas' rhetoric and cringed at the girl's response. Todd guessed that she was exactly the type of person Abbas was complaining about.

"The majority of people in this country hate what's different from them and aren't pleasant in expressing it. I'm always being tested, so my nine here is the answer key." Todd gulped and felt a shiver course down his spine. He knew that if he was caught there would be no reasoning with Abbas. He was the shoot-first-walk-away type.

"Well, I hope I can make amends for the way you've been treated," the girl said. Todd could hear the gun slide across the table, followed by the sound of little kisses.

"Be careful with that," he heard Abbas warn in between kisses that sounded like they were getting longer and more intimate. Todd struggled to hear what was going on over the loud beating of his heart. He thought he might pass out and willed himself to stay conscious.

"Have you ever used the gun?" the girl asked sensuously. "Have you ever shot someone?" She didn't wait for an answer. "With this you hold another man's life in your hands," she continued. "That's so hot!" Todd could hear a zipper being pulled down, then more little kisses followed by gentle moans. The intensity of both increased steadily.

Slap!

"What the fuck?!" Abbas bellowed. Todd heard the slap that was missing when he called her out of her name earlier.

"What the fuck is right!" she yelled back, matching his intensity. Todd wondered about the lunacy of a person who would slap an unstable man with a gun within his reach. He sent a prayer that the couple hadn't heard the sound he made when he flinched.

"What is this?" she yelled

"Keep it down," he said. "My parents are home and I don't want them to know I'm in here having sex."

"Who said anything about us having sex?" she snapped. "Why else would I bring you here?" he asked.

"I'm not a hoe," she snapped. "I actually *liked* you."

"I mean, I like you, too" Abbas replied, softening his voice.

"So then what. in. the. HELL. is. *this*?!" she exclaimed, her tone still intense.

"It looks like your condom," he responded, annoyed. "Now let's use it," he added gleefully.

"Why is it here?" she asked.

"I mean, it's too early to talk about having kids," he answered playfully. "But I like your style." Smooth, Todd thought, judging Abbas' attempt at getting out of trouble.

"It's not. *mine*," she said through gritted teeth. "I don't walk around with condoms in my hand waiting to use them with every guy I kiss. Am I just another notch in your belt?" Her voice sounded more pained now. "How many bitches do you bring in here?" she asked, louder. Todd could tell she was crying. He couldn't tell if the tears were out of anger or heartache.

"You're the only bitch – I mean girl – I've brought here."

Slap!

Todd flinched again, then heard the door swing open and the girl rush out of the motorhome with Abbas hopping behind her, still trying to pull up his pants.

Todd escaped the tiny shower prison and let out a huge sigh of relief. He now understood why the damsel in distress would always fall in the woods while being chased by the killer. In life or death situations, you freeze up in fear, a million thoughts racing through your head. Once your body is told to move again your muscles turn to jello.

"Amani!" Todd whispered loudly. Then he froze again. Twelve feet away from him, sitting on the table before him was the gun Abbas had left behind, glistening in the moonlight. This was the first time since Boy Scouts that Todd had seen a gun up close. He was just as intimidated by its power as the girl had been turned on by it. Its potential to take another's life frightened him.

Suddenly, the door flew open again, and with no time to react Todd knew he was a sitting duck. He just stood there in the open as Abbas ran inside the motorhome. Being this close, Todd could feel Abbas' malevolent energy. Abbas grabbed his gun and froze in place. This is it, Todd thought, fearing Abbas could hear the drops of cold sweat hitting the ground from Todd's face. He tried calculating his next move, but none made sense. Should he dive through the window like he saw in the movies? Maybe I can talk to him and explain the situation. No… Abbas was not a reasonable man, and as soon as he recognized Todd he was bound to shoot him.

Abbas readjusted his pants and tucked the gun into its waistband, then turned to pursue the girl. Todd fell to his knees, his nerves shot. He knew it was divine intervention that had kept Abbas from seeing him. Amani knew it, too. She ran to him and held him tight. Neither spoke. They just counted their blessings silently.

Todd turned down his street and cut off his headlights. His heart was still pounding. He'd driven 30 miles an hour the whole way home, his hands clutching the steering wheel tightly. He loved Amani with everything in him, but he didn't want to die because of her.

As he coasted up to his house he was thrilled to see all the lights still off inside. He parked the car and ran around to the back. He was surprised when he noticed he'd left the sliding glass door slightly ajar. He entered through the door and shut it firmly behind him.

Still too worked up to sleep and knowing the only things on television were infomercials, Todd decided to grab a snack. He grew less cautious now that he'd snuck out of and back into the house successfully.

Making his way to the kitchen, Todd froze. A sound caught his attention as he walked past the bathroom. He stopped just outside the bathroom door. The noise stopped. Brushing it off as nerves, Todd kept heading for the kitchen. He heard the sound again, this time louder. With the lights off, Todd wondered who or what might have snuck into the house while he was gone. A wild animal? Someone who'd tied his family up? The house was eerily quiet. Todd could feel his blood pressure rise as his anxiety levels boiled over.

Another thought crept into his mind. What if Abbas had seen him, beat him home, and was waiting to shoot him? He couldn't identify the sound. It sounded like a dog lapping water out of the toilet, but they didn't have a dog. Todd crept to the bathroom door. It was open slightly. His instinct told him to leave whatever the noise was alone; he had seen far too many scary movies to know that chasing after danger leads to bad things. Fight or flight, he told himself. Todd wanted flight but his legs wouldn't move.

Todd flung the door open, his arms flailing, his legs kicking, hoping to connect with whatever danger was on the other side. The glow of two sinister-looking eyes stared at him, bringing Todd to the point of panic. A giant raccoon. As if it knew it wasn't supposed to be there, the raccoon walked past Todd to the back door. It turned to Todd as if to say "can you open this for me?" Todd obliged and watched the raccoon run away.

I'm done, Todd thought. He abandoned his desire for a snack and headed upstairs to bed.

Chapter 32

"Todd!" his dad yelled from downstairs. "Telephone!"

Todd was shocked that he didn't hear the phone ringing. He was even more surprised that he'd slept as late as he did. Whoever was calling did him a favor; Todd was due at work in about an hour.

"I got it!" he yelled to his dad, while picking up the phone. "Hey, beautiful," he said.

"Nigga, what?!" responded the voice on the other end. It was Rob.

"My bad, Rob," Todd said, laughing. "I thought you were my girlfriend."

"Sure you did, County Boy," Rob said. "Look," he continued. "My car died last night so you're on your own getting back to school."

"No problem," Todd replied. "I'm sure I can find a way back."

Todd poured himself out of bed. Last night's events had drained every ounce of his energy. He wished he hadn't agreed to work this weekend. He was ready to go back to school. Ready to go back to sleepy, boring Jefferson City, especially since he hadn't studied a single subject outside of his brief calculus lesson on Friday. Hopefully it'll be slow today, he thought. Give me an opportunity to get some classwork done, but also to settle my nerves.

Todd's wish was granted. Outside of an early breakfast rush of mall walkers and church goers, the rest of the day was pretty quiet, so much so that Todd had a good three hours of uninterrupted homework time.

"Hey Todd, your girl's here," Dave joked, breaking Todd's concentration on a calculus problem. Expecting to see Amani, Todd was let down when he saw it was just Sasha.

"Where's Amani?" he asked.

"Well hello to you, too," she answered, perturbed.

"I am so sorry," he apologized. "Please, have a seat," he said, gesturing for her to sit down. "How have you been?" he asked, forcing himself through the pleasantries.

"That's better," Sasha said. "I came as a messenger. Amani told me to tell you she's laying low after last night but wants to see you tomorrow before you leave. She also said some sappy 'I love you blah blah blah' crap."

"Please tell her that I love her dearly and miss her already," Todd said. He was a little annoyed that Amani didn't deliver the message herself, but he understood her need to not call undue attention to herself or her activities, especially if they meant leaving the house.

"Can you also tell her I would love to see her before I head back to school?" Todd asked.

"Got it," Sasha said. Todd doubted she would deliver his message with the heartfelt delivery Todd intended. "By the way," she said, stopping and turning around. "What happened last night?" she asked. "We saw the police on our street. Apparently there was an argument between a couple and people sneaking around people's yards. It's not safe out there anymore," she added with a smirk, heading for the exit again.

Todd finished his shift along with all his homework. He felt accomplished and ready for his Spanish and Philosophy tests. The icing on the cake was having gotten it all done while he was getting paid double.

The sun was still out when Todd got home from work. It was too beautiful an evening to spend indoors. He grabbed his glove and a ball from out of his trunk and popped his head inside the house.

"Hey Dad, do you want to play catch?" When Todd was growing up, his dad always made time to play catch with him, no matter how busy he was or how rough his day had been. In fact, both parents had always been there for him.

His dad put on his sneakers and headed for the backyard. Todd wasn't sure he wanted kids of his own, but if he ever did, he hoped he'd have moments like these. He may be too hard headed to follow his dad's advice, but he'd always follow the example his father had set for him in spending time with his children.

Todd's love for the game of baseball may have started with his grandfather, but his dad was the one who'd nurtured it. No matter how poorly he played – and there had been some bad years – his dad always made him feel like a superstar. Todd knew he'd cherish this memory forever.

They tossed the ball back and forth for a bit, and then his dad broke the silence. "Todd?" he asked, "do you know the secret to happiness?"

"You always say it's to not piss Mom off. Happy wife, happy life," Todd joked. "Or was it if you want to be happy for the rest of your life, never make a pretty woman your wife?" he teased, reciting lyrics from a Jimmy Soul song. They both chuckled.

"Those are both good pieces of advice," his dad said, "but the true key to happiness is never hold in a fart." Todd held onto the ball and looked at his dad for a moment. Everything his dad said to him usually had a deeper meaning to it, but Todd was baffled by what this statement's lesson could be. Did it have something to do with his intestines, he wondered.

Reading his son like a book, Todd's dad could see the hamster in his brain had fallen off the wheel. "Son, when you keep something bottled up, it doesn't disappear, it just festers, leading to stress and anxiety. It affects your mental and physical health until one day the littlest thing sets you off and you look like a psycho. So let it out. Sometimes releasing that tension results in a stinky situation, and sometimes it leads to just a lot of noise, but in the end you'll feel better that you got it out of your system."

"You've looked a little stressed this weekend," he continued. "Let it out." Then he farted, smiled, and walked away.

Todd stood there, amazed at how his dad could turn something as small and insignificant as a fart to something with deeper meaning. Heading back into the house, Todd contemplated whether he should head back to school after work tomorrow or wait until early Tuesday. There really was no benefit either way. His home of eighteen plus years felt less like home every day, but there was no better sleep than the sleep he got in his own bed at home.

The taste of freedom he'd experienced had outweighed his distasteful dorm room conditions. Being able to come and go as he pleased, clean up when he wanted, and sleep in when he wanted outweighed even the comfort of his own bed. Then there was his family, Amani included. He missed them. He maybe even missed Tiffany. Maybe. College didn't include his dad's wit or his mom's unconditional love and cooking. School also didn't include Amani.

He could feel himself falling deeper in love with her every day, no matter how often his life was put in danger. He knew he needed college if he wanted to do something with his future, but what that something was was still unclear. But he could feel himself changing, even though he was still doing dumb stuff like sneaking out of his parents' house. In the past, he would go into dangerous situations blindly. Now, he was able to at least recognize how dangerous those situations were and to analyze them, for whatever good that'd do him if someone was shooting at him.

He decided to go back to school after work tomorrow. He figured he could use the time to study with no distractions.

Chapter 33

Todd was thrilled to find Amani waiting for him when he got to work. He'd planned to see her before he left for school but didn't know how or when.

"I don't have much time," she said sadly, wrapping her arms around Todd.

"I figured as much," Todd pouted in response.

Amani loosened her grasp, studying his face. "The other night has taken its toll on you, hasn't it?" she asked. She didn't need to wait for the answer she already knew. Todd remained silent. Yes, hiding in the shadows, fearing for his life *had* taken its toll on him, but not on his love for her. "You're lucky," she said.

"How so?" Todd asked, puzzled.

"At least you get to marry whoever you want."

"Not if she's not you," Todd responded without hesitation.

"Will you continue to write me?" she asked.

"Every day," Todd promised. Amani kissed him sweetly.

"I love you," she whispered, and walked off. A tear fell from Todd's eye. He felt a heavy pull in his chest as he watched her walk out of the restaurant.

Todd's shift felt like an eternity, and a punishment. Once again, they were unbearably slow. The only solace Todd took from working the Labor Day holiday was that he was being paid triple, though working with a lonely heart made the day three times as long.

After his shift was over, Todd hurried home to pack and hit the road. He filled his car with most of his winter clothes in case he didn't make it back home before Thanksgiving. He kissed his family goodbye, gratefully taking half-the-refrigerator, and an abundance of snacks his mom packed so he'd "have something to eat."

The trip back to school was smooth sailing. Not having to worry if his car was going to make it, or if he was going to land in prison alleviated much of his stress. Static replaced the music from the radio when he got out of the range of the station's signal but he didn't notice. His mind was focused on what Amani had said: "At least you can marry whoever you want." Had she been arranged and was too afraid to tell me? Nah, he tried to convince himself. She would definitely tell me. Right?

Todd was so focused on his thoughts that he almost missed the exit to school. As he pulled his car into a parking spot in front of his dorm, Todd marveled at how the arrival of students after a holiday mimicked that of the night before the first day of class.

"Mutha fucka you didn't think I'd be out already, did you?" roared an angry voice several parking spaces over. Todd was relieved the aggression wasn't directed at him, but he was surprised he could hear it over the festive environment around him. Students were unpacking their cars, talking about how they'd spent their weekends. As difficult as it was, Todd tried to ignore the abusive rhetoric being hurled at a group of male students.

"Bitch! Don't get mad at me because you got caught!" Todd instantly recognized both parties. Diamond was in attack mode. Her victims Rob and Big J. Todd would normally have walked away so he could honestly tell anyone who asked that he didn't see or hear anything, but today was different. Today he saw and heard a violent slap as Diamond smacked the both of them unmercifully. Todd giggled. It was comical that two men who portrayed themselves as thugs were being manhandled by a scorned, slightly more aggressive, gangster.

Todd hurried away from the commotion just in case she had a slap ready for him, too. He found a pay phone and called home collect. He recorded the caller as 'I made it safely.' His parents declined the call as expected. This was a free way of letting his parents know he'd arrived safely without having to use his calling card and being charged for a long distance call.

Chapter 34

Over the next couple of months, Todd fell into a comfortable routine. He went to the gym early in the morning to workout, then go to practice. He'd have breakfast, go to class, back to practice, study, do homework, and write Amani. Enclosed in each letter was two dollars so she could call him at lunch. When word got out Todd had a car people would offer him two dollars to run them around town, mostly to the liquor store, and mostly on the weekends. The trips were an escape from studying or playing the Sega gaming system as mid-Missouri was devoid of excitement on the weekends.

One evening, a banging on the door interrupted Todd's weekly recap letter to Amani. "Open up, Todd!" yelled a voice from outside. He had just finished telling Amani how much he missed her and couldn't wait to see her Thanksgiving weekend. He opened the door, finding Big J on the other side.

"What's up, Dollar Bill?" Big J said. Todd liked having a nickname among the guys; it made him feel relevant. But he didn't like the fact that he'd gotten it based on the dollar bills he received taking people places. He wanted to be called something in reference to baseball. He'd tried giving himself the nickname Ice, mostly because he played on a baseball diamond and ice was another name for a diamond, but apparently one can't come up with their own nickname and have it be considered legitimate.

"How's it going?" Todd asked, turning around to finish his letter.

"I see you writing yo girl again," Big J said. Over the past couple months, Todd, Big J, and Rob would hang out in each other's dorm rooms playing video games, listening to music, or talking sports. "Hey man, can you run me up the street? I need to get some Alize and condoms. I got this girl coming to the room, and you know what that means."

Todd chuckled. Big J and Rob were always bragging about the girls that were coming over to their rooms. It always seemed like the same story. This girl came over and we blessed the bottle of whatever it was they were drinking. It seemed like Big J drank Alize and Rob Hennessy. The story always ended with sex and the girls taking the walk of shame the next morning.

"Dog! I'm telling you," Big J started, "with yo' ride I can hook you up with dozens of girls."

"I can't," Todd said. "I have a girlfriend."

"Yeah, I know," Big J sighed. "*Every*body knows. You talk about her or write to her all the damn time." Todd shot Big J a sideways smirk. "Isn't yo' girl still in St. Louis?"

"Yes," Todd answered hesitantly. He knew there was something shady behind that question.

"Then it doesn't count if you hook up with another girl."

"Say what?" Todd asked, rolling his eyes at what was sure to be another rendition of Big J's hood logic.

"Because you're in different zip codes," Big J explained.

"That's the dumbest thing I have ever heard," Todd began before being interrupted by another knock at the door. "It's open!" Todd yelled.

The door flew open. It was Rob. "What're y'all up to?"

"What's up with the aggression?" Big J asked, closing the door quietly.

"Oh my bad," Rob said. "You know dark liquor makes me hype."

"I was just listening to Big J telling me it's not considered cheating to hook up with a girl here because Amani is in another zip code," Todd said.

"It's true," Rob agreed. "Just like it's not cheating if you pay for it because it's a business transaction, not pleasure."

"And it's not cheating if you pretend that it's your girlfriend," Big J added.

"And if it's bad sex it's not cheating," Rob said.

"And it's not cheating if it's your first time cheating," Big J exclaimed.

"How's that?" Todd asked curiously.

"Because, Rookie, everyone gets a freebie," Big J explained.

"It's not cheating if you don't know their name, either," Rob continued. "You clearly don't give a hoot about this person; you're just satisfying a physical need. It's like eating or breathing or pooping. It's just got to be done."

"Are you two done?" Todd asked.

"No!" Big J exclaimed. "You came to college to learn, so we're dropping knowledge. It's not cheating if you're in the military," he continued.

"Why?" Todd asked. Even though he wasn't taking either of them seriously – who with at least one functioning brain cell would? – he found them incredibly entertaining.

"Because you kill for our freedom, so you've earned the right to screw anyone you want," Big J explained.

"That's it," Todd said, rolling his eyes. "Lesson over. Do you still need a ride?"

"I'm coming, too!" Rob exclaimed.

As they headed for Todd's car, Rob and Big J continued their "it's not cheating" one-upmanship. *It's not cheating if it's in the shower because Pert Plus washes all sins away*, etc. Todd turned on the radio to drown them out.

"What are we listening to, Todd?" Rob asked, annoyed.

"My Tracie Spencer cassette," Todd answered without hesitation.

"Umm," Big J said, "you're playing a love song called *Tender Kisses* with two other **guys** in the car. And you were singing along. Man! That's like you're serenading us. Maybe we should be trying to hook you up with guys and keep the women for us."

"I like to think of it as a concert. I should make you pay admission," Todd joked.

"Todd, don't let this man hook you up with any of his so-called girlfriends," Rob advised. "His last girl was so ugly she needed prescription makeup."

"Oh yeah?" Big J countered, "well your girl…"

"Stop!" Todd interrupted, laughing. "I can't listen to you two going back and forth anymore."

As they drove, Todd listened distractedly as Rob told about his latest conquest. This one began with him not knowing her name and ended with him throwing her out of his dorm room without her clothes. Todd feigned a chuckle but was horrified that someone could treat a woman so disrespectfully. He also wondered why Rob got involved with so many girls who had self-esteem issues. Each tale started with how they were upset about something, how he consoled them, how they'd slept together, and how he would then drop them like a bad habit.

Rob bragged about how badly he treated these women, how they were like trophies for him. In his mind, if you treated them wrong enough, they would be too embarrassed to tell other girls, and you'd be free to continue to do what you were doing.

His latest victim had invited him into her dorm room. Things got serious, but stopped because they didn't have any condoms. "She was trying to give me blue balls!" exclaimed Rob, describing the scene from the back seat of Todd's car.

"So what'd you do next?" Big J asked excitedly.

"I went MacGyver on her ass!" Rob shouted.

"You what?" Todd asked, unfamiliar with the concept but not sure he really wanted to know.

"I grabbed a plastic grocery bag, hair tie, and baby oil," Rob explained.

"That *worked*?" Todd asked

"She'll be aight," Rob said. "I got mine, ya' know what I'm saying?" he bragged.

"Didn't that cause cuts and friction burns?" Todd asked. He was by no means a sexual pro, but after his first time he learned that not using the proper prophylactic can lead to injury and possible infections.

"What are you, the president of the women's rights coalition?" Rob asked, annoyed that Todd wasn't delighting in his triumph. Todd didn't say a word. He was relieved when he pulled into the parking lot of the liquor store. He needed a break from his two passengers trying to outdo one another in their tales of dating mishaps.

Todd waited in the car as Rob and Big J ran inside the store. As many times as Todd had been here he hadn't yet been inside. He had no reason to since he didn't drink. His dad had always told him that if he didn't have any business being somewhere then he shouldn't go.

Time ticked slowly as he waited. Todd wondered what was taking them so long. He figured an unsuspecting female was involved. Another ten minutes passed. Rob and Big J had been inside for over thirty minutes. There weren't enough condoms or alcohol in the world to justify how long they were taking.

Todd turned off the ignition to conserve gas. Should I go in and hurry them up, he wondered? They came out just as he was finishing his thought. Always playing, Todd thought. They were probably racing to see who was going to ride shotgun, he thought. Until he saw their faces. They looked scared. Did they steal their drinks? Then he saw what they were running from: six guys were chasing them.

Todd turned the ignition back on so they could make a quick getaway. He saw Big J hurl a brown bag at their pursuers but miss. Unfortunately, he didn't miss the store; its glass door exploded into hundreds of shards of glass.

"Todd! Grab the gat!" Rob shouted. Oh crap, Todd thought. Unarmed, and with no clue as to what was happening, Todd pretended to search for a weapon. He detached the face of his radio, hoping that, in the dark, the black plastic might look like a gun.

He hopped out of the car, trying to make himself look like he was carrying, but the store's lights made it clear he was not. Outnumbered and confused, Todd readied for a fight. He prayed his ruse would be intimidating enough that it didn't lead to to an actual fight. These guys didn't seem like they were playing. "That conjecture became fact when Todd watched them bare their teeth and raise their shirts to reveal they were carrying something a little more intimidating than his radio face. Once again, Todd was at the mercy of someone with a gun. How did this keep happening to him?

Rob and Big J ran behind Todd. So much for them being big tough guys, Todd thought. He wasn't one, either, so he was shocked they'd hidden behind him. But he stood his ground, staring intently at the posse in front of him. He wasn't being brave; he just couldn't move. He prayed he'd make it through yet another situation he'd gotten himself into, but he wondered if maybe this would be the time God stopped listening, or stopped caring to save him from the boneheaded moves he made.

"Later for you, bitches," the group's ringleader declared, kicking the front of Todd's car. He stared at it as if he was storing its description into his memory for later.

Suddenly, Todd could feel the heat from a patrol car's spotlight on his back. He thanked God for answering his prayer, knowing he should've found better friends the last time these two had gotten him into a situation that involved the police. Todd turned around slowly, beyond relieved to see the officers.

"On the ground!" one of them shouted as another one flipped on the car's red and blue lights. "You stay there!" he demanded of Todd, then he grabbed Big J while the other one grabbed Rob.

Just then, the store clerk came out of the store. Surveying the damage to his door, he called one of the officers over to him. After the cops got statements from both Rob and Big J, they were placed in the back of the squad car. Todd was surprised at how calm he was. Was he becoming numb to these situations? He told himself he had nothing to worry about; he was an innocent bystander. Right? Then he remembered that he'd been part of the destruction of private property, causing a disturbance of the peace, and brandishing a weapon of some sort; he could be in just as much trouble as Rob and Big J.

"Your turn," one of the officers said. "Come over here." Todd gave his side of the story, overembellishing how he got out of the car to see what was going on.

"College student," the officer snickered.

"Yes sir," Todd answered nervously.

"From St. Louis or Kansas City?" the cop asked.

"St. Louis County," Todd replied, trying to sound as innocent as possible.

"I see it all the time," the officer began. "You kids come into town from the big city thinking you own the place, that we townies should revere you or something. Well," he continued, "one of the townies pulled your card. And he's not one to mess with." He paused. "Kid, it's not where you're from, it's where you are now. You and your friends can pull that hood shit in St. Louis and get away with it, but here where they have nothing to lose and everything to prove it could turn deadly. You're lucky we happened to be patrolling the area when we happened upon you. You and your crew were about to become statistics. I suggest you stick to working on getting your degree and stop bringing toys to a big boy fight. Not only are you and your friends provoking *real thugs*, you're introducing a world of legal problems into your life." He glanced at the detachable radio face still in Todd's hand. "Really kid? Brandishing that thing as a gun? Penal Code § 417.4 PC makes it a crime to draw or brandish an imitation firearm in a threatening manner, such that it places others in fear. You could be looking at a minimum of thirty days to six months in jail. Try working on a degree behind bars," he said sarcastically. "Oh. And your two "gangsta" buddies? The clerk told us how they bragged about being from the tough inner city. Notice how they pulled you into the fracas? Notice how they were hiding behind you when we showed up?"

He made a gun gesture with his hand. "Don't you know the driver's the first one to get popped in these circumstances?"

He was right. Rob and Big J had almost sacrificed Todd to the wolves. The officer could tell Todd was hearing his message. "Remember this, kid: you will always be an extra cast member in the story of another person's life. You are expendable to others. Stop thinking that because they call you a friend that they'll be loyal to you when the shit hits the fan. Most 'friends,'" the officer, said, "will sell you out at the drop of a hat. A *true* friend wants you to succeed in every aspect of life; they won't put you in the kind of harm that these guys just did."

Todd was astonished by the revelation. His words almost mirrored what his dad would say. His dad wouldn't have called him an extra, but would have said he would always be a pawn in another person's game.

"Thank you, sir," Todd replied, extending his hand. He was truly grateful for the older man's wisdom.

"Your friends are going to be cited for property damage and disturbing the peace," the officer said, shaking Todd's hand and walking away. Todd made his way back to his car, inspecting it where it had been kicked. "I'm sorry Opie," he said, calling it by the name he gave all his inanimate possessions. Thankful that no harm was done, he sat down in the driver's seat. He was mad. It was his property that had been kicked, his life that had been placed in danger, and his freedom that had been placed in jeopardy. He turned the engine over and drove off, leaving his so-called friends in his rearview.

Chapter 35

"Welcome home," Todd's mom said earnestly.

He was so happy to be there. It was the day before Thanksgiving, a time for celebration. Thanksgiving was Todd's favorite holiday. He loved the food aspect, of course, but mostly he loved it because it was near his birthday. Occasionally it would even fall *on* Thanksgiving.

Todd had more cause for celebration, too. His midterms revealed he was passing all his classes – *in*cluding Calculus, not barely passing like he had in high school. He had a high B average in most of his classes.

"I'll be back," Todd told his mom.

"Where are you going?" she asked. He could tell she was upset that he was leaving so soon after arriving.

"Probably to see his girlfriend," Tiffany teased, entering the kitchen.

"Say hi to your brother," their mom told her.

"Why?" Tiffany asked sarcastically. "I've seen enough of him for fourteen years."

"Because I know you missed him," their mom said, "and because if you don't, I'm going to make you two hug each other."

"What did *I* do to get punished?!" Todd joked.

"Now!" mom demanded.

"Hi, Todd," Tiffany sighed, and Todd was out the door. He had plans to meet Amani at the public library. It was a quiet rendezvous. They would be alone. Amani figured it was the safest place in the world, the last place she would run into a family member, especially her brother.

When Todd pulled into the parking lot he could see that Amani wasn't alone, there was another girl with her. Todd and Amani had been together for just under half a year; she'd never mentioned having any friends besides Sasha. But Todd hadn't ever asked, either. He'd only focused on Sasha since that was who he was sending all the letters to.

"Hi, Todd," Amani squealed, running up to Todd tightly and throwing her arms and legs around him. He lifted her off the ground, grateful for her warmth against the brisk November weather. He didn't want to let go. Her arms were where he felt comfortable, whole, and happy.

A tear fell from his right eye. Part of him had been missing since Labor Day weekend, like there was a hole in his chest where his heart should've been. Seeing her patched it up.

Amani kissed every inch of Todd's face. "Uhhmmm," Amani's friend said, clearing her throat in an attempt to get the couple's attention. They'd completely forgotten she was even there.

"Oh, I'm sorry, Dawn" a giddy Amani said to her friend. "Todd, this is my friend Dawn. She used to go to my old school."

Dawn was tall, slender, and attractive. Very attractive. Her hair was cut into a sleek, tapered pixie style with bangs. The back and sides were cropped close to the scalp, and the sideburns had been shaped into perfect triangles. Her artificial tan made her look sunkissed and lovely. "Nice to meet you," she said to Todd.

"Nice to meet you, too," Todd replied, his voice monotone. He was a little suspicious of Dawn. Why was she there, especially since his relationship with Amani was such a secret? He abandoned his line of thinking, though. Amani knew what was best.

Todd hadn't taken his eyes off Amani and was still holding her hands. He'd longed to see her for so long; he was determined to make up for lost time. He drew her close to him again, kissing her.

"Down, boy," she giggled. "I, uh," she said, clearing her throat and changing to a more serious tone. "I mean, you and Dawn have so much in common," she said, "I thought you should meet."

"What for?" Todd asked nonchalantly, still trying playfully to get a kiss.

"You know," Amani began, gently pushing him away from her. "Get to know each other, go out."

"Wait," Todd said, confused. "What are we doing?" He let go of her hands. Had he heard her right? Was his *girl*friend hooking him up with another girl?

"Excuse me for a moment," Amani said to Dawn.

"No problem," Dawn said. "By the way, you were right. He *is* cute."

Amani pulled Todd away from her friend. She could see the hurt and confusion in his eyes. Wiping a tear that had fallen from his left eye, she pulled him close, stood on her tiptoes and gave him a kiss on his forehead. This can't be good, Todd thought. "I feel bad that we can't ever go out on dates," she confessed. "You deserve a girlfriend you can show off and experience life with, someone you can go to movies and dance with. I just want you to be happy."

"I *have* that," Todd argued. "Happiness! I don't need anything else. I don't need to go out to dinners and movies. Just being next to you is enough. I don't need to show the whole world I have a girlfriend, I just need a girlfriend that makes me whole and means the world to me. I have that in you. I just want you." Todd meant every word he was saying but still felt like he was rambling. He was desperate to find words to stop Amani's doubt.

"No relationship is perfect, but the love we have for each other is perfect. Or at least I thought it was." Todd began to shiver, and not because of the cold wind blowing around him. He simply couldn't stand the thought of being without her. "I love you, despite the fear and uncertainty of our future. I'm here, and I'm willing to see all of it through as long as you're by my side," he continued. "Amani. You're as essential a part of me as breathing and eating."

"Just do this for me," Amani pleaded. "They say absence makes the heart grow fonder. If you let it go and it comes back to you it's meant to be."

"Amani, I don't want a relationship with you built on cheesy cliches," Todd said. "I just want you."

Amani took a deep breath and a tear fell from her eye. "Todd, I just want to know you have somebody in case we can't be together." Her words lacerated Todd's heart. He knew what she was asking, but he just didn't understand why she was asking it. Had she given up on the one thing Todd was fighting for?

"Don't make me do this," he pleaded.

"Habibi. *Please* do this for me."

There was that damn pet name, Todd thought. He couldn't resist when she called him that. Amani turned back to Dawn. "It's settled. I want you to go out Friday."

The next day and a half was tortuous. Thanksgiving was ruined because he didn't have an appetite. A marvelous meal of turkey; baked mac and cheese; collard, turnip and mustard greens; ham; sweet potato casserole; and homemade yeast rolls was spread out in front of him but he was too upset to eat any of it. He'd struggled to get out of bed, even into the afternoon. He lied to his parents when they showed concern, telling them he was a little under the weather. "My throat is tender," he'd said, immediately wishing he'd just said his head hurt, then she wouldn't have made him drink her cure-all elixir.

For as long as Todd could remember, his mom would make him and Tiffany drink a disgusting combination of lemon, honey, ginger, and turmeric that she brewed into a tea. Even if he wasn't sick, he'd have to drink it as a precaution if Tiffany was. Each sip made him gag.

"You're probably sick from leaving the house without a coat and a hat," his mom scolded him. That was his mom's go-to when Todd got sick in the winter. "All your body heat escapes from your head and leaves you susceptible to illness," she'd say.

Todd knew this wasn't a cold, though. His uncertainty about his relationship with Amani made his affliction dire, and her love was the prescription he needed.

"Drink this," his mom demanded, shoving the tea into his hand. Todd took a tiny sip and wanted to gag. "Drink it!" she repeated.

"It's hot," he whined.

"I know," she replied, "it heals best when it's hot. Now drink up and go rest."

Todd spent the entire day and most of the next in bed. He tried to find a rational reason as to why Amani was setting him up with her friend. He tried to be angry at her so he didn't feel so bad for going on the date, but he kept coming back to her sacrificing her happiness so Todd could be happy. These thoughts relieved some of the sadness, but not much. Todd couldn't imagine not spending his life with the woman he loved.

"Look who's finally awake!" his mom announced as Todd joined his family in the family room. "Hopefully you're well-rested!"

"I'll see you guys later," he said. "I'm heading out for a while."

"Out?" his mom questioned. "We've barely seen you the past couple days!"

"Where are you going?" his dad asked.

"My girlfriend asked me to go on a date with another girl, so I'm taking her to the movies." The blank stares on his parents' faces were all the validation Todd needed to substantiate how insane Amani's request was. As he headed out the door, he heard his dad say to his mom, "Don't ask. It's the nineties; we wouldn't understand."

Todd had agreed to meet Dawn at the dollar theater to see *Single White Female*. Todd didn't know anything about the movie; it was a flick Dawn was eager to see.

Todd guided her to their seats. Todd sat away from her, leaving an empty chair between them. "Look," Dawn said sweetly. "You are *very* attractive. You're someone that I'd like to get to know. I love Amani," she confessed, "and I'd do anything for her. That's why I'm taking part in this ridiculousness. So let's just make the best of it."

Todd smiled at her and nodded, but he was hollow inside. The girl who made him whole had just discarded him like a puppy that was being dropped off to the mill.

The movie was long, or so it seemed to Todd, who was just eager to get the date over with. Afterward, Todd walked Dawn to her car, turning down an opportunity to grab a bite to eat with her. Dawn opened her arms for a hug, but Todd extended his hand for a shake.

"She's lucky to have you," Dawn offered and drove off. Todd felt bad about the way he'd treated her. He would be lucky to have her in his life. Amani was right: he deserved to go out with someone he could show off at parties, dinners, movies, and dances. It would be nice to be in public holding hands like most couples do without the worry of being caught by someone who might harm them. Dawn could be that one, but Todd was in love with her friend. If he ever dated Dawn seriously she'd never be anything more than a consolation prize. He was a little resentful of how the world worked but also thankful for his imperfect relationship. He headed home, excited to complain to Amani.

The next morning, Amani called, sounding upset. "Can I see you?" she begged. Her voice lacked its usual eagerness at wanting to spend time with him.

"The library?" Todd asked. His tone matched hers, mostly out of defensiveness and anxiety. The last time they met he was being pushed toward another girl, so he shuddered to think of what today had in store for him.

"The library is fine," she said, and then hung up without saying 'I love you.' This worried Todd even more.

He got to the library early, hoping it was just going to be the two of them. He was visibly upset when Amani arrived and could see she was upset, too. He was mad. How could the love of his life treat him like an object to be handed off when she no longer had any use for him?

"How could you do that to me?" he asked her now. Amani put her hand up to hush him.

"First things first," she barked. The scowl on her face said she was ready for a fight. Then it softened, and she put her hand down. She hugged Todd and gave him a kiss on the cheek. "No matter how mad we are at one another, love always comes first. I promise to always give you a kiss when I see you," she said. "No matter how much you disappointed me."

"Disappoint *you*?" Todd thought, puzzled. "I love you," he said.

"If you loved me, you wouldn't have gone on a date with Dawn," Amani snapped. Her scowl returned, as did her angry tone.

"I went because I *do* love you," Todd snapped back. "I would go to hell for you in a Speedo, if you asked me," he continued. "I was *in* hell because *you* asked me to be. But it's my fault because I would go anywhere in the world and do anything for you, because *you* are my world."

Amani began to cry. She dropped to her knees, defeated. Todd knelt on the ground next to her. He felt horrible now for getting angry at her. "I'm just scared that I can't give you the life you deserve," she confessed. "It's the start of the holiday season for you, a holiday I don't celebrate."

"Stop!" Todd interrupted. "You can give me a million reasons to give up on us, but I only need one reason to hold on." He looked deep into her eyes and then drew her to him, holding her tight. "Fuck Christmas," Todd whispered in Amani's ear. "It's just one long, overdrawn baby shower, anyway" he joked. He would miss Christmas, but he would miss her more. Besides, it wouldn't be much of a celebration if the love of your life didn't celebrate it with you. Todd began to feel differently about the holiday. It purported to celebrate the birth of his Savior but it was everyone else who got presents. It seemed an odd way to celebrate.

Todd and Amani held their embrace for a while, Todd wasn't sure for how long. Time stood still when he was in her arms.

"I have to go," Amani said. Four words Todd never wanted to hear. Todd gave her one last kiss before she left then headed to the Plaza to meet with Tim and Rick to secure a job over the Winter holiday .

As he entered the Plaza, Todd was amazed that Christmas decorations had already taken over the mall. Thanksgiving was just two days ago but it was already a blur in the minds of the shoppers rushing around in search of a bargain.

Todd was astonished to see how packed the restaurant was as he walked in. There was even a line of customers waiting! The hostess looked overwhelmed, and Todd found himself grateful that he wasn' working today, even though he could use the money. If they were this busy *now*, he wondered how busy he'd be working here for the holidays.

Todd joined the back of the line and waited patiently so as to not anger those who'd been waiting in front of him.

"How many, sir?" the hostess asked.

Todd was a little sad that he didn't recognize a single face working, but he wasn't surprised. It'd been two-and-a-half months since he'd been there, and with no customers there to give tips most of the time it would be hard to make a living. Employees were constantly coming and going.

"Oh, I'm here to see Tim and Rick," he said.

"Ummmm… okay," she responded, seemingly unsure as to whether she should leave her post or not.

"I'll go find them," Todd said. The hostess looked relieved to have one less "customer" to contend with. "Oh! By the way, is Emily, I mean, Erica still working here?" Todd was embarrassed that he still couldn't get her name right.

The hostess dropped the clipboard, a stunned look on her face. She began to turn pale.

"I just wanted to apologize to her because I always call her by the wrong name," Todd said with a smile. The hostess took a step to her right and looked down at the counter. Todd followed her gaze and almost dropped to the floor. There was a coffee can on the counter with a picture of Erica taped to it. They were raising money for her funeral expenses. Todd was flabbergasted. She'd looked fine the last time he'd seen her! "What happened?" he asked.

"Murdered," she mouthed. Todd could feel the blood rushing from his face.

Everything turned purple.

When Todd came to, he realized he was in the office in the back of the restaurant. A waitress was holding a bag of ice to the back of his head.

"Welcome back," Tim said. "Do I owe you money or something?"

"What happened?" Todd asked, confused.

"That's what we're hoping to find out," Tim said. "I came out from the back to find you sprawled across the floor."

"Mall security helped carry you back here before you scared away our customers," Rick added.

"I–uh," Todd began, "I–uh came to see if I could work during my holiday break," he replied, trying to gather his thoughts. "Then I saw the coffee can."

"Oh. Yes," Tim said. "Tragic story. But we don't talk about that here."

"So young!" Rick added.

Todd thought about how he'd put his own life in jeopardy lately. Until now he never thought it would or could happen to him or someone he knew. It always happened in other neighborhoods or cities. Not in his world. She was his age and had her life taken from her. What made him so special that it couldn't happen to him, too? From the time Dave warned him about Abbas to the incident at the liquor store he had been careless with his life. Even the fact that he didn't have a plan for his future was an example of taking his life for granted. Life truly was precious, short, and unpredictable. Erica was an example of this. He hadn't known her well, hell he could barely get her name right, but he was deeply affected by her loss, maybe because he was assuming she was an innocent victim, or maybe because of the wake-up call her death offered.

"Yep. Life is a precious gift, Todd," Tim began, "live your days wisely."

CHAPTER 36

"Freedom!" Todd shouted, running toward his car to celebrate the winter holiday. He was going to be away from school for over a month. The past sixteen weeks hadn't been easy but he'd gotten through it successfully.

He didn't have any holiday plans outside of working at Green Leaf Kitchen and seeing Amani. He was sorry now that he'd asked to work because he knew it was going to be busy. Christmas shopping at the Plaza was like an all-day adventure. The mall had close to one hundred stores anchored by four department stores that each had several floors. All this meant that Green Leaf kitchen was a welcome break for weary shoppers. Unfortunately, that made for long, hard, busy days. Todd would be working noon to 10 Thursdays through Saturdays and 10 AM to 7 PM on Sundays.

When he pulled up in front of his house, Todd was surprised to see a car he didn't recognize parked in his spot. It was a lime green, 1983 Mercury Colony Park station wagon with a black vinyl roof and hidden headlights. It seemed so out of place on their street, and Todd was annoyed that the hideous thing was in his spot. But then the door popped open and Amani hopped out.

"Hey, stranger!" she said. "Need a ride?"

Todd's demeanor changed instantly. The Mercury was a lovely car he'd happily have in his spot.

Amani ran up to Todd and jumped in his arms, kissing him as fiercely as a wrestler trying to pin his opponent to the mat. She tasted his tongue hungrily, taking charge as she held the back of his head firmly.

She bit his bottom lip playfully, then whispered, "Come with me." She grabbed his hand and guided him towards the behemoth of a vehicle.

"Where are we going?" Todd asked, struggling to open the heavy door.

"It's a surprise," Amani said.

"How are you here?" Todd asked. "Shouldn't you be in school?"

Amani cleared her throat and deepened her register. "I told the school Amani was sick," she said, sounding like Todd imagined her father might.

"Bravo!" Todd said, applauding.

"Then I told my mom I missed the bus and asked if I could drive to school and now I'm here!" Todd could see the back seats were folded down and several blankets were placed about neatly. Amani could see that Todd had caught on to her plan and grasped his hand, interlocking it with hers. They both smiled.

Amani drove to a secluded spot in a park down by the river. It was extremely cold outside, too cold for anyone to walk by their spot. Still, Amani made sure to park somewhere with lots of gravel so they could hear anyone who might be approaching.

"I'll be right back," Amani said, exiting the vehicle. Todd could hear the hatchback of the station wagon's door open and turned to see what was going on. "Uh uh!" Amani teased, "Don't look!" Todd turned back toward the front of the vehicle. It was a gloomy, overcast day. The wind was howling, and the only noise was the sound of scampering leaves skittering along the pavement.

"I'm ready," Amani declared from the back of the vehicle. Todd turned to see his girlfriend completely nude and laying invitingly on the blankets. On her breasts were two red bows. "Come open your belated birthday present," she giggled. Todd was almost out of his clothes before he leapt over the seat.

They spent the next several hours exploring one another and holding each other close. As wonderful and fulfilling as the sex had been, holding Amani in his arms was the greatest part. Todd basked in her essence, astounded that he alone was allowed to have this treasure. The heat their bodies generated by their bodies parallelled the intensity of their love. It was as great a birthday celebration as Todd could have ever hoped for. He knew nothing in the next month would measure up to this magical evening.

As he drove back to school three weeks later, Todd reflected on that perfect outing. It had been the only time they hadn't been rushed or interrupted. Todd couldn't imagine how he'd ever have a better moment than that one. Everything else would pale in comparison.

CHAPTER 37

"Glass! I want to see you in my office. Now!" Coach Hunter barked. "The rest of you hit the showers. We have six games in three days," he continued, "and I don't have to express to you that we have to win damn near all of them if we want to make it into the playoffs."

Todd was worried about what this impromptu meeting was about. He'd been working his butt off in practice, so much so that he was nowhere near one of the last teammates to finish in hill running. Unfortunately, none of his hard work had paid off; he had yet to see any action minus pinch-running duties.

Todd was still sitting on the bench behind Eli, who was only having a decent season, so he took the time to work on becoming a switch hitter. A natural righty, Todd worked vigorously from the left side. The thought occurred to him after recalling a conversation with Dave that batting left-handed would give him a better chance of hitting more line drives instead of pounding the ball into the ground right-handed and trying to use his speed to reach first base safely. He forgot the reasoning Dave had given, but it made sense at the time. To further justify this move, Todd told himself that a left-handed hitter was one step closer to first than a right-handed hitter at the plate. Todd was willing to do anything for an advantage; he was dying as a bench player. Highly superstitious, Todd emulated major league ballplayers' unique strategies from peeing on his hands like Moises Alou to eating the same breakfast of two eggs, two pancakes, and then another egg before he left like Stan Musial. He even reverted to eating only green M&M's during games because of a commercial he once saw that said the green ones help you hit home runs. It hadn't helped yet, but he's due.

Todd knocked on Coach Hunter's door. He was nervous. The coach hadn't said two words to him since Todd dismissed his advice at the beginning of the school year almost 9 months ago. Todd feared this meeting was to inform him they were rescinding his partial scholarship after scouting for his replacement.

"Come in! And shut the door behind you," Coach Hunter said gruffly.

"How's it going?" Todd asked, trying to keep his voice from shaking. He felt a chill course through his body when Coach

Hunter looked up at him, as if it pained him to talk to this freshman. Here it is, Todd thought, the end of my baseball career.

"I need you to stop attacking the balls that're hit directly at you," Coach snarled. "When you stop, you're stuck and have to overcome all your inertia to regain lost momentum going toward your target. You need to take a step to get around the baseball and let your momentum help guide your flow. Every second counts, and you're wasting time fielding the way you do."

"Yes, sir, thank you for the advice," Todd replied, trying to sound appreciative and coachable. The coach was unimpressed.

"You can go now," he directed. Determined not to draw the ire of his coach, Todd turned to leave quickly. Not quick enough, though. "One more thing," Coach Hunter said.

I knew it wasn't going to be that easy, Todd thought, releasing the door handle. His shoulders slumped as he turned to face his coach.

"We'll be facing several right-handed pitchers this weekend," Coach began. "As a lefty, I plan to plug you into the lineup throughout the games. I don't have to stress their importance to you, not only to our season but to the future of our program. As a university without the financial benefit of a football team, our baseball program operates at a loss. We rely heavily on boosters. Boosters want to see a return on their investment, which means a winning program. We have a chance to do something this program has never done before: make it to the postseason. It's time to show me what you've got. Don't make me regret playing a freshman over a seasoned player."

Todd could barely contain his excitement at hearing that he was going to get to play. And not only play, but start in meaningful games. He wanted to do flips, to shout for joy from the highest of mountaintops, though he knew better than to show emotion in front of Coach Hunter. He tried desperately to act as if he'd been a starter before, and he had, but never at the collegiate level!

"Yes, sir," Todd responded stoically. Fearful the facade was going to crack soon, Todd left the office, waited for the door to shut, and then lost it. He jumped for joy, did the moonwalk, and fell to the ground and did the worm.

"Coach must have told you that you are starting in my place," said a voice behind him. Todd looked up to see Eli standing above him. Embarrassed, Todd stopped immediately, stood up, and put a serious look on his face. "It's never a good thing to celebrate your successes in front of someone who's suffering because of them."

"I'm sorry, Eli," Todd said. "Coach didn't tell me I was taking your spot."

"It's alright, kid," Eli responded. "It's part of the game," shrugging sadly. The once-arrogant second baseman was a shell of his former self. "I was like you once, you know," he began. "I was the best in my northern Nebraska town, but playing in college is a whole other beast. College!" Eli took a long pause and sighed. "Todd, you haven't earned enough status to be on this team. I mean, you practice with us, you travel with us, you play with us, but you haven't proven yourself one of us," he said. "You ain't shit yet, kid," he continued. "To us, you're a broke-dick 18-year-old freshman puppy yapping on the porch, but you're out here playing with big-dick dogs: 22-, 23-year-old men who've been off the porch for years." He paused again, allowing Todd to let his message sink in a bit.

"Let me put it this way, slick," he continued. "In little league, hell, in high school everyone wants you to succeed. They give you oranges, trophies, and a letter to iron on a jacket, just for participating. And they do it to pump your little ass up. They want you to feel *special*," he said mockingly. "Here, though, it's a whole different ball game. Literally. Here, it's a job. A business. You're not a ball player; you're a brand. Don't think you're starting over me because you're better, because you're not. You're still a piece of shit, Todd. Just a shiny, new piece of shit. They want to show the boosters the future is bright."

"Don't worry. The shine on you will fade, too," he continued. "If it doesn't, don't look to be celebrated by any of your teammates. Every good game you have at this level is you taking a scout's attention off someone else. We're not a team on that field," he emphasized, "we're nine individual LLC's trying to succeed. And if you want to succeed here, it's time for you to toughen the fuck up mentally. You aren't a kid anymore. Like that TV show says, it's a different world than where you come from. You can have your little dance fever here in the hallway if you want," he cautioned, "but out there, it's Division 2 collegiate ball. It's time to work harder to not only advance, but to prove that you belong, and to stave off the next shiny turd waiting to take your place."

Eli turned to go, then paused. "And remember, Mr. Freshman: no matter how far you advance here, there's a whole other division higher than you. Division 1 is full of elite players all with the same goals as you. Fewer than 7,000 people between 1909 and 1993 have ever played in the majors. The competition to make it is stiff. You celebrate your achievements *after* your career is over. Like the guy whose spot I took, you'll have a lifetime of regrets that outweigh your achievements. I'm glad it's over."

Todd stood there wondering if Eli truly *was* happy that his career was over. Todd had always imagined that his own baseball career would end in a blaze of glory, celebrated with fanfare. Eli had shown him how most careers actually end: by being replaced by a newer, possibly better version.

"I tried my damndest this year," Eli confessed, "but no matter what I did I wasn't able to break out. Good luck, kid," he offered, walking away. Todd wondered if he was going to cry. He wanted to cry for him. He'd despised Eli at times, but now he felt sorry for him, mostly because he was the cause of his demise.

Todd paused to take in everything Eli had just said. He never quite thought of succeeding in baseball as a job. One thing was for sure, though, it was time for Todd to prove that he belonged. But first he needed to write to Amani and let her know the good news.

CHAPTER 38

Todd's nerves were wreaking havoc on his stomach. It wasn't nervous energy; it was bottled up excitement. He couldn't wait to get to the fields to play a double header against the Pumas from Southern Indiana University in Terre Haute, Indiana. Two other programs would be in Terre Haute doing the same thing, and Lincoln would be playing several games against others before heading back home to battle a conference rival to close out the regular season. The coaching staff refused to inform the team how many games they had to play and who needed to win or lose what in order to secure their postseason berth.

The bus ride to Terre Haute seemed like an eternity, and when they were still an hour away the coaching staff made the decision to pull over for breakfast to allow the congested morning rush hour traffic to thin out.

"Don't fill up too much," one of the assistant coaches said. "We have two games to play today." Two games! Music to Todd's ears. He couldn't wait to get breakfast over with.

"What are you having, sweetie?" asked the waitress.

"Two eggs, two pancakes, and an egg to go," Todd said, just like Stan the Man.

"What are you?" the waitress asked. The only answer to her question were the blank stares from Todd and his team. "Are you a band or a team?" she clarified, annoyed that she had to ask the question again.

"We're a baseball team," Elijah said, standing up and proudly displaying a blue and gray t-shirt with the words 'Blue Tigers Baseball' inscribed on the front. "We're from Lincoln University in Jefferson City, Missouri," he bragged, speaking loud enough so everyone in the restaurant could hear. "We came to Southern Indiana to do two things," he declared: "Kick Indiana baseball teams' asses," he cheered, "and chew bubble gum."

Elijah spit out his gum in dramatic fashion. "I'm all out of bubble gum!" he announced. Todd and his teammates clapped, cheered, and banged on the tables. The waitress rolled her eyes and walked away to put in the team's order. The rest of the diners mumbled under their breaths.

Breakfast took an eternity to finish. Todd listened to the coaches' strategy while the older players tried to hype up the younger guys. He was pumped full of energy; he didn't need to be hyped up. If he knew where the fields were he'd run to the campus. He was beyond ready to go.

"Let's head out, boys; traffic is clearing," the bus driver yelled. The patrons shot them dirty looks as Todd and the team walked out, and Todd quickened his pace so that he'd be the first on the bus.

After another hour on the road, Todd swore he could still see the restaurant in the distance. The combination of construction, an accident, and yet more rush hour traffic had the bus at a stand still. Todd wondered if a college team had ever had to forfeit a game due to traffic. A gurgle in his stomach made him think that he may need to find a restroom soon.

"Hey, Coach, how much longer 'til we get to the fields?" he asked.

"Glass," Coach Hunter snapped, "aren't you a little old to be asking 'are we there yet'? Your only concern at this moment is reviewing the scouting report we handed you, not worrying about where we are." Well *that* went just about as well as I expected it to, Todd thought. He wondered if Coach Hunter could ever just answer a question politely.

Todd gazed out the window at an endless supply of empty fields. It did little to take his mind off having to go to the bathroom. Ten minutes later – which seemed like an eternity since the bus was moving ten feet every ten minutes – the gas bubble in Todd's stomach (and his need to use the restroom) had grown to near urgent levels. He moved around in his seat nervously, trying to settle the uncomfortable feeling brewing in his bowels.

"Dude, sit yo' little ass still," Eli snapped. "Coach said to go over the scouting report."

"I'm trying to get comfortable," Todd said. He did *not* want the entire bus to know he had to go to the bathroom. He could hear their reactions now: 'You should have gone before we left.' 'Do you need a diaper?'

"Well *I'm* trying to rest," Eli shot back, "but I can't with you bouncing around like a spoiled ass kid. I need to be ready to jump in at a moment's notice when your freshman ass messes up," he added.

Ignoring the snide comment, Todd began bouncing his leg up and down rapidly. Anything to take his mind off the fact that he needed to go. And soon. He started to sweat, desperately trying to hold in what was sure to erupt. *That* wouldn't be pretty. He doubled over, feeling the breakfast he had begun its uprising. It was going to come up, or it was going to come out. He prayed that it would come up. Throwing up out a window would be much more pleasant than the alternative.

Todd celebrated the bus' every burst of movement. Twenty feet. Yes! One hundred feet. Right on! That's one hundred twenty feet closer to a bathroom. Still doubled over, Todd contemplated passing gas to relieve the pressure in his gut, but he worried that the smell would be unbearable to those around him. Well fuck them, he thought. Dad always said holding in a fart can kill you. He tried to let the gas out quietly but failed. It was going to be a wet one. Todd was at the end of what he could stand.

"Coach, I need a bathroom. Now."

"Todd, do you see a restroom anywhere near here?" the coach asked. Todd rolled into a fetal position. His teammates – who'd chuckled when he'd originally asked to go to the bathroom – now seemed concerned. He was at the point of no return. He needed to get off the bus now. Right now. He jumped up and the bubble forced its way down; it was coming out and there was no stopping it.

Todd threw off his tennis shoes and ran to the front of the bus. "Glass!" Coach Hunter shouted. "Where do you think you're going?!" Todd ignored him completely. He was at defcon 1 and it was going to be nuclear. Something was about to be destroyed, and if he didn't escape the bus it was going to be his pants.

"Hey! Kid!" the bus driver yelled, watching Todd struggle to escape. The bus was still in motion – albeit not *fast* motion – but Todd didn't care. After another twenty feet, they stopped again. The driver opened the door and Todd burst from it the way balls did from a pitching machine. He ran through the field at a torrid pace, then a brisk jog, then a waddle through the empty farm land. He began removing articles of clothing as he got further from the bus. First his belt, then he unbuttoned his pants, but he was only able to remove his left leg and underwear. His bare bottom faced the highway traffic, and, for the second time since starting college, he was being catcalled mockingly by his teammates.

"Hey, Glass!" one of them yelled. "Time to shave that assfro!"

Todd could hear the cackling and teasing, of course, but the bubble in his gut became too much. Resistance was futile. He couldn't crouch down fast enough before his breakfast escaped in a waterfall of brown waste. Cars on the highway honked their horns, and his teammates went from laughing at him to gasping in horror to groaning in pity. Todd just stood there convulsing as the waste exited his body, but he finally felt free of the excruciating pain.

Ten seconds later, Todd was able to stand up. He felt better than he had in a long time, but he was terrified to turn around. He took off one of his socks, inspected it for a clean spot, and used it to clean the exit point of his waste. He discarded the sock right where he stood. He freed his right leg from his pants and underwear and began wiping where the waste had splattered on him, once again discarding the article of clothing where he stood.

His feeling of relief was short-lived as another movement from his bowels consumed him. When the ordeal was over, Todd stood tall. He prayed the bus would leave without him. He was at his most vulnerable state and couldn't turn to face his teammates. He glanced over his left shoulder and saw the bus was still there. He looked at the field in front of him, took in a deep breath, and turned to face his audience. As he started walking slowly back toward the bus, passengers in the cars still stuck in traffic took pity on him, offering what they could to help: wipes, tissues, socks. Then, to his ultimate surprise, Eli ran out into the field and helped Todd back onto the bus. The ordeal had taxed his body tremendously. He was sweaty, yet cold. Still bare from the waist down, he made his way to an empty seat and lay down in a fetal position. He began to doze off.

After a few minutes he heard a commotion from several other teammates as they, too, began to feel ill. Selfishly, Todd was happy that he wasn't alone in his misery. He wasn't sure how long he rested before he felt a tap on his shoulder. It was Coach Hunter offering him some water. Todd waved it off as the coach laid a towel over him. "Drink up. Now," the coach demanded. Even as he tried to show compassion, Coach Hunter's voice was still gruff and authoritative. "You lost a lot of water back there. You're dehydrated." Todd gulped down the water fearfully, scared of putting more contents in his system that might result in more bowel movements. He was cramping, but empty. He dozed off again.

"Wake up, Glass," Coach Hunter said. Todd wasn't sure how long he'd been out this time, but it must have been quite a while judging by the drool he wiped off his face. "Get a move on," Coach barked, tossing Todd a warm pair of pants and clean socks. "You're lucky the facility had a washer and dryer nearby." The experience *must* have been draining if it knocked him out long enough that they not only arrived at their destination but also long enough for clothes to be procured and laundered.

Todd cleaned himself with a package of wet wipes and hopped gingerly off the bus, still not sure what his body's limits were. He joined the team in the middle of Coach Hunter's speech.

"Maybe next time," the coach snapped, looking directly at Elijah, "you shouldn't talk shit about an opponent when you're in an opponent's *state*." He shook his head as he looked at his players, all of whom were in one state of disheveledness or another. They looked like some kind of MASH unit, moaning and groaning, doubled over in pain.

No one seemed ready to play. All the extra energy he'd stored up was gone. No excuses, he told himself. "Fuck this!" he yelled. His teammates ignored his outburst, moving along gingerly.

"Hey!" Todd shouted, kicking the back of their dugout. His teammates and coaches stopped to see why Todd was having a temper tantrum. He'd never been the vocal teammate to give a motivating speech, but Todd continued, anyway. "We worked too hard to get this close to have Flo from Mel's Diner sabotage our efforts. We are going to go out there, kick ass, and then go back there and tell her to kiss our grits," he continued, doing his best with the references to *Alice*.

"I came here for two things," he continued, stealing the battle cry Elijah had used earlier: "to chew bubblegum and win every damn game this weekend. And I'm all out of bubble gum. Who's with me?!" The fanfare from the restaurant was absent this time around. Todd rushed onto the field for warm-ups alone. He was hyped…for a minute. Mother nature was calling again, and he urgently needed to find the bathroom.

CHAPTER 39

"You did good, Glass," Coach Hunter told Todd as he grabbed his bat en route to the on-deck circle. Todd beamed at the coach's words of acknowledgement and appreciation. Todd had had three hits in four at bats, with one sacrifice. His team was trailing by one run with the tying run on third, and the go ahead run on second base with one out. This was the type of scenario Todd wished for. He wanted it to all come down to him. He wanted to be the hero. Todd made his way up the dugout stairs.

"Whoa! Whoa! sport," Coach Hunter shouted. "Me telling you good job means your day is done. Time to hit the showers" he concluded matter of factly. Todd had a blank 'I don't understand' look on his face. "I'm pulling you," he informed Todd. Realizing Todd still was't comprehending what he was saying, Coach Hunter sighed deeply before explaining further. "They're warming up a left-handed pitcher to close the game out. If Javier doesn't bring in a run to tie the game, then it will come down to you. Lefty versus lefty, the pitcher has the advantage," Coach Hunter explained. "Maybe if this wasn't your first rodeo," he continued. Todd could feel his dream of being the hero on the baseball diamond slipping away.

"But Coach," Todd began to argue.

"Shit!" the coach yelled, stomping his foot. "That was inside! Javier, if it's close next time, swing the damn bat instead of standing there striking out!" he ordered. "Brown, get ready. They're bringing in Smith."

Todd's teammate Ronald Brown slowly made his way toward the bat rack. He, too, had suffered the effects of this morning's breakfast.

"Coach!" Todd began again, "I'm not a lefty!"

"Could've fooled me," Coach Hunter replied, brushing off Todd's admission.

"No seriously, I'm a natural righty."

"I don't have time for this," the coach snapped. "Brown! Get up there!" As the coach approached the umpire to announce the change in the line up, Brown threw up all over the lineup card.

"We need a batter!" the umpire yelled at Coach Hunter.

Coach Hunter turned around to see Todd standing there, grinning from ear to ear. He knew the coach was out of options. "Don't screw this up, kid," he threatened, grabbing Todd by the shoulders and drawing him in close enough that Todd could smell the Skoal chew on his breath. Todd winced in pain. The coach's grasp felt like a Vulcan death grip.

"Smith is a pro prospect, and we both remember how you fared against the last pro prospect you faced," he said, letting Todd go. "He leads the conference in saves and is a strikeout type pitcher. The pitcher you faced earlier in the game was a pitch-to-contact type pitcher." Todd, still tender from where Coach Hunter had grabbed him, was focusing more on whether or not he would be able to swing the bat than what the coach was saying.

"He likes to attack the lower half of the plate with his slider. He'll pitch you up and away with his fastball. Watch the shift. If they shift toward left field, wait for a middle to outside pitch to drive toward right. And don't get fooled by his curve; it has a nasty 12 to 6 bite." Todd had no clue what the coach was saying.

He was getting nervous. He was a reactionary hitter; he just wanted to go up to the plate and swing away.

"Got it, Coach," he lied. He didn't get it, but he was willing to say anything to get away from the coach.

"Kid!" the coach yelled again. "Even if you *get* a hit there's still a hill with your name on it in mid-Missouri for waiting until now to tell me you're a natural righty."

The home crowd rose to its feet. They smelled blood. They could sense the game was near its completion in their favor. The energy from the few hundred fans was electric. It was by far the largest crowd Todd had ever played in front of. The environment was intimidating. Todd could make out very few words that the hecklers rained down upon him, but 'bum' and 'bench rider' were among them. A couple of people said things about his genitalia or lack thereof, but mostly it sounded like noise. Lots of noise. Todd was mere feet from home plate. He took a deep breath, followed by a couple of practice swings from the left side.

"Wrong side, Glass!" Coach Hunter yelled. Todd had been practicing being a lefty for so long it had become second nature. He turned and walked to the other side of the plate.

The crowd erupted in laughter. The cheers against him grew louder. More hecklers chimed in after realizing Todd's snafu. He took a deeper breath and tried in vain to block out the noise. He could hear words of encouragement from his teammates and coaches, but they were drowned out by the crowd. Todd gripped his bat, raised his right shoulder, and dug in his right leg in anticipation of the pitch.

Straddling the rubber, Smith checked the runner at third base. He placed his right foot down firmly in front of his left. He kept his glove up and the ball hidden behind his back leg as he received the sign from the catcher. He shook off the first couple signs from his set position. He brought his right foot back and his hands to the center of his body. Smith's knees were slightly bent, his feet parallel. Finally getting the sign he wanted, he held his position for a couple seconds then began his windup.

Todd waited for the pitch. His bat perfectly still, Todd kept his head up and his chin tilted down toward his front shoulder. He didn't blink, his head didn't move; he was ready to track the ball all the way from the pitcher's hand to the barrel of his bat. His hands were raised slightly, level with his pectoral muscles and the bat raised diagonally behind his head. His back elbow was in a straight line to his shoulder, parallel to the ground.

As the ball left Smith's hand, Todd saw what looked like blurred vertical railroad tracks. He immediately recognized the pitch as a two-seam fastball. He swung hard but missed the pitch. The already electric crowd was even more energized. Only two strikes away from victory.

"That was ugly," Todd told his bat. "We can do this." He stepped back into the batter's box for a moment and barely had enough time to get into his stance before the next pitch was on its way. Todd analyzed the spin of the ball. He saw a red dot around two o'clock as the ball spun down and away. Todd watched what he recognized as a slider sail out of the strike zone. The crowd's moaning filled the air and boos rained down on the umpire for his call.

"Come on, Blue! Stevie Wonder could see that was a strike!" one fan yelled.

"Check your answering machine, Ump! You missed a call!" another one said.

Todd heard his teammates shout "Good eye!" and "Way to hang in there!" He stayed put in the batter's box, focused, feeling as if he was in good shape after one ball, one strike. He guessed an off-speed pitch was next, something that would keep him off balance.

He was right. The curveball's seams were coming at him at a ten- to four-o'clock spin. Just like the previous pitch, it dropped just out of the strike zone. Ahead on the count, Todd's confidence grew and so did the smile on his face. Smith looked annoyed. The catcher ran to the mound to calm him down. Todd looked at the batterymates, trying to catch a hint as to what was coming next, but these two were professionals and covered their mouths with their gloves.

The umpire went to the mound to break up the impromptu meeting. Todd took a couple more practice swings and was ready to go. The runners danced off the bases, hoping to distract the pitcher. The crowd noise grew louder as Smith began his windup. The ball flew from his hand but there didn't seem to be any movement to the ball. To Todd it looked like a reddish brown blur. Four-seam fastball! He knew instantly Smith was trying to challenge him with brute strength. Todd swung with all his might.

CRACK!

He could tell by the sound and feel of the ball hitting the bat that he'd made good contact. He couldn't have said where the ball was headed; his focus was making it to first safely. But he could tell by the exuberance of the runner at third that he'd just tied the game. He saw the first base coach waving him on to second and sprinted harder. Had he just helped them take the lead?!

As he rounded first base heading for second, Todd could see the play unfolding in front of him. The center fielder was fielding the ball with the left fielder covering him. Once he secured the ball, the center fielder threw a rocket to the shortstop, who was the cut-off man. The second baseman ran to the second base bag.

"I need to pick up the pace if I don't want to be thrown out," Todd thought. He gave it all he had, but he was running on empty. His morning on the side of the road had taken almost everything out of him. He slid into second base feet first as the second baseman received the ball and tagged his thigh.

"Safe!" the umpire yelled. Todd was ecstatic. He wanted to celebrate but couldn't. He mustered all his energy to get up and tried to act stoic in the presence of success. He wanted to present himself as someone who delivers in the clutch often in case a scout was in attendance. "Act like you've been there before," his dad would tell him. He would say personal success should be expected, so don't act as if it came as a surprise to you or anyone else. Wait until he sees my report card, Todd thought of his academic success.

Todd brushed himself off and waited at the second base bag for the next pitch. He was ready to jump up and down, scream, and throw Gatorade on Coach Hunter but refrained since his team still had three more outs to get. The top of the inning ended with a strikeout, but his Blue Tigers were up by one.

"Three up! Three down!" the team yelled as they took the field.

"Ball four!" the umpire shouted after the fourth pitch sailed out of the strike zone. What seemed like an inevitable win was turning into a heartbreaking ending. Todd could only look in horror as a pitch rocketed into the left field corner. The tying run jumped on home plate. The crowd that had been silenced just a half inning earlier was at a fever pitch.

The next pitch was a line drive at the shortstop for the first out. The shortstop looked the runner back to third. The pitching coach came to the pitching mound to talk to the entire infield. "We're going to walk the next hitter," he said. "I want you guys at double play depth," he told them.

The umpire walked out to the mound, breaking up the meeting. Todd's assignment was to play back and toward the second base bag. Elijah, the first baseman, played back and covered the line to protect against a double.

After the walk there were runners on first and third, but only the runner on third mattered. Todd saw the catcher call for an outside slider to the right-handed batter. Todd cheated slightly toward first base, away from where he should have been.

SMACK!

A check swing sailed the ball up the line past Elijah. Todd had a head start since he was cheating that way. He sprinted for the soft line drive. "Oh crap," he thought. "This is going to be close." If the ball lands foul he wouldn't be able to catch it because the runner could tag up, head home, and probably score since all of Todd's momentum was carrying him away from making a strong throw. He would have to let it go, giving the batter an extra life. If it's fair, he'd have the same issue, only he'd need a miracle on a throw he'd have to make.

He could see the ball was going to land just fair. Unfortunately, it was sailing over his head. Todd dove to try to make the difficult over-the-shoulder catch. He watched the ball land just on the top webbing of his glove. The force of his body hitting the ground stung fiercely. He popped up as if he'd belly flopped off a trampoline and, in one motion, fired a rocket toward home plate.

At the same moment, the runner on third was tagging up and heading for home. The catcher blocked the plate while anticipating the throw. The ball and the go-ahead runner met the catcher at the same time. He flinched as the runner's batting helmet and the catcher's mask flew off in a horrendous collision. Todd, who had dropped to his knees from the abdominal pain caused by too much activity and his belly flop, waited anxiously for a call from the home plate umpire. The crowd was silent.

"Safe! Safe! Safe!" the umpire yelled, pointing to the dropped ball. Todd was angry that all his effort, his amazing catch, his perfectly-thrown ball had been wasted. He quickly changed his tune, though, when he saw his catcher getting up slowly after that collision. Todd knew he probably wouldn't have been able to hold onto the ball, either, after being plowed into by a grown man running full speed.

What a roller coaster of emotions, he thought. He'd gone from jubilation from his hit to torment as he stood there watching the home team celebrating in front of him. He'd failed. If only I'd run faster; I could have thrown the ball harder, he thought. If only I'd had more power and hit the ball over the wall and not to it. Todd didn't want to face his teammates.

"Watch them celebrate," Elijah said, coming up to him. "Let the pain you're feeling drive you to be better. Let it inspire you enough in your performance that no one will ever celebrate in front of you again. Let the anger fllloooow through you," he added in a very *Star Wars* emperor voice. The two chuckled.

Todd looked up at Elijah to see several tears escape. Todd felt bad for him. His one wish, to make the postseason his senior year, was not going to come true. Will this be my fate, too? he wondered. He'd spent the past four years celebrating in front of others. What if this was it? It wasn't going to be. He wouldn't let it. He was going to work hard to make himself a better player. How could he not? He had the love of a good woman who'd been turning him into a better man. Imagine what he could do if he, *himself,* put in some effort? Like his dad would tell him: the effort you put forth in whatever you do is directly proportional to the results you produce. Dad had some great advice. I wonder why it took me so long to listen.

CHAPTER 40

Todd was over the moon. Even though his team had failed to make the postseason, he'd given his coach and boosters something to be excited about for the future. Him! He was so excited to tell Amani about his performance. He rushed into his room and sat on the edge of his bed. He went into his bag and grabbed his bat and glove. "Thank you, thank you," he said to them. Todd was seriously superstitious. He believed wholeheartedly that a result was due to a specific action, that his success wouldn't be due to months of hard work and practice but rather to the fact that he'd found a spot on the bed for his bat and glove and had been rewarded for it. At least he hoped that was the reason and not the horrible experience with breakfast. Tucking the two objects under the covers, Todd leaned over and placed a kiss on each. He stood over them, admiring both as if they were a newborn child.

Todd turned his attention toward his desk. He wanted to pen every detail about the game to Amani, from the smell of the popcorn to the distinctive sound the ball made as it came in contact with the bat. Mostly he wrote about how well he'd done. He wrote with vigor, partly to fill Amani in, but mostly to relive his experience. He had a zest for life, and he owed it all to her. His motivation in everything was due to her. He was finally able to reach his potential, something his parents and teachers claimed he's had since he was a preschooler. A life with her was his motivation for getting his shit together.

It was finally happening. Todd's actions were becoming those of which he could be proud, unlike all those years of hiding report cards and progress reports. With finals just about over, he was more than assured of being placed on the dean's list. For the first time ever, Todd was excited to receive his report card. He actually couldn't wait to show it to his dad. He might have to have a defibrillator on hand because his dad was going to fall out in disbelief, quite the contrast to his last year in high school when Todd blithely meandered through the semester on fumes. Now he was blazing through his first year of college amassing accomplishments.

Todd nearly jumped off his seat when the phone rang. He was ecstatic to hear it was an outside call. He tossed his letter aside. Why write when I can tell her everything? he thought. He bounced merrily over to the phone.

"Hey love," he answered. His voice was full of happiness.

"I am going to fucking *kill* you!" shouted the voice on the other end. Todd pulled the receiver away from his ear, trying desperately to place that voice. He looked at the time and saw it was when Amani had lunch, but this was not Amani. Very few people were aware that she even called Todd let alone during her lunch break. Shocked as much as he was confused, all Todd could think to say was "Hello." It sounded more like a question than a salutation.

"You killed Amani!" the girl screeched into the receiver. A lump the size of the Statue of Liberty stuck in his throat. He looked at the receiver as if it were defective. He knew the voice now. It was Amani's younger sister Amna.

"Huh?" was the only response he could muster. Is this some kind of sick joke? he wondered. Had he heard her correctly?

"You selfish asshole!" she screamed. The intensity with which she spoke convinced Todd it couldn't be a joke. She would have to be better than Meryl Streep to perform this well for a joke.

Todd's knees buckled and he hit the ground, his mind spinning. He couldn't understand anything he was thinking.

"You selfish bastard," Amna continued. "You tricked my sister into dating you. You deflowered her. You *knew* she wasn't allowed to date outside of her religion, that it was a death sentence if anyone found out. I read the notes. I know what you two did. I hope you rot in hell."

"Dead?" Todd asked. But how? And how did Amna get ahold of the letters? Amani was supposed to have burned them! And if Amna had read them, had her dad and Abbas read them, too? Was Todd's life in jeopardy? Did he need to run and hide? He was shaking, his skin like ice. This can't be happening, he thought. His heart pounded so heavily in his chest he thought he was going to have a heart attack. His stomach churned so rapidly he vomited violently all over himself. He wanted to run away.

Amna was sobbing uncontrollably on the other end. Todd wanted to cry, too, but the pain was so deep he couldn't. He didn't care what happened to him; he cared about Amani. Why did she have to be taken from this world? The one person he would turn to when he was lost, upset, hurt was gone. What was he going to do? He *needed* her. She'd made him strong when he'd been weak. She wasn't just a piece of his heart, she **was** his heart. Maybe Amna was wrong. Maybe Amani wasn't gone. He prayed with all his heart that she wasn't gone. He'd read about miracles in the Bible. Well he needed one. Now.

The sound of Amna crying told him there would be no miracle. Was he really everything she said he was? Was he so selfish that he'd ignored the dangers of his and Amani's love? Did he unknowingly exploit her? Had he taken advantage of her love for him, pushing her down a path toward death? He was in anguish, then angry. He'd always believed she was a gift from above. The feelings they had for each other could only have come from heaven. Why had it been ripped from him?

In an instant, Todd became a shell. Baseball, school, life… none of it mattered anymore. How could he continue in this world without the person he was building a life with? The reason he had for living was dead. He knew he should say something to console Amna, but he didn't have anything to offer. Whenever something bad happened his first thought was to turn to Amani for advice and comfort. Without her, he was nothing. He *had* nothing.

Todd stayed on the floor for hours. He wasn't sure when Amna hung up; he just knew she wasn't on the line anymore. It was late. The rumbling of thunder outside let Todd know a spring storm was approaching. He was partially convinced the pain in his heart had brought the storm on. The cold linoleum floor was painful after sitting in one spot for so long, but he didn't have the energy or the aspiration to get up. He needed the pain. He was numb. Maybe physical pain would distract him from the emotional torment he was in.

How do you continue to live when the one thing you're living for is gone? He asked this question over and over again. Then came the why? Why continue living with such pain? With such unbearable hurt?

It was almost midnight. His eyes were swollen and painful from holding back tears. The smell from the vomit he still had all over him tickled his nose. Gingerly, he lifted himself off the floor, feeling outside his body the entire time. He walked out of his room, forgetting to shut the door behind him. He exited the dorm. The campus had lost power while he'd been on the floor, but Todd hadn't noticed.

Without the street lights, the only source of light came from the sky. Lightning danced above him as the clouds opened after a deafening clap of thunder. The ground rumbled, car alarms sounded. Tornado sirens were going off in the distance. Sheets of rain flooded treacherous streets. The sky was pitch black, but still too bright for Todd. The pain in his chest had become unbearable. He fell to his knees. He couldn't walk, couldn't stand. Even if he'd wanted to. Todd didn't care that he was outside in the middle of a thunderstorm; he barely even noticed.

Finally, the tears began streaming down his face. The heaviness of Amani's death paralyzed him as he knelt there getting drenched. Each raindrop merged with his tears, as if the heavens were trying to wash away his pain. But there was no stopping grief like this. Todd opened his heart in prayer, begging for a miracle, but his call to the heavens went unanswered. He felt even more abandoned, more lost. Desperate, he pined for something more forceful, more extreme. Something that would match the anguished turmoil within him.

Todd turned his gaze from the darkened sky to the saturated ground. No longer in prayer, he wished for a bolt of lightning to strike him dead. He needed to be released from this torment. The sirens in the distance were now on top of him, and he longed for a tornado, ruinous and catastrophic, to strike him. Anything to whisk him away to where his pain would be replaced by peace.

As the storm intensified around him, he remained where he was, as did his pain. His heart heavy, he closed his eyes and accepted his fate. He knew he would never escape this pain; it would last forever. He knew he would never rise above the torment that drowned his soul. Time may eventually mask the suffering – though he couldn't then imagine how – but he would be forever unable to escape the death his actions had caused .

Hunter publication

Bringing the world a new generation of entertainment

Acknowledgements

This is a work of fiction. Unless otherwise indicated, all names, characters, businesses, places, events, and incidents herein are either the product of the author's imagination or used in a fictitious manner. Any resemblance to actual persons, living or dead, or actual events is purely coincidental.

World's Apart: Volume One written by Kenneth J. Hunter
Cover art by Kenneth J. Hunter
Developmental and content editing by Laura Neeter

Look for *Worlds Apart: Volume 2*
Coming Soon

www.ingramcontent.com/pod-product-compliance
Lightning Source LLC
LaVergne TN
LVHW011941060526
838201LV00061B/4170